Tell Me a Story

Tell Me a Story

Sharing Stories to Enrich Your Child's World

ELAINE REESE

OXFORD
UNIVERSITY PRESS

OXFORD
UNIVERSITY PRESS

Oxford University Press is a department of the University of Oxford.
It furthers the University's objective of excellence in research, scholarship,
and education by publishing worldwide.

Oxford   New York
Auckland   Cape Town   Dar es Salaam   Hong Kong   Karachi
Kuala Lumpur   Madrid   Melbourne   Mexico City   Nairobi
New Delhi   Shanghai   Taipei   Toronto

With offices in
Argentina   Austria   Brazil   Chile   Czech Republic   France   Greece
Guatemala   Hungary   Italy   Japan   Poland   Portugal   Singapore
South Korea   Switzerland   Thailand   Turkey   Ukraine   Vietnam

Oxford is a registered trademark of Oxford University Press in the UK and certain other
countries.

Published in the United States of America by
Oxford University Press
198 Madison Avenue, New York, NY 10016

Library of Congress Cataloging-in-Publication Data
Reese, Elaine.
Tell me a story : sharing stories to enrich your child's world / Elaine Reese.
p. cm.
Includes bibliographical references.
ISBN 978-0-19-977265-0
1. Storytelling.   I. Title.
LB1042.R44 2013
808.5'43—dc23
2012042588

1 3 5 7 9 8 6 4 2
Printed in the United States of America
on acid-free paper

To Benjamin and Dylan, the main characters in my favorite stories. And to Adele, Mary Nell, and Joseph Reese, for sharing their favorite stories with me.

Contents

Preface and Acknowledgments

Some of my earliest and best memories are of family stories.

One is a memory of cuddling in the crook of my mother's arm as she read me a story. I don't remember the book. All I remember is the faint smell of coffee on her breath and the warm encircling feeling of absolute safety.

Later, I remember my grandmother Reese's thrilling stories of homesteading in Florida in the late 19th century, and my father's hair-raising, funny, and at times sobering stories of the triumphs and trials his single-parent family faced in the midst of the Great Depression. These stories of other times and places connect me to my family's past, just as my stories of growing up in Texas connect my New Zealand "Kiwi" children to their American ancestry.

When I started graduate school at Emory University in the late 1980s to explore the science of memory, I was fortunate to work with Dr. Robyn Fivush, who introduced me to the fascinating study of family stories. It seemed too good to be true that I could turn my love of family stories into my life's work. At the time, we suspected that family stories would turn out to be important for children's memory development, but we (or at least, I) did not anticipate the far-reaching consequences of family story reading and storytelling for children's language, emotional development, and adolescent well-being. The main reason I wrote this book was to share with other parents my passion for family stories and the benefits they can confer for children.

My gratitude for the making of this book extends far and wide. I'll start by thanking the New Zealand families who have so graciously shared their lives over 15 years. My deep respect and admiration go out to you for raising such eloquent and balanced young people. I also thank the Marsden Fund of the Royal Society of New Zealand for funding the early childhood phase, and the Division of Sciences at the University of Otago for keeping the study going over the years.

Thanks also to my many students who have trudged around to all corners of Dunedin, braving fierce dogs and shocking weather, video cameras and recorders in hand, to collect the families' stories, and who later painstakingly transcribed and coded each and every word. Very special thanks go to Kate Farrant, Keryn Harley, Stephanie Read, and Sandy Sullivan for helping the study's inception, and to Amy Bird, Rhiannon Newcombe, Rachael Brown, Rebecca Brookland, Gabe Trionfi, Emily Cleveland, Fiona Jack, Jessica Glen, Naomi White, Donna Anderson, Helena McAnally, Bridget Forsyth, and Joanna Parry for following the children as they started school and entered adolescence. Adell Cox, Nicola Brown, Sarah-Jane Robertson, Yan Chen, Federica Artioli, and Shelley MacDonald, thank you for your illuminating work that I have included here. Jessica Johnston, I appreciate your hard work over the summer helping with the final stages of preparing this book.

Of course, I would not have written this book without the mentorship and support over the years of Robyn Fivush, who began as my PhD supervisor but who is now a trusted colleague and treasured friend. Other colleagues, and students-turned-colleagues, with whom I've had many spirited conversations and e-mail exchanges about family storytelling include Alison Sparks, Diana Leyva, Tia Neha, Qi Wang, Mele Taumoepeau, Carole Peterson, Allyssa McCabe, Stuart McNaughton, Karen Salmon, Harlene Hayne, Judy Hudson, Katherine Nelson, Wendy Grolnick, Rachel Barr, Tilmann Habermas, Bill Friedman, Kate McLean, Amanda Barnier, John Sutton, Elizabeth Schaughency, Catherine Haden, Peter Ornstein, Lynne Baker-Ward, and Patricia Bauer. Lyn Tribble and Merata Kawharu, please accept my sincere thanks for your expert editorial and cultural advice. I am fortunate to have you as colleagues at the University of Otago. Kathy and Jeff Hirsh-Pasek, thank you for getting me off to a good start.

To Sarah Harrington, Andrea Zekus, and the superb team at Oxford, thank you for believing in this project and for providing expert, steadfast advice and encouragement throughout.

Finally, my deepest thanks extend to my family and friends who have stood by me, behind me, and over me as I worked on this book, and who offered valuable advice at every critical juncture. Mother, Jennifer, Andrew, Steve, Roy, Mary Ann, Casey, Betty, Fernando, Ros, Ruth, Rachel, Sebastian, Tamara, Janice, Jane, Jon, Caroline, Moto, Isabelle, Geoff, David, Rowena, Jed, Saskia, and Louis—I don't think you all realize how much you've helped me to persevere "in the face of extreme difficulty," as one of the mothers in our study so aptly put it. Most of all, thank you, Ben and Dylan, for your willingness to share your stories, and for endless enthusiasm in cheering me on to the finish line. We did it!

Elaine Reese
1 December 2012
Dunedin, New Zealand

Introduction

What Is Story Sharing?

Four-year-old Allie and her mother are walking in the parking lot of the supermarket when a plane flies overhead. Allie points and says, "Grandma's plane!" Allie's mother replies, "That's right, Grandma came to visit us on a blue plane. What was your favorite part of Grandma's visit?" Allie thinks and then offers, "Going to the zoo." Allie's mother asks, "We saw lots of animals at the zoo. Which animal did you like best?" Allie answers, "The panda bears, because they were so tute (cute). But I didn't like the monkeys." "Why didn't you like the monkeys?" asks Allie's mother. "One threw fruit at me." Allie's mother agrees, "No, I didn't like that very much either, because later I had a hard time getting the stain out of your shirt. But then we had a picnic lunch by the flamingoes, and they looked really funny." "Yeah," said Allie. "I nearly dropped my chocolate chip cookie but then I caught it." Allie's mother responds with, "Oh yeah, I had forgotten that part." and then ends the conversation with, "Let's call Grandma today and tell her how much fun we had at the zoo." They enter the supermarket and start shopping.

It is nearly impossible to get through a single day as a parent without a story. Most of our everyday stories are small ones, such as the conversation Allie and her mother had about Grandma's recent visit. Other stories of the day are longer and more obvious, such as the chapter of *Huckleberry Finn* that you read at night to your 10-year-old, or the tale of *Cinderella* that your 3-year-old daughter watches on DVD again and again and then reenacts later in full costume, despite the ridicule of her older brother.

Stories large and small pervade our lives and the lives of our children. At first glance, small stories about our everyday experiences do not seem to have much in common with the grander tales found in books and in movies. Most parents don't think twice about these short conversations about everyday life. Few parents even think of them as stories, certainly not in comparison to a beautifully illustrated children's book or a full-length film.

It may surprise you to learn that these small stories are every bit as beneficial for your child's development as the grand tales told around campfires or contained in books. No doubt you already know the benefits of reading to your child. Teachers, doctors, librarians, even ads on the city bus all tout the value of reading books to young children. It's almost as if reading books with your children is a magic cure-all for their learning and development. And reading books with children *is* important—I will argue for the value of continuing to read books with children past the time most parents think they should, as long as both parties are willing. But what most parents, doctors, teachers, and librarians may not know is that other forms of conversation with children have many of the same benefits as book reading. For instance, family storytelling helps children's language, cognitive, and social skills. What's more, family storytelling is an activity that can be practiced virtually any time and any place, with your toddler as well as with your teenager. It's free, completely portable, and the main characters are the people you love the most. Best of all, everyday storytelling is something that all parents already do, whether they realize it or not. Parents vary, however, in how effectively they tell these stories. This book is about how to read and tell stories with children of all ages in ways that research has shown will help them the most.

Parents who tell and read stories in a rich and responsive way have young children with advanced language, memory, and emotional development, and they have adolescents with a healthy sense of identity and well-being.[1] Parents' stories also lay the foundation for children to have strong reading skills. My aim in this book is to show you these new ways of sharing stories to enrich your child's world.

Traditional techniques of book reading and family storytelling place the adult in the lofty position of "reader" or "teller" and the child in the passive position of "listener." This traditional storytelling stance evokes a lovely image of a child sitting spellbound at an adult's feet, listening raptly, mouth slightly agape, to every word of the book or story. The child is either completely unquestioning, or politely waits to the end of the story to ask a single question. The adult answers, and the child is satisfied. *The End.*

The only problem with this dreamy image is that it rarely exists in real life with real kids. If you try to read or tell a story to your children in this way, you will soon find them interrupting, gazing around the room, wandering off, or, depending on the age of your child, climbing on the couch cushions. Of course, as you know, it is completely normal for toddlers to be highly active. Why, then, do we cling to this soft-focus view of storytelling when we know it is unrealistic? This nostalgic view of storytelling arises from past generations when adults wanted to think of children as seen and not heard, a time when teaching and learning were viewed as a process of shunting knowledge from one generation to the next. This view of learning simply doesn't apply to most children of our current generation growing up in Western cultures, who are encouraged to engage, to question, even negotiate with others when they learn.

My goal is to create a new image of story reading and story telling that I hope will become even more comfortable and comforting for you and your child. Imagine instead a parent and child talking together about a book or a story. They may be sitting side by side with a book on their laps, or at the dinner table, or walking and talking—as in the conversation that Allie and her mother had about Grandma's visit on the short walk from their car to the supermarket entrance. They are having a conversation about a book or about an experience. They are both asking questions and offering information, pointing to interesting pictures or landmarks, listening, laughing, even disagreeing. They are *sharing* a story.

It is this conversational method of sharing stories that is most effective for children's development in today's society. It is a method that is adapted easily for children of different ages, for different kinds of books and stories, and for all kinds of children and families.

You are probably already using elements of this conversational method. Do you...

- Ask your child open-ended questions about the story, like "What's that one called?" or "What's happening here?" when you are reading a book?
- Praise your child's responses to your questions?
- Follow in on your child's response with a related question?
- Talk with your child about everyday experiences such as when you went to the science museum last week?
- Talk with your children about longer-ago events such as the day they were born, or of events in the family's history that occurred before they were born?

If you answered "yes" to any of these questions, then you are already using some of the elements of the approach that I will share with you. What you will learn from this book is how to fine-tune these techniques to maximize the developmental benefits for your own child.

I won't ask you to shatter your cozy image of your child listening to stories and throw it away forever. There will still be a time and a place for story listening—but it will be rare, probably restricted to a bedtime story with an older child, or the first telling to your children of a family story from past generations. After trying the techniques that I'll teach you for **story sharing***, you won't miss the old ways. Your child will respond in such a positive way to the new methods of story sharing that you will be richly rewarded for the change.

STORYTELLING AROUND THE WORLD

The pervasiveness of stories in our society is not new or unusual. Every culture has stories. As Ursula Le Guin claims, "There have been great societies that did not use the wheel, but there have been no societies that did not tell stories."[2] However, the means of experiencing stories are more numerous today than ever before. Children hear stories small and large from their parents, grandparents, aunts and uncles, teachers, even from their friends and older brothers and sisters. They hear and read stories from books, view stories on video, and create stories themselves on computers and in role-playing video games. Researchers are beginning to discover how all of these different forms of stories are affecting our children, for better or worse.

We are also beginning to understand how parents in cultures around the world share stories of their traditions with their children. In contemporary Tongan families in New Zealand, for instance, Bible stories form a primary source of parent-child reading. Tongan parents use Bible stories as a means of passing down moral messages and encourage children to learn passages by heart.[3] Children may benefit from having this store of cultural and religious knowledge in several ways: They develop a strong sense of community and tradition; they may also be strengthening their memory skills, along with their moral development. Because all of these stories are outside children's own experience, however, there is less opportunity for interaction and for the child to contribute. Thus, these stories play less of a role in children's language development, but may be important in other ways. Children can benefit from all sorts of stories.

It is also true that some cultures prize storytelling more than others. In New Zealand, where I live, Māori culture has strong oral traditions.[4] For instance, Māori children may learn a basic *mihi* to introduce themselves to others, narrating their tribal identity, perhaps including their connections to ancestral leaders and landscapes such as their mountain, harbor, or river. As they get older, Māori children may then learn more of their *whakapapa* to ancestors two or three generations before them, if not also to founding tribal ancestors. In some now exceptional cases, they may learn of their connections to the ancient voyaging ancestors who came to Aotearoa New Zealand in migratory canoes some 1,000 or so years ago. Māori children brought up in a Māori environment also hear and learn a diverse range of speeches, greetings, blessings, and prayers, all with special rules for telling, especially in *marae* (ceremonial courtyard and ancestral meeting house) contexts.[5]

Other examples of cultures with rich oral storytelling traditions, past and present, include some African cultures, Native American cultures, indigenous Australian cultures, Indian cultures, and South American cultures.[6] These cultures differ in the exact forms of story-telling, and in how much elaboration on the facts is encouraged. These cultures share a love of story, however, and all use stories to entertain and to remind others of whence they came. As one 6-year-old child from the indigenous Brunka tribe in Costa Rica reported, "We eat, and we go to bed, turn off the lights, and they tell us a story."[7]

In many cultures, telling stories to children serves another important purpose besides informing them of their lineage and meta-physical origins. In some Chinese families, for instance, parents tell elaborate stories of their children's past misbehavior, with the goal of helping their children develop appropriate behavior in the future.[8] These types of moral stories are in line with Confucian values, such as respect for elders. Parents in indigenous Latin American communi-ties accomplish a similar goal of getting children to behave through telling fictional stories. For instance, one vivid oral legend that par-ents in the Brunka tribe of Costa Rica tell their children is about la Llorona, a weeping woman whose children drowned in the river that she now haunts.[9] Parents tell this tale in a clear effort to scare chil-dren from going out after dark, when la Llorona may kidnap them. Perhaps this tale also warns children of the dangers of getting too close to rivers or lakes.

This use of storytelling for moral lessons may appear strange, even damaging, from a middle-class Western point of view. Most Western middle-class parents do not want to focus unduly on a child's misbe-havior. Instead, they deal with the undesirable behavior at the time and then prefer to put it behind them. Bringing up a child's misdeed after the child has already received a consequence for that behavior would be seen as "revisiting the past" and as poor parenting in the eyes of Western culture. Nor do Western parents tend to tell scary fictional stories as a way of keeping their children safe. They prefer to tell realistic stories about dangers to their children, but they are care-ful not to make these stories too vivid for fear of traumatizing their children and creating nightmares. For instance, my own children Ben and Dylan spend a lot of time around (and in) New Zealand riv-ers. With a father who is a professional fishing guide, teaching them about water safety is essential. Besides investing in swimming lessons and delivering the usual lectures and admonishments, I noticed that I have told them several times a story from my childhood of two sisters at my elementary school who drowned in the aptly named Devil's River in south Texas. The girls were in a boat with their father but the boat overturned in the current and he couldn't save them. I still remember the shock I felt when I heard the announcement at school on a grim Monday morning. This tragedy made a lasting impression on me about the unpredictability of rivers, and now I pass on this cautionary tale to my own children.

Of course, Western society has its own versions of moral tales. In Judeo-Christian traditions, reading and telling children Bible stories serves this purpose, and in previous generations, Aesop's fables were a popular method of passing down moral messages. For the youth of today, moralizing comes in the form of major Hollywood children's movies. In *Finding Nemo*, for instance, the moral is to stick close to your parents, who love you even if they seem to be smothering you. In *Shrek*, children are told to look beyond appearances to find beauty and happiness. And in *Rango*, children are taught the ethos of sharing scarce resources.

These different stories, and ways of telling those stories, are not inherently good or bad for children. They exist because they serve a function in the culture. Parents in different cultures vary dramatically in the goals they have for their children. In Puerto Rican culture, for instance, parents prize respect (*respeto*) and proper demeanor, whereas middle-class Anglo parents instead hope that their children will be self-reliant and creative thinkers.[10] These different goals for child-rearing affect the types of stories parents tell their children, as well as the way they tell them. Parents in cultures that emphasize obedience and respect for elders adopt more of a "sit still and listen" approach to storytelling. Parents in a culture that prizes independent, creative thought instead prefer a "give and take" style of story sharing in which children's contributions are valued and expanded on from a young age. In Western middle-class cultures, the "give and take" style of story sharing is the one that is most clearly linked to benefits for children's development, so that is the main style that I will profile in this book. I will introduce you to styles of storytelling from other cultures, though, as a fun twist on your typical storytelling style.

A word of caution: A very important finding across all the research on reading and telling stories with children is that children's enjoyment of a conversation or a book determines its benefits. In other words, parents' storytelling and story reading can only make a difference when children are interested in hearing the story. Children like some stories or books more than others, so it is vital for parents to attend to their children's interest in the conversation or the book. Armed with the knowledge that having conversations about everyday experiences can produce many of the same benefits as storybook reading, you can relax and stop force-feeding your children with books that they are supposed to like but simply do not. Think of it as the adult equivalent of allowing yourself to admit that you really didn't enjoy reading *War and Peace* (or even that you never actually finished it!).

PRACTICAL NOTES

In the first five chapters of this book, I will tell you about the ways that sharing books and family stories matters for children of different ages. I begin with toddlerhood, not infancy, because it is when children start to talk that these story-sharing methods are easier to implement and most effective. Of course, story sharing will be most effective with toddlers if you have been talking to and interacting with your baby from the first few days of life. I will present evidence that story sharing starts out by being most important for toddlers' language development, but these effects quickly translate into benefits for children's social and emotional lives by the preschool years. For older children and preteens, strong oral language skills also spell success in reading and school achievement. Moreover, parents who share stories about their children's positive *and* negative experiences have older children with stronger self-esteem. In adolescence, families who share stories have teenagers who are better able to cope with difficult life events, and who have a stronger sense of identity.

Ultimately, the best story sharing is geared to your child's current narrative level, or his or her own ability to understand and tell stories. In each of these first five chapters, I will first tell you about children's own story development at each age. Here I include excerpts from real stories that children in my own research studies have told us. In one of these studies in New Zealand, my students and I have been following the storytelling and language development of over 50 children from the time they were toddlers and into their teens. Anna, Charlie, and Tia are pseudonyms for three children from this study whose stories exemplify narrative development from toddlerhood to the teenage years, and whose parents illustrate the positive story-sharing techniques I would like to teach you.

Anna, Charlie, and Tia all entered the study as talkative and engaging toddlers. At age 16, all three are well-adjusted, happy, and hard-working teenagers who are doing well in school, have many outside interests in music, culture, and sports, and enjoy close-knit family relationships and healthy friendships. Anna and Charlie are each in two-parent families with one other sibling (Anna has an older brother, Nick, and Charlie has a younger sister, Jessica). Anna's parents both have university degrees and work as professionals, whereas Charlie's parents both have technical degrees and work in service industries. Tia has experienced more change and challenge in her life than either Anna or Charlie, at least on the surface. Her parents, both of whom have a high school education, separated soon after she started school. At age 9, she moved to Australia with her mother, new stepfather, and younger brother Paul. Her family returned to New Zealand for her to begin high school. Despite the considerably more complex events with which Tia has had to grapple, her resilient spirit shines through in the stories she tells about her life.

With my students and colleagues, I have also conducted numerous other studies on family book-reading and story sharing as related to children's language, self-concept, and emotional development. I include story excerpts from children in these other studies to illustrate the main points about children's narrative development and their parents' storytelling styles, again using pseudonyms to protect the identity of the children and their parents.

To help you enrich your own child's development, in the final parts of Chapters 1 through 5 I will reveal the types of book-reading and family storytelling that matter most for children of each age, as identified by the latest research findings. It's okay to skip straight to the chapter for the current age of your child, but I suggest that you read the adjoining chapter for children who are slightly younger or older too. Children develop storytelling skills at different rates. Particularly if your child is an older preteen (ages 10–12), I strongly urge you to read the adolescent chapter (Chapter 5) as well as the preteen chapter (Chapter 4). Many older preteens these days have already entered puberty and will be acting (and telling stories) more like teenagers. You will know you are in the right chapter if the story examples sound similar to your own child's stories.

Does it matter for story sharing if your child is a boy or a girl? Or if you are a father or a mother? When I first started studying family stories in Atlanta in the 1990s while in graduate school at Emory University, my PhD supervisor, Robyn Fivush, and I were initially surprised to find that mothers *and* fathers consistently told richer, more detailed family stories with their daughters than with their sons, and preschool girls in turn told richer, more detailed stories than did preschool boys.[11] In this day and age, why are parents having different conversations with their sons and daughters? This gender difference was less apparent when I did similar research in New Zealand, which after all was the first country in the world to give women the right to vote. However, the differences between girls' and boys' storytelling still existed even in egalitarian New Zealand.[12] The message I want to convey to parents of sons is to be persistent in your story-sharing efforts, even if it isn't always easy. I know this lesson from personal experience with my own boys and from hard experimental evidence. When we coached parents in telling more elaborate stories with their sons, boys benefited just as much from the enriched storytelling as did girls.[13]

It is obvious that boys eventually learn rich ways to tell family stories, because many of them grow up to be fathers who tell these elaborate stories with their children. However, boys may need some extra help from their parents in order to tell richer stories at younger ages. Worldwide, boys are falling behind girls in their reading achievement.[14] Because we know that reading is based on strong oral language skills, one explanation for this difference lies in girls' early language advantage, and in parents' richer conversations with daughters than with sons. Family stories offer one way to strengthen boys' language development and their sense of belonging. If your son is not yet a book-lover, then telling family stories together is one way to strengthen his language skills, which in turn will help boost his reading.

Children with less developed language skills, and those with attention difficulties, will also need extra help in their storytelling. I have devoted Chapter 6 to these individual differences in children's storytelling. In this chapter I help you adapt the basic story-sharing techniques for children in all kinds of families and cultures. I also highlight the importance of grandparents' stories in this chapter. In my view, grandparents are a wonderful but often untapped source of family stories. We can take a note from many cultures with rich storytelling traditions and find ways to encourage grandparents to share more family stories with us, their adult children, as well as with their grandchildren.

In Chapter 7 I offer many practical tips on times and places for storytelling to help you get those stories flowing. The main idea is to become more flexible and thoughtful in your storytelling, but always to take your child's interests and abilities into account.

In Chapter 8 I conclude that parents can continue to share stories even as their children grow up and have children of their own. After all, our children's development never really ends.

STORY-SHARING TECHNIQUES THAT WORK

You will notice throughout the book that I distinguish between tips that are solidly supported by research and those that are what I call "parent-tested" in what is perhaps the toughest lab of all. I am a parent of two sons as well as a researcher, and some of the story-sharing techniques I will feature are those that I have developed with my own children or that other parents have shared with me. I offer these "parent-tested tips" to other parents who are looking for practical storytelling techniques. I also offer up these tips to fellow researchers in the hope that they will subject these ideas to rigorous study. Throughout the book, I have tried to avoid technical jargon, but I have bolded a few **technical terms*** in the text, and defined them more fully in the glossary.

And while on the topic of technical details, the research I selected to profile in the book is all of the very highest quality. You may already know the difference between correlational and experimental research designs, and the conclusions that we can draw from each.

Correlational studies capture naturally occurring patterns between parents and children, either at a single moment in time, or over months, even years. Let's start with a simple example of a correlation: We observe that children who eat breakfast are more successful in school. We are tempted to claim that eating breakfast *causes* children to achieve at higher levels. But with a correlational design, many other interpretations are possible. Children who eat breakfast every day may also be more compliant in other ways, and their compliance may help them learn more easily from their teachers. Parents who make sure their children eat breakfast may have more resources in general, and they may use these resources for tutoring and special help that ensures their children perform well in school. Or perhaps parents who provide breakfast on a daily basis are more highly educated themselves, and their higher education levels mean that they have higher academic expectations for their children, and are also able to help their children more effectively with their homework. With a correlational design, it's important to consider as many of these other interpretations as possible. If we take into account parents' education levels and income, as well as children's personal characteristics at the start of the study, and we still find that children's breakfast eating is linked to their school success, then we can be more confident that breakfast is playing a part in children's academic achievement.

But even with the most carefully designed correlational study, we still can't claim that eating breakfast *causes* children to perform better in school. For that claim, we would need to design an experimental study, in which we intentionally improve some children's breakfast eating habits while leaving other children to eat, or not to eat, breakfast as they normally would. The first group of children would form the "experimental" group. In developmental psychology, this group of children and their parents would receive help in improving breakfast habits. The other group of children would form the "business as usual" or "control" group. We would measure all the children's academic performance before and after providing breakfast help to the experimental group, and we would also measure all the children's compliance, parents' education, and family resources to make sure the two groups of children were similar in these other ways. IF the children in the experimental group improve in their academic performance after following the special breakfast regime compared to children in the "breakfast as usual" group, and IF the two groups of children and their parents started out the study looking similar to each other in all other ways, THEN we can claim that our breakfast program did indeed help children's performance in school.

Experimental studies are considered the "gold standard" in research, because only with an experimental study can we claim causality. However, that doesn't mean that correlational studies are without value. Instead, correlational studies are worth their weight in gold (and they do take considerable time and labor), because without correlational studies, we wouldn't know which techniques are the most promising candidates for creating growth in children's development. For instance, we might believe that a technique for parents to use when reading picture books is beneficial for children's language, but without the backing of careful naturalistic evidence, we might waste parents' and children's time by trying out a technique that doesn't work at all, or that parents are unlikely to ever use in real life. In the worst-case scenario, we might inadvertently try out a technique that could actually slow down children's language development or turn them off reading books entirely.

And even when we do test out a technique experimentally that proves to work, often we need to return to correlational studies to figure out WHY it works, and for whom. Rigorous qualitative research, in which we interview parents directly about how and why they are reading and telling stories with their children, further complements our understanding. With this knowledge, we can test out new reading techniques with parents and children from different cultures, language levels, and personalities to get a better idea of which children will benefit the most.[15]

Suffice it to say that we need the highest quality correlational *and* experimental evidence to gain the most comprehensive picture of how children develop, and to know how to optimize children's development. Throughout the book, I will be careful to point out when the field has achieved the gold standard in research design, and when we are at a less conclusive point in the knowledge cycle. I will tell you now that we have highly robust and established evidence for how to read and talk with young children growing up in monolingual English-speaking households. The research base on how to read and talk with bilingual children, older children, and teenagers is still developing. We already have some very good ideas, however, of what might be the best ways to share stories with older children and teenagers. I am sharing these tips with you now because of the important role that I believe family stories will prove to play in protecting adolescents from some of the risks and dangers they face in today's society. If we can strengthen children's core sense of who they are, and help them learn to talk with others about their triumphs as well as about their trials, then perhaps as teenagers they will be stronger in the face of challenges.

As the Native American proverb goes:

> *Tell me a fact and I'll learn.*
> *Tell me a truth and I'll believe.*
> *But tell me a story and it will live in my heart forever.*

Happy story sharing!

Tell Me a Story

1

Sharing Stories with Your Toddler

Ages 1–3

Anyone at any age is able to tell the story of his or her life with authority.

~ E. L. Doctorow

The two most obvious tasks that toddlers must master are walking and talking, and not necessarily in that order. Stories don't matter at all for children's physical development, although going on a walk with your older child is a wonderful way to get the stories flowing (see Chapter 7). Stories matter a great deal for your toddler's language development, however, whether the story is from a book or about everyday experiences.

The sheer amount of time that we talk to our toddlers is a startlingly strong predictor of their language development. And the *way* we talk to children matters just as much as the quantity. Parents who use diverse vocabulary and different verb tenses have children with better language skills, even after taking into account how much they are talking to their children.[1] It's not just what parents *say* that matters for children's language, either. You can also enhance your child's language development by noticing what you are *doing* as you are talking. When an adult focuses on what children are looking at before labeling an object, toddlers learn new words from parents' speech at a much faster rate.[2] This phenomenon is called *joint* or *shared attention*.

Imagine an invisible triangle between your eye gaze, your child's eye gaze, and an object. When the parent checks in to see where the child is looking, and then labels the object that the child is paying attention to at that moment, it's much easier for the child to attach a label to the object and remember it. If instead the parent tried to get the child to switch her attention to a different object from her current focus, and then labeled that new object, the new word would not be as likely to stick in the child's memory.

Although all talk with these special qualities—diverse vocabulary, a sentence structure that is just beyond the child's current abilities, and shared attention—will help children's language, stories are an especially important way for children to learn language. One reason that stories are special is that parents use higher quality speech when they are reading and telling stories than when they're talking about what's happening at the moment. Parents' talk during storybook reading is more complex and rich with new vocabulary compared to how they talk when playing with their children, or during everyday activities such as feeding, dressing, and bathing.[3] When parents are shown how to read books more effectively with their toddlers, storybook reading has even greater benefits for children's language skills.[4]

Your child's language is, in turn, vital for nearly every aspect of their thinking and even their social and emotional development. As a baby, your child developed basic concepts about the world, but the advent of those first words fundamentally changes the way a child thinks. Eventually nearly all their thoughts and memories and imaginings—their inner lives—become filtered through language.[5] Strong language skills also lead later to strong reading skills, especially in terms of how much children understand of what they read.[6] When your children enter school, language is the medium through which they learn virtually all their academic subjects, even math. Try doing math problems in a foreign language and you will understand the degree to which language pervades nearly every aspect of thought. Because sharing stories with your toddler helps her language skills, and especially her vocabulary growth, stories are more than simply a nice way to pass the time with your toddler—although stories are also that.

And as if helping your child's language growth weren't enough, we are now finding that sharing stories helps your toddler's growing social and emotional skills. Even at this young age, language is important for building friendships. The friends children make as toddlers may not be lifelong, but they are nonetheless important for learning social skills such as sharing and accommodating to others. As children get older, communication is essential for building and maintaining relationships with others.[7]

Toddlers with better language skills are also better able to put their passionate feelings into words, which can help them to control those feelings and to develop the all-important skill of self-regulation.[8] Take the extreme example of a toddler who bites. We've all encountered one of these toddlers at a playgroup or at preschool, or perhaps that toddler is your own. Many toddlers who bite and show other aggressive behavior have low **expressive language*** skills. They can't express their emotions verbally so they get their point across in another way—and believe me, they do get a reaction. Teaching a toddler words for his emotions at a young age can help him to channel those emotions more constructively.

At first, toddlers start to talk about their own desires (*wanna, like*).[9] This talk of desire quickly segues into talk about emotions (*scared, mad, sad*), first their own and then other people's. A few months later, toddlers also start talking about their own and other people's thoughts and beliefs with words like *think* and *pretend*. This armory of **mental state words*** is fundamental for children's understanding of themselves and others, and it is the foundation for how well children communicate with and get along with others later in life. If you think about the invisible nature of mental states, it's pretty amazing that toddlers are able to grasp this concept at all.[10]

Once again, it turns out that sharing stories is a very important way that adults can teach children about their own and others' mental and emotional states of being. I will teach you some techniques for fostering your toddler's language and social understanding through story sharing, but first I need to give you a better idea of where toddlers are in their own understanding and telling of stories. That way you can gear your use of the techniques to the story level of your own child to maximize their effectiveness. The "Developmental Snapshot of a Toddler" (Table 1.2) at the end of this chapter also gives you a sense of where most toddlers are in terms of their language, cognitive, social, emotional, and physical development, as well as why these developments matter for their story understanding and storytelling. Bear in mind that toddlers vary hugely in the age at which they reach different milestones. Some toddlers talk before they walk, and others are running before they can put together a sentence. Almost always, this variation is perfectly normal. If ever you are concerned about your child's development, talk to your child's doctor for advice.

THE STORIES TODDLERS UNDERSTAND AND TELL: FROM BOOKS AND FROM PERSONAL EXPERIENCES

Stories from Books

Toddlers' contributions to traditional storybook reading are limited. If you attempt to read a storybook to a toddler without asking any questions, she will say very little, if anything.[11] More likely, she will lose interest completely and wander away or start bouncing on the sofa cushions. Most toddlers don't yet have the attention span to sit and listen to a story if you read it straight through, nor can they understand a storyline without help from you. Toddlers don't deal well with monologues except when those monologues are their own! However, toddlers *can* become engaged in storybook reading if you are highly interactive. And the more often you share books together, the more your toddler's interest in reading will grow.[12] Later I showcase all of the techniques that you need to make storybook reading most effective for your toddler's language learning.

Stories from Personal Experiences

In contrast to their limited contributions to stories about characters in a book, toddlers love to tell stories about themselves. To a toddler, it really is all about "me." Linguist Jacqueline Sachs documented her daughter Naomi's first forays into talking about her past experiences.[13] From around 1-1/2 to age 2, Naomi's "stories" were about events that she had just completed (*I did it; I throwed it*). Not coincidentally, this is around the same age that most toddlers start to talk about themselves with their own name and with the pronouns *I, me, my, mine,* or my personal favorite, *mines,* and to combine words into simple sentences (see "Developmental Snapshot").[14] From ages 2 to 3, Naomi began to talk about her past experiences in a more complex way (*I played toys with Kimberly; Yestermorning I maked a tiger*).

I also kept a diary of my first son Benjamin's talk about his personal experiences in the past.[15] Similar to Naomi, Benjamin began to talk about the past at around age 1-1/2 by saying "Choo-choo" as we drove over a bridge where the day before we had seen a train. Like many young boys, Benjamin had a passion for trains, which I'm sure contributed to his memory and speech for this particular event. Benjamin's reference to the absent train allows us to infer that he was talking about a memory of the train—in other words, he was seeing an image of the train in his mind. This development represents an important advance in children's thinking.[16] From this point on your child is capable of thinking and talking about things that are not in his immediate environment—the starting block for abstract thought. We know from other research that even babies as young as 6 months are capable of remembering events,[17] but of course at that young age they are not capable of putting those memories into words.

As children's thinking and their language skills progress, they start to tell what I like to think of as their first stories. Now, these early stories don't seem like much on the surface, and some other researchers would not glorify them with the term. Here's an example for you to decide for yourself.

Hand. Door.

At 17 months, Benjamin toddled over to his Uncle Steve in the living room and uttered these words while showing his uncle one of his fingers, pointing to the door, all the while with a pained expression on his face. You had to know the context to understand what he was saying, which was that six days earlier, I had accidentally pinched Ben's finger in that same door while closing it. Now Benjamin was sharing that painful experience with his uncle.

What makes these early words a story? I argue that they have at least some of the basic elements of a story, although most of the elements are implied. And what are the basic elements of a story? Well, you need characters. The main character in most toddlers' stories is themselves, and often they leave this element unstated. Next, you need a plot. If there aren't any actions, you have a scene or a vignette, not a story. It turns out that actions are what toddlers do best, in their stories and in everyday life. What happened to Naomi's toy? She *throwed* it. In Ben's story, the action was expressed nonverbally when Ben showed his finger to his uncle and pointed to the door. Finally, you must have a point to a story. Why are you telling it? For toddlers, usually the point of the story is to express an emotion that they feel strongly. For Ben, it was the memory of pain. Emotions are expressed early in toddlers' tales, and often the emotions expressed are negative. In psychologist Peggy Miller's research with working-class toddlers in South Baltimore, over half of the stories that 2-year-olds told were about negative events.[18] This pattern will become a theme throughout the ages of storytelling. Stories of negative experiences can be more interesting to tell—and to hear—than stories of positive events, and perhaps are also more therapeutic. Every good story needs emotion; every good story needs conflict. Fiction writer Robert Olen Butler put it best when he said, "Story is a yearning meeting an obstacle."

Other topics that toddlers bring up on their own, however, can be mundane and devoid of emotion, at least from an adult's perspective. In a larger diary study,[19] I asked over 50 New Zealand mothers to write down each time their toddlers (aged 2 to 2-1/2) brought up a past event on their own. The mothers in the study willingly complied with this request: When their toddlers were 2, mothers recorded two to five memories over one week. When their toddlers were 2-1/2, mothers reported 14 to 20 memories per child over a week. Note the explosion in toddlers' memory talk over this brief 6-month period, an indicator of the dramatic advances after age 2 in children's speech and in their memory abilities. This transformation is what happens when memories collide with language. Almost without exception, however, the events that toddlers brought up on their own were not very interesting to adults. For instance, one toddler talked about throwing two milk jugs out the window. Another toddler brought up seeing a Thomas the Tank Engine toy in a shop window. Other events the toddlers talked about were simply funny, such as a child talking about seeing the family dog bite Homer's bottom on *The Simpsons* (see Box 1.1 on the controversial topic of toddlers watching TV). Still other events were no doubt remembered because children received a reprimand, such as when 2-1/2-year-old Jasmine said, "Pegs not lollies." When she saw a pink plastic clothespeg (clothespin to Americans), it reminded her of her mother's words 8 months earlier when she put a clothespeg in her mouth and her mother reportedly told her they were "pegs, not lollies (candy)."

Box 1.1 A Few Words about Toddlers and Screentime

Use with extreme caution! Scientists still don't know the effects of TV and other screens on toddlers' brain development. The American Academy of Pediatrics discourages screentime for children under 2. For young children over 2, the AAP recommends only small amounts of carefully selected programming. [20] I know all too well how tempting it is to sit your active toddler in front of a screen so that you can have a few blessed minutes of peace to drink a cup of coffee, have a shower, or even just to go to the bathroom (all by yourself). It's difficult to resist, especially in the face of the explosion of TV programming and DVDs targeted at babies and toddlers. First it was only *Teletubbies* and *Baby Einstein*, but now parents have an overwhelming selection from which to choose, most of which claims to be educational.

Toddlers do enjoy these programs, without a doubt. Babies and toddlers look more often to programs specifically designed for them than to programs designed for adults.[21] But are they actually learning anything from the screen? Could screentime even be harmful for their brain development? These are the questions that parents of young children urgently need answered.

Fortunately, we are starting to get some answers to both of these questions. First, on the positive side, several researchers

(*continued*)

Box 1.1 (*Continued*)

have now conducted careful experimental studies of the potential benefits of screentime for toddlers' language development and for their learning. The findings are crystal-clear. Toddlers can learn to imitate an action from an adult model on TV as early as 6 months, and after age 2 they are able to learn new words from commercial TV programs. Up to age 3, however, toddlers do not learn as well from a screen as they do from a live interaction, called the *video deficit* effect.[22] One reason for this video deficit appears to be the 2-D nature of the screen. Toddlers also have difficulty learning from other 2-D media such as picture books when the pictures are less realistic, or more distracting, as when the pictures are designed to pop out of the page.[23] Younger toddlers simply do not have the cognitive skills to transfer effectively what they see on the screen to real life. They are also easily distracted by other standard features of programming for children, such as music, voice-overs, and fast cuts to new scenes. When it comes to toddlers' language development, toddlers still learn best from interactions with real live adults than from TV.[24]

If you do choose to allow your older toddler to watch limited amounts of screentime, then it is also clear that some children's programs are better than others for potentially enhancing children's language development. High-quality, interactive programming such as *Arthur, Blue's Clues, Clifford, Dora the Explorer,* and *Barney and Friends* are all linked to higher expressive vocabulary in toddlers, even after controlling for other important factors such as family socioeconomic status.[25]

The jury is still out in response to the second question about the potential harmful effects of screentime on toddlers. For ethical reasons, we cannot systematically increase toddlers' exposure to screens and then watch for decreases in their attention and behavior. We do know that toddlers who are exposed to a great deal of screentime have problems with attentional control 3–5 years later. This effect held, however, only for their levels of exposure to adult programming or to children's shows and movies that are designed to entertain, not to educate (e.g., *Rugrats; The Lion King; Power Rangers*). The amount

(*continued*)

Box 1.1 (*Continued*)

of educational children's programming that toddlers watch is NOT linked to later attention difficulties.[26] These studies are careful to take into account other factors that are linked to high doses of screentime, such as family income, education levels, even maternal depression and parental conflict.

Given the current high rates of exposure to screentime of most toddlers in developed countries, these findings should make parents think carefully about their toddlers' screentime. One study in the United States, for instance, found that babies and toddlers are watching around an hour of TV every day, and that nearly 40% of homes with young children have a TV on in the background for most or all of the day.[27] Background TV could be an even greater problem for babies and toddlers than their direct screentime for two reasons. First, they are being exposed to a greater quantity of adult programming when the TV is turned on for much of the day. Second, when a TV is turned on, even in the background, toddlers play for shorter periods and are less engaged in their play, and adults talk less and are not as actively involved in play with their toddlers compared to when the TV is off. These effects of background TV occur even when toddlers do not appear to be paying much attention to the screen.

My own children were young around the millennium, which coincided with the explosion in children's TV programming. I confess that I let my boys watch TV as older toddlers and pre-schoolers more than I now like to admit: *Teletubbies* and *Barney and Friends* were Ben's favorites, and Dylan loved *Dora the Explorer* and *Clifford*. True, I was always in the room with them while they watched TV: folding clothes, paying bills, or doing any of the other myriad things that full-time working mothers do in their time "off." I would occasionally chime in on a song, answer Dora's questions, or ask a question or two of my own. Ben learned not to waste water from one of those interminable *Barney* songs, and Dylan learned his first few words of Spanish from *Dora*. When adults watch TV with children and interact with them during the program, using the same types of questions and comments that help children draw knowledge from book-reading and storytelling, the benefits of TV watching are maximized, and the negative effects ameliorated.[28]

As you can see from these examples, toddlers' early references to the past do not qualify as stories in the classic sense. There is no clear beginning, middle, or end. Often the characters are left implicit for the listener to infer. Only someone very familiar with the toddler's life could understand these tales. There are emotions in the storytelling, however, and there are actions. And usually there is a point to the telling, as in Benjamin's urgent recounting of his pinched finger to his uncle. Certainly, these stories are longer and more complex than the stories that children are able to tell about books at this age. Sometimes, however, these stories seem to be told simply for the toddler's own delight, more of an externalized monologue of times past as they are replayed in the toddler's mind in the form of a memory, than a true conversation. Some toddlers enjoy rehearsing their speeches at night to themselves after they're put to bed. This talk is often called "crib speech." Not all toddlers do it, but some toddlers talk up a storm in a "party of one" every night before they fall asleep. Psychologist Katherine Nelson and her colleagues studied one toddler's nighttime monologues over a period of 15 months (from 21 to 36 months) via a tape recorder by her crib.[29] Emily was a verbally precocious child who at the start of recording was already talking in complex sentences such as "Then when Daddy done getting Mommy pretty soon then gets Emmy up."

Despite Emily's precocity, the content of her speech was mundane from an adult's point of view, much like the children in my larger diary study. Instead of talking about the arrival of her baby brother Stephen at 23 months, she discussed with herself the family's plans the following day to go buy diapers.

These early tales are best thought of as stories-in-the-making. They contain the seeds of a good story, but in their present form only a family member or very close friend can understand and appreciate them. That's why it is up to you to fill in the gaps to create a full-fledged story, which I will tell you how to do next.

HOW TO SHARE STORIES THAT MATTER WITH YOUR TODDLER

Stories from Books

Some parents have a completely unrealistic picture in their minds of what it will be like to read books with their toddler. The vision: the two of you cuddled up together in a comfy chair, your toddler staring intently at a beautiful picture book, hanging on your every word. The reality: If you attempt to stick to this rosy vision, your toddler will probably be climbing down every few seconds, pawing the book, even (gasp) tearing the pages, so that the idyllic vision soon turns into a frustrating experience for you both. The solution: Book-reading, or rather, book-sharing, at this age *must* be highly interactive and brief if you want to engage your toddler. Toddlers are just beginning to understand that the two-dimensional, static, often highly stylized pictures in books are representations of reality. That's why it's best to choose simple books with realistic pictures to share with young toddlers. They learn new words more readily from books with realistic drawings or photos than those with cartoons. Pop-up pictures also appear to distract toddlers from word learning.[30]

Toddlers' understanding of categories can be extremely narrow or overly broad at this age, and their words for objects reflect this limited knowledge. They may use "duck" only to refer to their rubber duck bath toy, and not for the ducks at a pond. Or they may use "duck" for every bird they see. Extrapolating from pictures to real life is even harder for toddlers. A watercolor picture of a poodle may look very little like the weimeraner next door. Toddlers will need help linking the poodle on the page to the real dog, as well as help linking both breeds to the general category of "dogs."

As hard as it is to create an exciting book-sharing experience, the rewards for your toddler's language development are astounding. Under the right circumstances, toddlers can and do learn new words from books. Books also offer word-learning opportunities that can be hard to capture in everyday life. Imagine trying to teach your toddler about elephants without the help of a book (barring an expensive trip to the zoo).

How do you create a book-sharing environment that is optimal for language learning? First, choose the right time. This point may seem obvious, but you would be surprised by how many parents of toddlers only attempt to read books at bedtime. Book-reading as a bedtime ritual is a lovely habit to start at this age, or even earlier, but don't limit yourself to bedtime. Many toddlers are so tired and frazzled by bedtime that they will be nodding off or overstimulated at this time, not absorbing and practicing new words. You know your toddler's rhythms best, so choose a time when you know your toddler is alert and receptive, neither raring to run or overtired. After a nap or an outing to the park, during bathtime (with waterproof books), while waiting for the doctor—if you have a supply of books in most of the rooms in your house and tuck a few into the diaper bag, then any time can be book-sharing time.

Don't worry either if these early book-sharing sessions are short. You don't need to complete an entire book at a sitting for your child to benefit.

Now you're set with all of the ingredients of a successful book-sharing experience: a rested toddler and plenty of sturdy books with interesting, simple pictures and not much text (see Box 1.2). How do you do it? What do you say?

Box 1.2 Attachment Security and Story Sharing

All of the techniques that I will share with you for story sharing will work better if your child is securely attached to you. Nearly all toddlers become attached to their caregivers, but not all of these attachments are what we call "secure."[31] A child is securely attached if she trusts that her caregiver will meet her needs. Can she depend on you to care for her when she is hurt or ill, to respond to her when she cries or talks to you? Do you provide just the right amount of stimulation, not too much or too little? You can tell if you are overstimulating a toddler if he consistently turns his face away from you, or in extreme examples if he turns his whole body away when you attempt to interact. Or, when a toddler is unsure whether you will respond or not, she may approach you with a toy but then turn away just as she reaches you—and not simply because she has suddenly become interested in another toy. Around one-third of middle-class toddlers are insecurely attached to their parents. The good news is that secure attachment can be developed. Secure attachment can also be recaptured. The main ingredient is consistent, loving, responsive care that is not intrusive.[32] If your toddler can depend on you in times of need, then he is also more likely to enjoy and learn from story-sharing sessions with you.

Perhaps the most extensively tested method of sharing books with toddlers is called **Dialogic Reading***.[33] Dialogic Reading, my version of which is called **Rich Reading*** (see Table 1.1), was developed from principles that speech-language therapists use with children who have language delays, but it works just as well with children whose language is developing typically, and even with toddlers whose language is faster than most.

The basic principles of Rich Reading with toddlers are simple:

1. Treat the book-reading session as a conversation or *dialogue* with your child, instead of thinking of yourself as the reader and your child as the listener.

2. You can start by reading the text on each page, but you don't have to read the text at all, and you should never simply read the text and then turn the page. The most important part of the technique is to *ask questions* on each page. Whenever possible, these questions should be open-ended, *wh-* questions. Notice your child's interests by looking where he is looking. For instance, when reading *The Very Hungry Caterpillar* with your toddler, you could ask the following questions:
   What's that? (point to caterpillar)
   What is the caterpillar eating now? (strawberries)

Avoid or limit questions that only require the child to point (*Where's the caterpillar?*) or give a yes/no answer (*Do you like the butterfly?*)

3. *Pause* for longer than you might think necessary after asking a question. It takes time for a toddler to formulate a response. Think how much time you would need to answer in a language you had just learned several months before, and then double that time! Research shows that these pauses are nearly as important as your questions in creating an effective book-sharing experience.[34] If your child doesn't respond, supply the answer for him—"It's a caterpillar."

4. *Confirm and praise* your child's response with a "Yeah," "Good!" "That's right," and by repeating what they just said. *Yes, that's a caterpillar. You're right!*

5. *Extend* your child's response in your next question or statement.
   What's the caterpillar doing?
6. Respond, then start the cycle again with a new question.

Following up with a new cycle is very important for extending your child's language. Recently as I was sitting in a doctor's waiting room, I noticed two mothers talking to their toddlers. The first mother showed her son a book. He excitedly pointed to a picture of a car and said, explosively, "CAH!" The mother responded with praise and expansion, "Well done! It's a car." Then the interaction fizzled and the toddler turned to a playhouse with a real car. This would have been the perfect opportunity for the mother to take it one step further, as the second mother in the waiting room did. "Lion" her toddler said, looking at a book. "You're right, it's a lion. A big lion, and what is the lion doing?" the mother replied. "ROAR" said the toddler. "Yes, the lion is roaring. Why is he giving such a big roar?" This mother was following in on her child's interests, just as the first mother did, but she was extending her daughter's language by modeling more complex sentences and eliciting more diverse vocabulary. Both toddlers were currently at the one-word stage of language development, but I would place bets that the second toddler's language will progress much faster than the first toddler's. The more you focus on a single topic, the more practice your toddler will get at putting thoughts into words. Also, following in puts you in a better position to ask higher-level questions, such as "Why?" Your toddler may not be able to answer these questions yet, but you can supply an answer if she can't.

Talking about Emotions and Thoughts during Book-Sharing

With younger toddlers, the best way you can talk about emotions with them during book-sharing is to discuss their own current desires, likes, and dislikes (*Do you* <u>*want*</u> *an apple for snack, like the boy in the book? Do you* <u>*like*</u> *this book? You* <u>*don't like*</u> *the part about the spider.*). Toddlers learn the words for desires before they learn the words for emotions and thoughts (see "Developmental Snapshot"). Labeling your child's own desires is the best way to help her learn words for emotional states because her own desires are extremely strong at this age. If you assign a label to a strong emotion that she is feeling *at that moment*, that label is more likely to stick. Remember that mental states (thoughts and feelings) are invisible; the only way your child can learn the words for these mental states is for you to label them and discuss them.

With your older toddler (age 2 and up), you can start discussing the book characters' emotions and thoughts and talking about your own thoughts. Older toddlers have a stronger self-concept, accompanied by a firmer understanding of their own desires and preferences, which puts them in a better position to learn about other people's desires and thoughts. In the above example, when the mother asks, "Why is he giving such a big roar?" she could supply the answer for an older toddler, "I think he's angry at the tiger." A 2-1/2-year-old toddler, who might already know the word "angry" as a label for her own emotional states, is able to learn about others' emotional states through a process of extrapolating from her own emotions to others' emotions, in this case the lion's. At the same time, she is learning about her mother's thoughts (*I think...*).[35] Toddlers need to learn about their own and others' mental states in order to communicate with others, interact with others, and form relationships with others.

Keep these early reading sessions brief and fun, even if you only manage to look at one or several pages of the book together. With time, your toddler will develop a longer attention span for books, especially if you keep these early sessions fun and interactive. Monitor your child's interest. Just as you wouldn't shove a spoonful of food into a baby's mouth if he's turned his head away, you shouldn't force a toddler to share a book with you. Psychologist and literacy expert Hollis Scarborough talks about a "broccoli effect" with reading: If children do not like books, should we force reading on them, similar to the dilemma of whether we should force children to eat broccoli even when they don't like it? Maybe not, but I'd like to carry this analogy further. If we continue to expose children to books (or broccoli) in a sensitive way, with time even a book-hater may turn into a book-lover, or at least a child who will like certain books.

(It might help if you think of Rich Reading as the cheese sauce of book-reading: with a little bit of cheese sauce, even a reluctant eater may be able to stomach some broccoli.) However, if you have a toddler who simply doesn't like books (or broccoli), even with cheese sauce, don't push him. Instead, take comfort in the knowledge that there are other ways to help his language development, as I will show you below.[36] The last thing you want to do is turn your toddler off from books at an early age.

What if you have the opposite problem and your toddler loves books so much that he wants you to read the same book over and over? If it's one that your toddler adores, then do this at his request, no matter how much it starts to seem like stale chewing gum to you. Following the principle of shared attention, toddlers are always going to get more out of book-reading when they've chosen the book than if you do, especially if you turn down one of theirs in favor of one you select. So if your child is choosing the same book over and again, realize that she must still be getting something out of it, even if you aren't.[37]

Stories from Personal Experiences

Because personal narratives of their past experiences are the first stories toddlers tell, these stories are a natural place to start helping toddlers' language development, even if (or perhaps especially if) they are not yet very interested in books. Talking about your child's personal experiences has many of the same benefits as storybook reading for children's expressive language skills and their emotional development, with the added advantage of being completely portable. Stories of your child's past are absolutely free and can be pulled out of the air and told anywhere—in the car, on the bus, while walking to the park, in the doctor's waiting room, even in the line at the grocery store. These stories deserve a special place in parents' bags of tricks to entertain and distract toddlers. Best of all, these stories always star your child as the main character, so they are almost always intrinsically interesting to your child.

Why create stories about *past* experiences instead of about the present or future? For one thing, past experiences are already completed, so they are easier to use as material for full-fledged stories.

When talking about the moment, there is only the ongoing present, not any clear beginning, middle, or end. Toddlers can also talk about the past before they can talk about the future (see "Developmental Snapshot"), so stories about the past are the best place to start. And, talk about the past extends your child's language development because it exposes them to diverse verb tenses: past and future as well as present. (*See that bird? It's like the one we saw at the zoo. Let's go to the zoo again soon.*)

You will be able to tell when your child is ready for you to share stories of her past experiences when she brings up past events spontaneously in her speech (see "Developmental Snapshot"). Is she using some personal pronouns such as "me," "my," "mine"? Is she listening attentively when YOU talk about a recent past event? Even if you are not yet seeing these signs, you can still talk about past events with your child, but you will need to gear down the conversations accordingly. Try talking about something that just happened rather than something that happened a week or month ago. For instance, talk about a recently completed action: "Oh, you ate that cracker all up! What kind of cracker was it?" Pause, but if your child doesn't answer, you can supply the answer yourself. "It was a rice cracker, wasn't it? And what did you have to drink?" In this short conversation, you are still using the same techniques of following in on your child's interests and activities, and you are using open-ended questions. Don't worry if you are doing most of the talking at this stage. As long as you are pausing long enough for your child to respond, it won't be long before you are rewarded with a one-word response, which you can repeat and then extend. "Cracka!" "Yes, it was a rice cracker ...." And so the cycle continues.

If your child is already bringing up past events in conversation, and is also showing signs of a maturing self-concept (see below), then he is ready for you to help him expand on his primitive stories of the past. My colleagues and I have solid research evidence that the best way to accomplish these fuller, richer stories of the past is by asking *open-ended wh-* questions when your toddler brings up a past event.[38] Each question should contain *new* information about the event. We call these "open-ended *elaborative* questions" because the question itself contains cues that will help your child formulate an answer. That way you're helping your child put their experiences into words, which is the first step to telling a good story. In our longitudinal research, we found that mothers who use more of these open-ended elaborative questions when their toddlers were 19 months (especially if their children were showing signs of a maturing self-concept at this age, see Box 1.3) had children who told longer and more complete stories to a researcher at age 3-1/2. This was true whether mothers adopted this strategy naturally or whether we taught them to use the new strategies.

Box 1.3 Toddlers' Self-Concept and Story Sharing

It will be easier for your child to understand the stories you tell about her past experiences if she is showing signs of developing a self-concept. A toddler's growing sense of self is legendary. Researchers measure a toddler's self-concept using a test of self-recognition in a mirror.[39] First, the researcher surreptitiously "marks" the child's nose by dabbing a bit of red rouge on it with a tissue in the guise of wiping a runny nose. (As all parents of toddlers know, nose-wiping is pretty much constant, so toddlers don't even seem to notice.) Then, a few minutes later, we place the toddler in front of a mirror and observe their reaction. Toddlers who do not yet have a solid self-concept play with their image in the mirror, usually laughing at their image and touching the mirror, but they don't seem to notice at all the bright red dot on their noses. To an adult this phenomenon is akin to the toddler ignoring an elephant in the room. Somewhere between 15 and 24 months, however, toddlers placed in front of the mirror will immediately and somewhat soberly touch the mark on their nose. Sometimes this nose-touching is accompanied by verbal commentary such as "Dirty" or with his own name, "Joseph." This dramatic change in toddlers' behavior is thought to mark the beginning of a sense of self. Before this milestone, toddlers may not have a sense of "me," or a visual image of what they normally look like.

Here's an example of Anna's mother talking with her at age 1-1/2 about a farm visit, with the open-ended elaborative questions underlined. Notice how Anna's mother accepts Anna's speech as real contributions to the conversation: She definitely gives Anna the benefit of the doubt here as she helps Anna turn her babbles into recognizable words.

Mother: <u>Can you tell Mummy about when we went to the farm?</u>

Anna: *Ahhhh.*

Mother: <u>What did we see at the farm?</u>

Anna: *Ah dadadadada um.*

Mother: *Little baby lamb, lamb. Clever girl.* <u>What did you do to the lambs?</u> (pause) <u>What did you do to the lambs at the farm?</u>

Anna: *Ahh.*

Mother: *lamb.* <u>How many lambs were there?</u>

Anna: *Do do do.*

Mother: *Two of the little baby lambs. Gertie and George.*

Anna: *He.*

Mother: *And they had little tails, didn't they?* <u>What did their tails do?</u>

Anna: *Wave.*

Mother: *Yeah they wiggled and wiggled.* <u>And what did Anna give to the lambs?</u>

Anna: *Fayah [unintelligible]*

Mother: *Baby lambs. Anna,* <u>what did you give to the lambs?</u>

Anna: *Is a baa aah.*

Mother: *baby lamb. Did you give them a bottle?*

Anna: *Yes.*

Mother: *You did!* <u>What was in the bottle?</u> (pause) *Mmmm?*

Anna: *Milk.*

Mother: *Clever girl. Milk in the bottle.*

Anna: *Milk bottle.*

Notice that at this young age, even highly verbal children like Anna aren't able to contribute much to a conversation about a past event. Typically, toddlers' talk about past events is simpler in structure

than their talk about ongoing events. For instance, if they are using
two- and three-word sentences in speech about ongoing events, they
might revert back to one- and two-word utterances when referring to
past events. You are telling the story but inviting them to participate
by pausing after each of your questions. And Anna does participate
by taking turns at the conversation and providing utterances, even a
recognizable word here and there. Her mother responds by assuming that Anna made a real contribution, which she praises and then
expands on through her use of elaborative questions and statements.
Eventually, the story of feeding the baby lambs is told, piece by piece,
together.

With older toddlers who have more advanced language skills,
you should be able to ask a few more open-ended questions and
cut down on your use of closed questions (those that only require
the child to answer "yes" or "no"), as in the following example of
Tia and her mother talking about her 2nd birthday party. Make
sure that you *confirm and praise* your child whenever they give a
response and then *extend* by following up with a new, related question or statement (underlined below).

> Mother: <u>What did you have at your birthday?</u>
> Tia: *Candles.*
> Mother: <u>Candles?</u>
> Tia: *Yeah.*
> Mother: <u>Where were the candles?</u>
> Tia: *Blow them.*
> Mother: <u>Were they on the   ?</u>
> Tia: *Mah. [blows]*
> Mother: <u>You blew them?</u> *Were they on the cake?*
> Tia: *Yeah.*
> Mother: <u>Cool. What sort of cake did you have? (pause) What</u>
>   <u>did your cake look like?</u>
> Tia: [unintelligible two words] *Blow them.*
> Mother: <u>What what sort of cake was it?</u>
> Tia: *Ah my birthday.*
> Mother: <u>Yeah,</u> *what did your cake look like?*
> Tia: *day a like a [unintelligible two words].*
> Mother: <u>Looked like a   ?</u>

Tia: *Teddy.*

Mother: *Teddy. It was a teddy cake wasn't it?*

Tia: *Yeah my birthday teddy.*

Mother: *And did he have buttons?*

Tia: *Yeah.*

Mother: *What were his buttons made of?*

Tia: *Lollies (candy).*

Mother: *Yeah. And who came to your birthday?*

Tia: *Lollies.*

Mother: *Who came?*

Tia: *[unintelligible two words].*

Mother: *Who came?*

Tia: *Uh.*

Mother: *Who came to give you presents? Tama and Tainui?*

Tia: *Tama and Tainui.*

Mother: *Who else came?*

Tia: *Linda and Mark.*

Mother: *Linda and Mark.*

Tia: *Elizabeth.*

Mother: *Elizabeth.*

Tia: *and Grandma.*

Mother: *Grandma and Grandad.*

Tia: *Grandma and Grandad.*

Notice how almost all of Tia's mother's speech consists of open-ended elaborative questions, confirmations, and extensions of Tia's speech. The few times she does ask a repeated question, such as "Who came?," she meets with little success until she adds more information, "Who came to give you presents? Tama and Tainui?," after which Tia responds with four more attendees. *It's very important that you avoid repeating the same question without variation again and again, even if the question is open-ended.* This strategy does NOT lead to better storytelling. In fact, it can quickly turn your child off from the conversation altogether if she perceives she hasn't given you the "right" answer to your question. Instead it's better to provide more detail in your next open-ended question or simply to supply some information yourself in a statement or closed-ended question, as Tia's mother did to great success.

By ages 2-1/2 to 3, your child will no doubt start taking the conversation in directions that you may not have intended to go. In the following example, 2-1/2 year old Charlie and his mother have slightly different aspects they want to discuss about their recent visit to a new mall with Charlie's dad and sister Jessica.

Mother: *Do you remember when me and Dad and Jess and you went to the new Meridian mall?*

Charlie: *Mm.*

Mother: *And who did we see there?*

Charlie: *Um Dandad.*

Mother: *Grandad? No, Grandad wasn't with us that time. Who was there?*

Charlie: *Diane.*

Mother: *Diane? Yeah. We saw Diane and Gail and who else was there? Who were we laughing at?*

Charlie: *Um Marcus.*

Mother: *Who? Marcus, yeah, but who was there, someone that we didn't know that we'd never seen before.*

Charlie: *Um Gail.*

Mother: *A big ___?*

Charlie: *Big tall man.*

Mother: *A big tall man on stilts. And what was he doing?*

Charlie: *Ummm.*

Mother: *Do you remember? (laughs) What was he doing? Was he making us laugh?*

Charlie: *Mm.*

Mother: *What did he look like? Did he did he have something on his face?*

Charlie: *Mm.*

Mother: *What did he have?*

Charlie: *Um a yoyo.*

Mother: *Did he have a yoyo?*

Charlie: *Yes.*

Mother: *Yes, he did too. And did we have an ice cream or something?*

Charlie: *Yup.*

Mother: *Did we? And what was your ice cream like?*

Charlie:	*A tall man.*
Mother:	*A what?*
Charlie:	*Tall man.*
Mother:	*A big tall man like a clown, wasn't it?*
Charlie:	*Mm.*
Mother:	*And what else do you remember?*
Charlie:	*A clown.*
Mother:	*A clown, yeah.*
Charlie:	*Um and Marcus.*
Mother:	*And Marcus. Who's Marcus?*
Charlie:	*Marcus Brown.*
Mother:	*He's a baby, isn't he?*
Charlie:	*He a baby.*

Notice how Charlie's mother validates his contributions (although she corrects factual errors—*Grandad wasn't with us that time*). Instead of going into more detail to discuss ice cream, a topic she introduced, she returns to elaborate on Charlie's preferred topics—the "tall man"*(a big tall man like a clown)* and "Marcus" *(he's a baby, isn't he?)*. It's important at all ages in these conversations of shared experiences to follow in on what your *child* wants to discuss.

At this age, you're telling most of the story of the personal experience for your toddler, but at the same time you are encouraging your toddler to supply more of the story than he would on his own without support. So ask questions you're pretty sure your toddler can answer, bearing in mind the missing pieces to most toddlers' stories: the characters, details of what happened, where, and how everyone felt. Don't focus too much yet about asking "when" the event happened. Toddlers don't have a strong enough sense of time to understand this question. I will discuss "when" questions in the next chapter for preschoolers.

Keep your questions short but packed with new bits of information about the event. Try to use a few words that you think might be slightly beyond your child's current vocabulary, including words for desires and emotions. If there's only one new word in a sentence, then your child will be able to figure it out from the rest of the sentence without you having to stop and define it.

Who went with us to the Boston aquarium?
What happened after we saw the turtles?
Where was the rugby game?
Who was scared of the bear mascot?

Notice how these main elements for sharing stories of everyday experiences—asking open-ended elaborative questions, pausing, confirming and praising, following in and extending—are identical to the basic elements for book-sharing. The only difference is that now you are helping your child elaborate on your family's past experiences instead of on a book character's experiences.

When my colleagues and I coached mothers in this technique of **Rich Reminiscing*** (see Table 1.1), it helped all the children to remember and report more about their personal experiences later.[40] Although we haven't yet tested this technique with fathers and toddlers, there's no reason why it wouldn't work equally as well (see Chapter 6).

How often should you use Rich Reminiscing with your toddler? I suggest that you start out having one or two short conversations about the past each day. Because we know from the diary studies that toddlers are naturally bringing up the past as often as several times a day, you should have plenty of opportunities to seize on this talk about the past and expand it into a true conversation. The most successful conversations will follow in on your child's reference to the past. That way you know you are talking about a topic your child wants to discuss.

For instance, when Jasmine's mother reported in our diary study that Jasmine said "Pegs not lollies," when she saw a pink clothespeg, she could have praised Jasmine's utterance, expanded on it, and then posed an open-ended question in response:

Mother: *You're right,* [confirm] *I told you they were clothespegs, not lollies.* [extend] *You tried to put a clothespeg in your mouth when we were hanging out the washing.* [extend] *What color was the clothespeg?* [open-ended elaborative question]

Jasmine: *Pink.*

> Mother: *Yes,* [confirm] *it was a pink clothespeg.* [extend] *What kind of lolly did you think it was?* [open-ended elaborative question]

However, if your child doesn't bring up the past on his or her own, you can initiate the conversation yourself. It's still best if you can follow in on your child's current focus and use that focus as a springboard to a related past event. For instance, if you're taking a walk together and your child points at a bird in a tree, you can start a conversation about the past by responding:

> Parent: *Yes, it's a bird up there. It's singing, isn't it?* (pause) *What kind of bird did we see at the zoo last week?*
> Child: *Ummmm*
> Parent: *What was the name of the bird that squawked at us really loud?*

Again, keep it short at this age, and talk about events that happened fairly recently, or at most 6 months to 1 year in the past if the event was really important to your child. That's about the extent of your child's ability to talk about past events at this age.[41] You can build up to longer conversations about more distant events whenever your child shows interest in continuing. For toddlers, it's best to have these short conversations in the course of other activities—while playing, taking a walk, giving your toddler a bath. Sometimes your child will initiate past event talk while riding in the car, usually when cued by something he sees, as when Ben said, "Choo-choo," or at a familiar place such as a park. Although it's best to have these conversations when you can share eye contact with your child, the car is a natural place for storytelling because you and your child may see cues for past events along the way, and because there's not much else to do in the car but to talk (assuming you are not using DVD players, iPhones, and other electronic devices in the car with your toddler—see warning above).

In encouraging parents to tell stories of the past with their toddlers, I agree with Doctorow's assertion at the beginning of this chapter that "anyone at any age is able to tell the story of his or her life with authority" but would add "with a little help from someone *in* authority."

Table 1.1 Tips for Sharing Stories with Toddlers		
What to Do	**How**	**Why it Helps**
1. *Share books with your toddler using Rich Reading techniques*	Reading with toddlers works best when it is a highly interactive conversation about the pictures in the book. Use open-ended questions (*What's that? What's happening here? What is the boy doing?*) to get your toddler started talking, and then praise and extend his responses (*That's right. It's a bicycle. Where is he going?*), following up with a new question cycle. If your child can't answer a question, supply the answer yourself—don't repeat your question.	Expands vocabulary learning, knowledge about the wider world, emotion understand-ing, comfort.
2. *Share past experiences with your toddler using Rich Reminiscing techniques*	Toddlers are ready to have these conversations when they start referring to recent past events on their own. Use Rich Reminiscing by following in on these events and then praising, extending, and asking a new open-ended question. Through your open-ended questions (*What did we see at the Botanic Gardens last weekend?*) and responses (*You're right, it was a choo-choo. What noise did the choo-choo make?*), try to create as complete a story as possible in terms of the what, who, and where, always gearing the length of the story to your child's attention span. A short, packed conversation is better at this age than a	Promotes vocabulary learning, memory, bonding over shared experiences.

(*continued*)

Table 1.1 Tips for Sharing Stories with Toddlers (*Continued*)		
What to Do	**How**	**Why it Helps**
	lengthy one in which you are continually repeating questions and switching topics in an effort to get your toddler to attend.	
3. *Use screentime thoughtfully*	If you do allow screentime for your older toddler, make sure it is limited to one or two carefully chosen programs a day. Watch the shows with your child and interact during the viewing. Use cycles of open-ended questions, praise, and extensions similar to your book-reading and past event conversation sessions. Encourage others in the household not to have the TV on in the background when young children are in the room. Media expert and parent Rachel Barr recommends that you invest in a DVR to record the programs you want to watch, virtually eliminating background TV.	Some vocabulary learning (but only for older toddlers over age 2).
4. *Parent-tested tip for conversation starters*	Keep a diary of the past events your toddler brings up, even for a day, or better yet for a week. It's fun! And it gives you great insight into your toddler's thoughts and passions, which in turn will help you figure out what your toddler *really* wants to talk about, even if it is a mundane topic from your perspective.	Helps you understand your child's perspective, thinking, and language skills.

Table 1.2 Developmental Snapshot of a Toddler[42]		
Domain	**What Happens and When**	**Why It Matters for Story Sharing**
Language Development	*First words* (8–18 months), *sentences* (18–30 months), *references to the past* (18–24 months), and words for *desires, emotions, thoughts* (22–30 months)	Children who understand and use language more proficiently can participate more fully in past event conversations and in book-sharing.
Cognitive Development	Beginning of *representational thought* about an absent object or action (6–18 months), *mental problem-solving* (10–24 months), and *sustained attention* to a goal (12-36 months)	A basic understanding of cause and effect, and the ability to hold in mind an image of an absent object or event, are prerequisites to understanding stories and participating in conversations about the past.
Self-Concept Development	*Self-awareness*: Children recognize their own image in a mirror (15–24 months) and start to use *self pronouns* (I, me, my, mine, myself) and own name (14–30 months)	Children with a stronger self-concept may have more solid representations of past events, and may more easily connect talk about a past event as something that happened to them.

(continued)

Table 1.2 Developmental Snapshot of a Toddler (*Continued*)		
Domain	**What Happens and When**	**Why It Matters for Story Sharing**
Social and Emotional Development	*Joint* or *shared attention* (7–12 months)	Children who can engage in shared attention are able to communicate with others about the world. Shared attention with an adult also promotes language learning.
	Attachment to one or more caregivers (6–24 months)	Children who are securely attached to a parent have more harmonious and elaborated conversations and book-sharing experiences.
Physical Development	*Activity levels*: Walking, then jumping, then running (9–36 months)	Because toddlers are very active, all forms of story sharing must be highly interactive.
	Brain development: A time of making new connections (synapses) between neurons. A large burst in frontal lobe activity occurs between 18 and 24 months, when toddlers start to use language to govern their behavior.	Brain development supports changes in toddlers' language and thought. In turn, toddlers' experiences with the world (including story sharing) help them to create new neural connections.

2

Sharing Stories with Your Preschooler

Ages 3–5

What kind of people we become depends crucially on the stories we are nurtured on.

~ *Chinweizu, Nigeria*

Compared to toddlers, preschoolers' worlds have widened dramatically to include school experiences, a larger circle of friends, and more exciting outings—by adult standards—to museums, amusement parks, and festivals. This change does not happen all at once. As my favorite parenting writer, Penelope Leach,[1] says about the transition from toddler to young child, "She becomes a child when she ceases to be a wayward, confusing, unpredictable and often balky person-in-the making, and becomes someone who is comparatively co-operative, eager-and-easy-to-please at least 60 per cent of the time." Preschoolers are more independent in all ways—toileting, dressing, feeding, playing. Their language is also flourishing. Preschoolers know literally thousands of words. They use these words in creative ways to voice their thoughts and memories, their dreams and imaginings, and their many strong feelings (see Table 2.2, "Developmental Snapshot of a Preschooler" at the end of this chapter). And it is for their language, thinking, play, and emotions that stories matter the most for preschoolers. If you successfully introduced your toddler to stories as a fun and engaging way to learn to talk, then as a preschooler, your child will be drawn to stories like a magnet (see Box 2.1). He will use stories as a way to understand and express his thoughts and feelings, to tell others about his experiences, and to pretend that everyday life is anything but routine. Preschoolers live, breathe, talk, and dream stories.

Box 2.1 Preschoolers: The Play's the Thing

If you ever want a preschooler to do something, the best way is to simply slip into a story. Want your preschooler to eat his snack? Pretend that you are a flight attendant on an airplane, your child is an unruly passenger, and offer him a choice of fruit or crackers. Want your preschooler to get into her car seat (now) so that you can buckle her up and get to the grocery store before picking up your older child at school? Tell her she is an astronaut and that you are buckling her into the spaceship for a trip to the moon. Things could get pretty interesting in the grocery store when she insists on floating through the aisles in zero gravity, but that's all part of the fun. And I guarantee that your shopping trip will be much less stressful.

I believe that preschoolers need stories almost as much as they need proper nutrition and physical activity. They turn to stories and thrive on them as a plant to sunlight. Stories help preschoolers make sense of and master their world.

What kind of stories do preschoolers need the most? The more diverse their story experiences, the better. They need stories of far-away lands, both real and imagined. They need stories of other children who are both similar to and different from them. They need stories of creatures of all shapes, sizes, and forms. They need stories of their own lives, from both recent and distant times. They are even starting to want to hear stories of *your* life.

In stories, children are being exposed to richer language than they typically hear in everyday conversation. They are learning new vocabulary and advanced language structures through stories.[2] Take the classic storybook for preschoolers, *Corduroy*, which begins[3]:

> *Corduroy is a bear who once lived in the toy department of a*
> *big store. Day after day he waited with all the other animals*
> *and dolls for somebody to come along and take him home.*

In this short excerpt, children are hearing new vocabulary, such as "department," accompanied by regular and irregular verbs in different forms and tenses (*lived, take, to come*). They are learning adjective clauses introduced by relative pronouns (*who once lived in the toy department of a big store*). They are introduced to literary phrases such as "Day after day," as well as temporal markers (*once*). And that's just in the first two sentences of a 32-page book.

Preschoolers are also learning classic story structure through books. Again using *Corduroy* as an example (which, as you might have guessed, is a personal childhood favorite that I later shared with my boys), children are first introduced to Corduroy as the main character. They learn the setting for the story in that first sentence too, which is the toy department of a big department store. Almost immediately they discover the problem that Corduroy faces, which is that *no one ever seemed to want a small bear in green overalls*. Soon after the problem is introduced, the reader meets other important characters, such as Lisa and her mother, who will prove to be instrumental in resolving the problem. But along the way, other exciting events occur, such as when Corduroy loses a button and decides to search for it that night when the shoppers have left. Adventures on escalators and with mattresses, floor lamps, and a security guard ensue. A happy ending follows in which Lisa purchases Corduroy with her own money, takes him home, sews on his missing button, and becomes his friend. This storyline of setting—problem—complicating actions—high point—resolution is a classic structure that forms the basic template for virtually all of Western literature.

Children are also busily learning story structure from the stories of their own lives. Take the event of a preschooler's injury on the playground. When a parent retells the story later to the child's grandparent, all of the elements of the classic storyline will be present: the main character (the child), the setting (the preschool playground), the problem (another child carelessly pushed him on the slide), the high point/low point (he went crashing to the ground and broke his arm), and the resolution (the teacher rushed him to the hospital, where his arm was put into a cast, and soon after he was reunited with his parents and got chocolate ice cream on the way home).

As preschoolers are learning about their own world, they are also learning about the wider world beyond their own experience. Stories offer them a way of grasping this wider world, including an understanding of other people's thoughts and emotions. During the preschool years, children's thinking, like their language, is growing in leaps and bounds (see "Developmental Snapshot"). Even toddlers can understand that other people have thoughts and feelings. But from around age 4, preschoolers can also appreciate that others' thoughts and feelings may be different from, and even in direct conflict with, their own. This ability to understand their own and other people's thoughts, beliefs, and emotions is called **theory of mind***, because children are starting to develop ideas, or theories, about what other people are thinking and feeling.[4]

One vital way that preschool children learn about others' thoughts, beliefs, and emotions is through stories, both stories about the lives of characters in books and stories about their own lives. For instance, mothers who use more words about emotions and about cognitive states such as "think," "know," and "believe" when reading storybooks have preschoolers with more advanced theory of mind 1 year later.[5] And in my study with colleague Mele Taumoepeau, we found that the same Rich Reminiscing techniques we taught mothers of toddlers also helped their children to develop an advanced theory of mind by the time they were preschoolers, especially for those children who had started out the study with lower language levels.[6] With preschoolers, all kinds of talk that parents can offer about mental states—the child's and other people's, about thoughts and emotions, from books and experiences—are helpful in promoting children's theory of mind.

All of these advances in children's internal life play an important role in their ability to get along with others (see "Developmental Snapshot"). With friends, preschoolers become capable of true interactive play that can get extremely complicated, with a storyline sometimes extending over days.[7] As you might expect, children with a strong theory of mind are better at negotiating play roles with others and planning out a fictional story. Preschool children may also have an imaginary or pretend friend, or even a cadre of pretend friends, on which to practice their storytelling when alone. Pretend play, in turn, is linked to advances in children's language and narrative development. My colleague Gabriel Trionfi and I discovered that preschool children with a pretend friend had more advanced storytelling skills, especially when it came to including references to time, cause and effect, and character information in their stories.[8] Tia was one of the 48% of the children in our study who had a pretend friend at some point during early childhood. In fact, Tia had an abundance of pretend friends, the most loyal of whom was Marka, who "sat" by Tia in an empty spot at the table for dinner each night. Children who tell stories with and/or about a pretend friend may be getting extra practice in their storytelling skills.

THE STORIES PRESCHOOLERS UNDERSTAND AND TELL: FROM BOOKS AND FROM PERSONAL EXPERIENCES

Stories from Books

In parallel to these broader developmental changes, preschoolers' story worlds have also widened and deepened. They can listen to a complex storyline from a book or on a CD and (mostly) sit still (see "Developmental Snapshot"). They can watch a full-length children's movie and (again, mostly) understand it. They enjoy fairy tales and folktales in addition to more realistic fare. When hearing stories from books, however, many preschoolers are still at the level of processing and remembering basic story events; they do not yet fully understand characters' intentions and motivations, nor do they always understand cause and effect in the storyline.

For instance, after we read to the children in our study the classic storybook *A Snowy Day* by Ezra Jack Keats when they were just over 4 years old, we asked them a series of factual and inferential questions about the book. Most of the children could remember the name of the main character of the story (*Peter*) and some of the events from the story (*What did Peter use to make another track in the snow? A stick. What did Peter bring inside? A snowball*). When we asked them inferential questions, such as, "Why didn't Peter join the big boys?" however, only a few of the 4-year-olds could give us an answer. In keeping with her advanced language development and story understanding, Tia replied, "Cause he was too little. Cause he's two."

Preschoolers' prodigious language progress is particularly evident in their storytelling. From the two-word stories they told as toddlers, they now burst forth with full-blown tales in complete sentences, filled with emotion, description, action, and even adventure. By the preschool period, children are liberally sprinkling their stories with words for time, cause, and effect, but they are not yet using those words in conventional ways (see "Developmental Snapshot"). They are referring to their own and others' mental states in their stories, but that doesn't mean that they fully understand mental states, either their own or others'. These stories are no longer limited to personal experiences, although I argue that their personal narratives remain their greatest storytelling masterpieces. Preschool children can now also tell a skeleton outline of a story they've heard in a book or seen in a movie (see Box 2.2).

Box 2.2 The Stories They See: Preschoolers and Screentime

As I mentioned in Chapter 1, the American Academy of Pediatrics recommends no more than 1 to 2 hours per day of quality screentime for preschoolers.[9] That's in total, so it includes TV shows, DVDs, computer time, videogame systems, iPhones, iPads, and yes—even educational electronics such as LeapFrog and LeapPad. The reason to be cautious is that scientists don't fully understand the developing brain, much less the effects of modern technology on the developing brain. The latest evidence all points to a need to err on the safe side. Even after carefully controlling for alternative explanations such as the effects of poverty and levels of parental education, children who watch more TV and videos in early childhood, especially when the programming is for entertainment value only, have lower academic achievement, more behavior problems, and

(continued)

Box 2.2 (*Continued*)

are more likely to be overweight or obese in adolescence and young adulthood. However, those preschoolers who watch more educational TV, such as *Sesame Street*, have higher math and reading achievement later on, so the answer is not simply to ban children from all forms of screentime.

I am not a purist about screentime. Electronic and digital media are part of our culture. Screentime *can* be educational, enlightening, and emotionally satisfying when used appropriately. Preschoolers have gone beyond the "video deficit" that I discussed in Chapter 1 for toddlers. They can now learn readily from screens, not just new words but also literacy skills, facts, causal connections, and narrative skills from high-quality children's programming such as *Sesame Street*, *Between the Lions*, *Blue's Clues*, *Clifford*, *Pinky Dinky Doo*, *Dora the Explorer*, and *Arthur*. For instance, in one well-designed study, researchers compared preschool children's acquisition of story skills from watching three different types of TV programs: traditional narrative programming (*Clifford*), nontraditional narrative programming (*Pinky Dinky Doo*, which contains a story within a story and later discussion), or nonnarrative programming (*Zoboomafoo*).[10] The children assigned to watch these different forms of TV were compared to a control group of children who did not watch any additional programming during the preschool day. The children who watched the narrative programming (*Clifford* or *Pinky Dinky Doo*) had higher story knowledge and storytelling skills 40 days later compared to children who had watched nonnarrative programs (*Zoboomafoo*) or no extra programs. The children in this study were from low-income families, though, so it is not clear whether children from middle-class homes, who are probably already getting many stories from books, would benefit as much from watching stories on video.

Other shows have not yet been tested for their educational benefits, but are promising candidates, as well as favorites of children of this age: *Curious George*, *Madeline*, *Eloise*, *Charlie and Lola*, and *Super Why*. Because these shows are adapted from books or retell favorite books, and all contain a narrative structure, I look forward to hearing the results of rigorous studies

(*continued*)

Box 2.2 (*Continued*)

on whether or not they benefit children's language, narrative, and early reading development.

Children develop emotional attachments to movies and movie characters just as they do to characters in books.[11] The very eye-catching visuals that hold a child's attention to a video we don't want them to watch are also responsible for allowing a child to pay attention to a full 90-minute story. Imagine what would happen if you tried to read a chapter book of *Finding Nemo*, without pictures, to your 3-year-old for 90 minutes straight. The session might last for 10 minutes on a good day. Then compare their attention span for hearing a story to watching a video of a story. Much to your dismay, perhaps, preschoolers can raptly attend to a full-length movie—often the same one over and over again. Just as it is good to indulge children in their requests to hear the same books over and over, it is also beneficial for children to watch the same shows and movies again—and again.[12]

Children find solace in stories via videos in the preschool years, well before they can read a full-length story to themselves and find solace independently from books. They are still dependent on adults to provide stories in all other forms available to them at this age—whether it is through reading or storytelling. Thus, movies provide preschool children with a full-blown story over which they have a greater degree of control and autonomy than the stories they hear from books. All but the most purist parents I know allow their preschoolers to pop in a Disney DVD on a near-daily basis. For Ben, it was the Disney video of *Aladdin*. For Dylan, it was *Hercules*. I think I must have watched parts of both videos with my kids at least 50 times. At age 9, Dylan still put on *Hercules* about once a year for nostalgia, usually when he was sick and home from school.

So what is it that young children are getting from watching movies, and how can we help maximize those benefits, while minimizing the possible detrimental effects of screentime? First, children are being exposed to a much more complex story form than they can get from a book or from storytelling at this age. The overall structure of the story is similar across media. All share a beginning that orients the listener to time and place

(continued)

Box 2.2 (*Continued*)

and to the main characters. All classic story forms introduce a problem to be solved. Think of the basic story structure of *Corduroy*. It is very similar to that of *Finding Nemo*, although of course *Finding Nemo* is much longer and more involved than *Corduroy*. Both contain themes of separation, loss, trust, and friendship. The main difference between the plot of a movie like *Finding Nemo* and that of a book like *Corduroy* is that the storyline and the characters can be developed in much more detail in a movie. The typical picture book has approximately 40 sentences and around 20 scenes, whereas a movie contains thousands of sentences and hundreds of scenes.

Yet no one has tested the linguistic, cognitive, and emotional benefits of movies for young children, and research on the narrative benefits of stories received in movie versus picture book format is nonexistent.[13] In our anxiety about the possible negative effects of screentime for children, we have failed to explore some of its potential benefits. Can children more readily identify with a character in a movie as opposed to a book, and through this identification, learn to understand others' thoughts and feelings? Do movies about a separated family help a preschool child to cope better with his parents' own separation than reading a book about the topic or talking about his experiences? Can children learn about causes and consequences of emotions and events more effectively by watching them in movie format, because they're happening closer to real-time? These are unanswered questions. It is my hope that researchers will start to look at the positives as well as the negatives of screentime in comparison to other methods of story delivery.

What we do know is how to ensure that your child benefits from screentime when he or she does watch it. Because preschool children haven't yet mastered complete story forms, they will learn more from watching a TV program or movie with you than without you. If you insert questions and comments at key points of the narrative, similar to the tips I give below about sharing stories from books and personal experiences with your child, they will benefit even more.[14]

Truly original stories, however, are still incredibly difficult for pre-schoolers. Their made-up stories are most often told in action as an integrated part of their play, or they are slightly scrambled variations on stories from TV, movies, or books. Preschoolers love to engage in role-play with others, either with friends or with indulgent siblings and adults. I spent long hours of pretending to be a dog called Sally, Spot's mum from the *Spot* books, with my older son Benjamin. Later, with Dylan, I was once again a dog (nameless this time around, and a role reversal as a puppy) while he was the somewhat bossy owner. Older brother Benjamin at age 7 also endured countless hours as 3-year-old Dylan's puppy. (Note that I finally wised up and got my boys a real puppy when they were 14 and 10.) My sister-in-law Betty, who has beautiful long blonde hair, patiently lived through endless Cinderella enactments with her two boys, and my sister Jennifer was a plucky Princess Leia to her son Sam's Luke Skywalker. With friends their own age who may be less willing to constantly play the supporting actor/actress/animal, preschoolers construct rambling and lengthy unscripted plays on real life—school, family, shopping, church—and fantasy themes: superheroes, monsters, Star Wars, Indiana Jones, Pokemon, Snow White, Cinderella, The Little Mermaid, and Madeline.

Stories from Personal Experiences

As charming as preschool children's stories during play are, their most coherent and fully formed stories at this age are still those that they tell from personal experiences. They are now capable of telling a story about something that happened to them in a way that a naive listener can mostly understand. In the following example, 3-1/2-year-old Jake tells a researcher about a parade he saw with his mother. I have taken out the researcher's prompts so that you can see the shape of the entire story.

> Researcher: *Do you know what else your mum told me about? She said you went to Forbury Park. Could you tell me about that?*
> Jake: *We saw um, a big um dragon going round with people on it and it. But I didn't go on it. Because there was too many people on it. Only was only have to be lots of people on because there's lots of seats. Umm. We saw a plane and*

sometime when we go back there um and the people um the plane will um shoot people out of the plane. We um um we saw um um horses going past. Lots and lots and lots and lots and lots. Mmm. And one kicked so mum taked me off the gate. Cause one kicked. And it nearly got me. Um, and the fire brades (brigades) go first and then some big big horses come past. And them all going brrmm brrmm brrmm brrmm brrmm. We didn't go on thing that goes way up high cause it's real scary. When I'm a bit older.

Note that Jake is now including critical details about the event that help make it understandable to the listener: what happened, even a bit of where and when (see "Developmental Snapshot").[15] These developments are important because they enable your preschooler to tell you stories about experiences that you didn't share with her, such as at preschool or at friends' or grandparents' houses. In fact, preschoolers actually provide longer and more detailed stories when parents ask them about these unshared experiences compared to shared experiences.[16] Perhaps because preschoolers are now more aware of what other people know and do not know, they understand that they need to do more of the work of storytelling when parents did not share the experience with them.

But what is especially striking about this short story is that Jake devotes a large proportion of the story focusing not on what happened but on what *might* have happened (*it nearly got me*), what *could* happen in the future (*when I'm a bit older*), and how what did happen made him *feel* (*it's real scary*). This is the interesting stuff of stories. These are the seeds of drawing meaning from life's experiences. Preschool children are by no means capable of insight into life's experiences, but these early stories show that they are on the path to insight.

The understanding that others may have thoughts and feelings different from their own is also reflected in children's narratives in the later preschool period, when they begin to negotiate points of disagreement with parents and to stand up for what they believe is the true state of affairs. Typically we do not see these negotiations or challenges from children until they are 4, although they have been referring to thoughts and feelings in their stories from age 2. When Rebecca in our study was 4 years old, she and her mother had an extended negotiation about what happened when they went to the circus.

Mother: *What else do you remember about the circus?*

Rebecca: *Um, we had candy floss (cotton candy).*

Mother: *Oh yes, we did, didn't we?*

Rebecca: *Yes. And Zinnia's friend—*

Mother: *(interrupts) No, actually, no we didn't have candy floss.*

Child: *Yes.*

Mother: *Not there, that was when we went to the gypsy fair. That was next door to the circus. We had something, we did have something else to eat, though, before we went to the circus. What did Zinnia buy for us? She had money to buy…?*

Rebecca: *Popcorn.*

Mother: *That's right. But the candy floss we had another day but it was right beside the circus, wasn't it? But it wasn't on the day that we went to the circus.*

Rebecca: *Yes, it was.*

Mother: *Not the candy floss, dear. No.*

Rebecca: *Yes, but they threw it over. Off the edge.*

Mother: *Ohhh, so they did.*

Rebecca: *Yeah.*

Mother: *How did we get the candy floss? You, you're absolutely right. Good girl.*

Rebecca: *'Cause they threw it over the fence.*

Mother: *That's right. (Rebecca laughs with delight) I went to hand it back to one of the performers.*

These negotiations about what happened at an event appear to be particularly effective for children's higher-level understanding of how memory works and for their understanding that other people can have different perspectives. In Rebecca's case, she learned that even parents have memory failures at times! Her mother's acceptance of Rebecca's version of the experience no doubt also helped Rebecca feel that her perspective on an event is listened to and valued.

HOW TO SHARE STORIES THAT MATTER WITH YOUR PRESCHOOLER

Stories from Books

All of the Rich Reading techniques that you learned in the last chapter—asking open-ended questions, pausing, praising, and extending children's responses—still work well with preschoolers when you are sharing picture books (see Table 2.1 for tips). Older preschoolers, however, are more advanced in their language, their thinking, their emotional understanding, and their attention spans. You can ramp up Rich Reading for preschoolers by asking more difficult questions about *what's happening, why,* and *how* everyone is feeling. Expand your book-reading strategies by asking more *challenging open-ended questions* to encourage your child to tell even more of the story, to make *predictions* about what's going to happen next, or to *infer why* a character did what she did. You can also help your preschooler *link* the story events to events in their own lives.

The best ways to ask these more challenging questions depend on your preschooler. If your child is still having difficulty attending when you read the story, then you need to be more interactive. Ask questions like "What's happening on this page?" to get your preschooler engaged in the book and talking. Whatever your preschooler's response, you'll need to follow up with the same cycle of *praise* and *extension* that you used when she was a toddler, followed by a new question cycle.

If your preschooler is absorbed in the storyline, you can save most of your questions until the end so as not to interrupt the narrative. In one study that colleague Adell Cox and I conducted with preschool children in New Zealand, a researcher read 2–3 picture books a week individually with 4-year-olds who varied in their language skill.[17] We read all the preschoolers the same set of books over a 6-week period, but we varied our style of book reading. With some children, we used a style similar to the version of Rich Reading that works with toddlers, in which we asked a question or provided a statement about the pictures at the end of each spread of pages. *What's that called? That animal is a hedgehog.* With other children, we used a more demanding style in which we didn't interrupt the story, but saved our questions and comments for before and after the reading. The questions in this style were more challenging, requesting that children predict what's going to happen or infer cause and effect. *What do you think Peter will do now with the chair? Why do you think Peter didn't want his chair painted pink?* Notice that the two styles were equally interactive, but the second style was more challenging and did not interrupt the storyline.

The two styles had different effects depending on the initial language levels and age of the children. For younger 4-year-olds with smaller vocabularies, the simpler, more interrupting style helped them grow their vocabularies. But for the older children with larger vocabularies, the more demanding and less interrupting style was most effective for increasing their vocabularies over the 6-week period. Older children are better able to gain new words from context—just by hearing the words in the text and later discussing key concepts—than younger children with smaller vocabularies, who may still need help labeling the pictures. This interpretation fits with other research showing that children with larger spoken vocabularies find it easier to acquire new vocabulary from print once they start reading compared to children with smaller spoken vocabularies.[18] If children don't know the meaning of a high proportion of the words they see in print once they start reading, it's harder for them to learn the meaning of new words simply from seeing them in a sentence. This effect is very much akin to adults' experiences of reading unfamiliar technical material. If we know only one noun in a sentence, it's very difficult for us to figure out the meaning, unambiguously, of the remaining words. But if we are familiar with all of the words but one, it's much easier to assign a fairly accurate guess about the meaning of that one word, even if no one has formally defined it for us.

The message is that if your preschooler is older or more advanced in her language, then you can ask fewer questions *during* the reading, as long as you still have a discussion at the end of the book about the story. You can also vary your book sharing style when rereading a favorite book, sometimes reading with fewer interruptions to allow your child to hear the rhythms and sounds of the language, and at other times engaging in more discussion and interaction.

Your preschooler can now learn new words about emotions and other mental states from books too. The most effective way to help a preschooler's theory of mind from storybooks is to explain or clarify why the characters act or feel a certain way.[19] In one study, when mothers clarified book characters' mental states, their preschoolers advanced faster in their theory of mind. *He puts all the makeup back so Mummy doesn't <u>know</u> what they've been up to.* And *He's getting quite <u>angry</u> 'cos dogs <u>don't</u> <u>like</u> cats.*

Now that your preschooler is starting to hold two or more things in mind at the same time, she can also understand and benefit from *linking* between the story world and her own world. An effective Rich Reading method with older preschoolers (4- to 5-year-olds) includes these connections between the book and the real world.[20] Drawing a connection between the book world and your child's world helps him to generalize beyond the book. These connections may be obvious to you, but they're not always obvious to your preschooler. If you can, frame the link in the form of an open-ended question: *<u>Who</u> has a blue car like that one in the picture?* Or simply point out a connection with a statement, *That boy walks to his preschool, just like you do.* By all means, if your child is the one who spontaneously brings up the connection, praise her response and expand on it, just as you would if she labeled a picture.

Child: *I've got a blue car like that one. [linking]*
Parent: *Yes, [praise] you've got a blue car with white racing stripes just like that one. [extend]*

In the interest of helping your child process the storyline, though, you will probably want to keep these conversations about connections brief, lest they take you too far off track from discussing the story.

Remain sensitive to your child's understanding of the book and you will be able to vary your book-reading style in a way that produces maximum benefits for your child. If you think that most of the vocabulary in the text is new to your child, or if his attention is waning, adopt a more interactive style, similar to your reading style when he was a toddler. If you're pretty sure most of the words and concepts are familiar to your child, and she seems absorbed in hearing the story, wait until the end of the book to ask a few key questions to extend her understanding. With older and more advanced preschoolers, you can also discuss their emotional reactions to the story afterward: *Did you like that story?* (pause and discuss) *Why did you like it?* (pause and discuss) *I liked the part at the end when Peter painted the chair pink for his baby sister. I think that means he realized how grown up he was. How do you think he felt about his sister at the end?* These evaluative, interpretive discussions are a very important part of the culture of school that they will soon experience. In the classroom, it will not be enough to say that they liked or didn't like a book—they will be expected to say *why* and to support their evaluation with specific details from the story.[21]

Expand your child's book-reading diet as well as the style in which you read to him. Preschool children are ready for a whole range of books beyond the simple picture books they enjoyed as toddlers. They are ready for much more complex storylines, realistic fiction as well as fantasies, fairy tales, and fables—the more diverse the better in terms of their narrative development. Don't forget about the tried and true children's classics. You may be drawn to the latest Caldecott winner, but your child may prefer the battered old copy of *The Three Billy Goats Gruff* that you got in a cereal box. In our study with New Zealand preschoolers, children's hands-down favorite books were *The Gingerbread Man* and *The Three Billy Goats Gruff*, despite our efforts to include the very latest in high-quality children's picture books. Children's fascination with the age-old themes of bullying, violence, betrayal, and "might doesn't make right" is revealing.[22] I have not yet met a child who asked repeatedly to hear a politically correct book like *The Paperbag Princess*. *Respect* your child's choice of book. It's okay to indulge her in her favorites, just as it's okay to round out those favorites with a wider range of options.

If your child prefers nonfiction, indulge him in his passion, whether it is dinosaurs, trucks, trains, or rocks. Preschool boys are six times as likely as preschool girls to have an intense, sustained interest in a single conceptual domain.[23] Children can still learn vocabulary, print, and book concepts from nonfiction books even if they're not being exposed to a storyline. And there are now some excellent nonfiction books available for preschoolers. In one study I did with colleague Sarah-Jane Robertson, parents reported that their children enjoyed a nonfiction book (*What Is a Fish?*) more than the fictional storybook that we provided (*Hemi's Pet*). In this study, mothers also reported enjoying fiction more in their own leisure reading, whereas fathers reported enjoying nonfiction more.[24] Whatever your own preference, be sensitive to your child's interests—your child may not share your preference. Perhaps some children prefer to get their stories from another medium altogether, such as watching movies or talking about their own experiences. Don't force-feed your child with fiction that he would prefer not to hear.

Stories from Personal Experiences

Hans Christian Anderson said, "Life itself is the most wonderful fairy tale of all." The stories you create with your preschoolers about their everyday personal experiences are the foundation for their personal history—the story of their lives. These stories of everyday events are just as important for your child's development as the stories that you share with your child from books. Just as you widen preschoolers' book diet beyond simple picture books, you can also broaden the types of past experiences you discuss with them: Shared experiences still dominate, but you can also start asking them about experiences you didn't share with them, as well as discussing events from their early childhood that they cannot personally remember.

Talking about Shared Experiences with Preschoolers

Because preschoolers are now capable of telling a short account of an event on their own, your task is to help them flesh out the story, and especially to include the critical elements that they typically neglect at this age. When using Rich Reminiscing with preschoolers, ask more *where* and *when* questions, and a few well-placed *why*s when constructing together a story of a shared experience, along with your well-practiced *what* and *who* questions (see Table 2.1 for tips). Try to weave the *where* and *when* questions in naturally near the beginning of the story to make it more coherent. The best stories quickly orient the listener to the *setting*, or the *who*, *where*, and *when* of an event.[25] Because you know what happened at a shared event, you can more effectively help your child to coconstruct the story.

At the preschool age, though, it's still important not to get too hung up on the *when*. Children's understanding of time is extremely primitive at this age (see "Developmental Snapshot"). There are more important story elements to master first, ones that are closer to their grasp cognitively. One of the most important is establishing cause and effect, both for physical and emotional experiences. Another important story element to master is basic chronology. The ability to order actions in time is beginning in infancy and toddlerhood, as discussed in Chapter 1. By the preschool years, children are starting to mark order in their narratives with sequencing words such as "first," "next," and "last," but mostly "and then" (see "Developmental Snapshot"). As with their words for time, they don't always get these words right. You can help by modeling these event-ordering words when constructing a story together about the past.

> Child: *We went to playgroup. We got ice cream.*
> Parent: *Yes, that's right, <u>first</u> we went to playgroup, and <u>then</u> we had ice cream. And what was the <u>next thing</u> we did?*

As always, following in on children's responses and filling in the gaps through open-ended questions will be your best tool for teaching your child advanced narrative techniques. When you're discussing *what happened*, it's okay not to be the authority all the time. Your child may have seen, heard, even smelled (!) parts of the event that you didn't, as in the following example of 4-year-old Anna and her mother discussing a visit to a new playground.

> Mother: *Do you remember when we went to the special playground?*
> Anna: *What playground?*
> Mother: *Yeah, it was mummy's old school. Wasn't it? Do you remember the name of the playground? (Anna shakes her head no) Do you remember some things that were at the playground?*
> Anna: *Slides.*
> Mother: *A pole to slide down, there was. Yes, it was quite tall that pole.*
> Anna: *I could still slide slides down it.*
> Mother: *Yes, cos I didn't know you could do that by yourself. And you could. Okay, what else was at the playground?*
> Anna: *ummm, a bridge.*
> Mother: *There was too. There was a bridge.*

Anna: *A wee house, two wee houses?*

Mother: *Were there? Ohh. What were the houses like? I don't remember them.*

Anna: *They were, one made, there was one made out of wood and one made out of tyres.*

Mother: *Oh right. I remember the tyre one. You went inside it.*

Anna: *It's stinky in there.*

Mother: *It was? Did Emily go on the slide? (Anna shakes head yes) Did she?*

Anna: *That's why she knew.*

Mother: *Oh, that's how she knew it was stinky. So did you enjoy that playground?*

Anna: *Yep.*

Mother: *We should go back there sometime, eh?*

Researchers call this type of reconstruction "metacognitive" talk because you are revealing to your child that part of every story from memory is constructed from what we know *must* have happened, even if we don't remember it directly. Children are also learning about the fallibility of memory, and about how we know what we know. When mothers in our study used more of this higher-level talk during conversations about past events with their young preschoolers, their children had better theory-of-mind skills 1 year later.[26] These metacognitive skills also become very important later on when children are trying to monitor how much they understand of what they read.

Because of preschoolers' advanced understanding of their own and others' thoughts and emotions, you can also devote time in your conversations about shared experiences to your child's emotional perspectives. One of the most effective techniques parents can use when talking about emotions is to provide a brief explanation of *why* they or their children might have felt that emotion, and the resulting consequences.[27] Parents who were taught to talk about their preschool child's past emotions in this way over a 6-month period improved their children's emotion understanding.

For instance, when Rachel in our study was 4, her mother had the following conversation with her about a minor injury:

Mother: *Can you think of a time when you felt sad?*

Rachel: *Um, when I fell over.*

Mother: *Yeah, you were a bit sad when you fell over, weren't you? And you hurt your hands, didn't you?*

Rachel: *This one went sliding like that, and this one went sliding like that.*

Mother: *Oh okay, and* <u>*that made you feel sad? You do feel a bit*</u> <u>*sad when you hurt yourself, don't you?*</u> *(Rachel nods) Yeah, and* <u>*what happened when you felt sad?*</u>

Rachel: *Um.*

Mother: <u>*What did you do*</u>*?*

Rachel: *You came.*

Mother: *I came, yeah.*

Rachel: *And Luke (big brother) said, "are you okay?"*

Rachel: *Luke looked after you? He did too, didn't he? He was good, wasn't he? And* <u>*what did you do*</u>*?* <u>*You cried, didn't you?*</u> *(Rachel nods)* <u>*That's all right. It's all right to cry when you feel sad.*</u>

Shared experiences are ideal for these explorations of the emotional landscape. You were there so you have a good idea of your child's emotional reactions, what precipitated them, and how the emotion was resolved. Even then, there may be some differences of opinion, as in the following example of 4-year-old Jessie and her mother discussing a dead bird.

Mother: *Do you remember what happened last, a couple of days ago, when you were playing in the sandpit?*

Jessie: *No.*

Mother: *Do you remember what happened to the bird?*

Jessie: *What? Yes, it died.*

Mother: *It died, didn't it? Well, how did it die?*

Jessie: *Because it hurt itself.*

Mother: *How did it hurt itself?*

Jessie: *It flew past it.*

Mother: *It flew past it.*

Jessie: *You, and it hit it. (break in conversation) ....*

Mother: *How did it hurt itself?*

Jessie: *Because it, um, it, it hit meself on the nose.*

Mother: *Yeah. It flew into the window, didn't it? And it got hurt. And then what did we do?*

Jessie: *What? Bury it.*

Mother: *We buried it.*

Jessie: *I li-, I don't like burying things.*

Mother: *No, <u>it was a bit sad, wasn't it</u>?*

Jessie: *I don't care if it's sad, because I hate birds.*

Mother: <u>*You were a bit upset, weren't you?*</u>

Jessie: *No, I wasn't.*

Mother: <u>*But then you decided you weren't upset.*</u> *Cos it was a bit much.*

Jessie: *No, I was only sad upset because I didn't want to um, put my red flower in the little place.*

Mother: *Yeah.*

Jessie: *Yes.*

Mother: <u>*It was nice that you gave him a flower though*</u>.

It's important for you to accept your child's current version of their emotional state rather than denying it entirely. Feelings can change with time, just as our perspectives on past feelings change—and preschoolers are only starting to become aware of these multiple perspectives on events. Gently lead them into understanding by proffering some alternative explanations and expanding on your child's reasoning, as Jessie's mother does in exploring Jessie's complex reaction to the dead bird. This process begins by labeling the emotion or emotions (*sad, upset, not upset*) but most importantly asking for and exploring the causes of the emotional reactions (*I don't like burying things, I didn't want to put my red flower in the little place*) and how the situation was resolved (*it was nice that you gave him a flower*) or could be resolved in the future.

Understanding emotions is absolutely essential for children to learn to regulate their own emotions and their behavior, and to get along with others. It is a lifelong process, of course, but it is one that parents can help boost in a dramatic way (see Box 2.3).

Conversing about children's own past experiences, in my view, has a definite edge over discussing stories from books in helping young children understand emotions. It's still extremely difficult for a preschool child to link a book character's feelings and experiences with her own. Psychologist Paul Harris suggests that children understand others' emotions by first understanding their own. And a book character is at least twice removed from the child: the character is an

---

Box 2.3 Attachment Security and Story Sharing with Preschoolers

In order to help your preschooler to benefit from discussing emotions during story sharing, your child should first be securely attached to you. Colleague Rhiannon Newcombe and I found that mothers' emotion talk made no difference for children's storytelling unless the children were securely attached. From age 1-1/2 to 4-1/2, the insecurely attached children did not adopt their mothers' style of talking about emotions, whereas the securely attached children progressively took on their mothers' emotional style over time. If a child hasn't developed a trusting bond with his parent, why should he adopt his parent's emotional perspective on an event? Remember that attachment security is malleable. You can still foster a secure attachment in your preschooler in much the same way that you did when she was a toddler—by responding to her sensitively and serving as a safe haven from life's failures, fears, and frustrations (see Chapter 1).[28]

"other" as well as a "fictional other." Discussing *past* personal emotions is especially effective, because, as psychologist Robyn Fivush pointed out, the child is no longer in the grip of the negative emotion but can recall her prior experience of that emotion.[29] Through conversing about past emotions, the child is learning to take a feeling and analyze it—*Why did I feel that way? How did I react to the feeling? How could I react differently the next time I feel this way?* Understanding one's emotions is critical to regulating those emotions. Separating negative feelings from our reactions to those negative feelings is key to developing self-understanding and healthy, respectful relationships with others throughout our lives.

Talking about Unshared Experiences

Preschoolers can be very interested in your requests for them to tell stories about events that you didn't share with them. By this age, they understand that they have privileged knowledge about these events. Sometimes they will provide you with even more information about an unshared event than a shared experience, as in the following example of 4-year-old Anna telling her mother all sorts of interesting details about the time she went to the airport with her grandparents.

Mother: *And now I want you to tell me about something really special that Grandad and Becky did with you and Nick when Mummy was sick. And mummy stayed home, and Daddy was away. Do you remember where Becky and Grandad took you? And they went and took you, on the way to their house, they took you somewhere special. On the way to their house, at Gore.*

Anna: *The where where those people were which were camouflaged and they were funny colours they were getting in grass and leaves.*

Mother: *They were camouflaged, weren't they? Why were they camouflaged?*

Anna: *I don't know.*

Mother: *Were they—*

Anna: *They didn't want people to see them in the grass.*

Mother: *No.*

Anna: *They had guns.*

Mother: *Yes, they did. It was the army. The army things were out there. Where were they? What was the place called, do you know?*

Anna: *I don't know.*

Mother: *Was it, what else was at the place?*

Anna: *Uh, a icecream van.*

Mother: *Oh, you didn't have an icecream, did you? (Anna shakes her head yes) Did you? Did Nick have one? Did Grandad and Becky have one? (Anna shakes her head yes) Did they? It was at the airport, wasn't it? At the little Taieri airport. And it's near—*

Anna: *Grandad and Becky's house.*

Mother: *Yeah, and someone works near there, as well.*

Anna: *Who? Daddy.*

Mother: *It's near Dad's work, isn't it? Were there some aeroplanes and things?*

Anna: *There was a wee tiny helichopter that was there was two of the little helichopters. What else was there? Ah when we were*

> *when we were with Grandad and Becky, we saw something that*
> *knocks down posts.*
>
> Mother: *Did you?*
>
> Anna: *Yeah.*
>
> Mother: *Knocks down posts. Was it a big machine? Mmm? And*
> *was it—*
>
> Anna: *And there was a big crane that has something heavy, that*
> *was knocking down the old light or something like that.*
>
> Mother: *You haven't told me about that before. Was this at the*
> *airport? (Anna shakes head yes) Was it?*
>
> Anna: *It was near the airport.*
>
> Mother: *Near the airport. And it was a big crane. Had a demoli-*
> *tion ball, big ball on the end. Was it?*
>
> Anna: *Yep. It had a square shaped ball, to crash down.*
>
> Mother: *Cool. That would be an interesting thing to see.*

Preschool children are eager to author their own experiences, especially when they're telling parents something they don't already
know. Indulge your child in spinning out stories about his growing
world apart from you. Soon enough you will be working very hard to
get any information at all about his private life, so enjoy these confi-
dences while they last.

Talking about Your Child's Earliest Experiences

Preschoolers are now ready to listen to and ask questions during a
story about an event they didn't personally experience or remember,
such as the story of the day he or she was born.[30] Children of this age
love to hear their birth stories. They will hang on your every word.
Don't think you have to sugarcoat it completely, either; it's okay to
leave in some of the gory bits. Let them ask questions, and on subsequent retellings, they may even be able to fill in bits and pieces of the
stories themselves. For instance, in the following example, 5-year-old
Eric, who was born prematurely, is engrossed by his mother's description of his not yet fully formed ears:

> Mother: *Well when you were in my tummy… like babies need to*
> *stay in mummies' tummies for quite a long time but you decided*
> *that you didn't want to so you and I had to go to hospital in an*
> *ambulance. Because you decided that you wanted to come into*

the world you see. So into the hospital I went in the ambulance
with you in my tummy and then the next morning you were
born. And do you know how big you were?

Eric: *No.*

Mother: *You weighed about the same as this. That heavy. You*
feel that. (gives child a paperweight to hold)

Eric: *Hmmm.*

Mother: *Yeah, you weren't very big and you know how big you*
were? You look at me. (shows with her hands) There you go. You
were about a foot long. And you were very sick.

Eric: *Why?*

Mother: *And you had to live on a big tray like this ... for the first*
week and you were so tiny and you didn't have hardly any ears
but you had some lovely red hair.

Eric: *Where where where where where where where—*

Mother: *At the hospital.*

Eric: *Where was my ear? Where was my ear?*

Mother: *Well they hadn't—they hadn't grown properly you see*
because you were so early. Because you wanted to come early
you see. And then do you know what happened? You started to
get bigger and better.

In telling your child the story of her birth or his earliest experiences, always remember that you are completely responsible for the way these events are framed and interpreted. You are filling in the first chapters of your child's life story, and in doing so you are shaping your child's self-concept. Be sure to highlight the positive aspects of his or her temperament or personality. It's much better to say "You were so energetic as a toddler that you climbed higher on the jungle gym than any other kid on the playground. And now you're one of the fastest runners in your class," than "You drove us crazy climbing up on the refrigerator every day, and that's when we first started wondering if you were hyperactive." It's okay, even good, to discuss negative things that happened, but be sure to resolve any negative emotions or negative events in a positive way. Notice how Eric's mother reassured him that he soon got bigger and better, even his ears, and Rachel's mother reminded her daughter that even if she gets hurt, other people will be there to help.

Table 2.1 Tips for Sharing Stories with Preschoolers

What to Do	How	Why it Helps
1. *Share stories from books and experiences*	Whether you are sharing a story from a book or about a past experience, keep using your techniques of *following in* on what your child is interested in, then *asking an open-ended question* with *new* information embedded in the question. *Praise* your child's response, and then *ask a new* but related question, or add new information in a statement form.	Advances memory, narrative, and vocabulary skills.
2. *Spin out the story*	Whether you're discussing a book or a past experience, try to engage your child in longer conversations about a single topic as opposed to brief question and answer about lots of different topics. You're going for depth.	Promotes telling longer and more complete stories.
3. *Ask harder questions about the story or the past event*	You can still rely on your staple "What" and "Who" questions, but start introducing some "Where" "When" and especially "Why" questions. Preschoolers are ready and willing to draw inferences if you help them to do so. Preschoolers are also keen to tell you about their experiences apart from you.	Helps narrative sequencing; understanding of cause and effect
4. *Expand the conversation beyond the book, past event, or movie*	"What do you think will happen next?" "That girl goes to preschool just like you. *How* is her preschool like/not like your preschool?" "What ride do you want to go on the next time we go to Disneyland?" "What other amusement parks have we been to?" Like toddlers, preschoolers are still most interested in stories starring themselves. For that reason, when extending stories of the past beyond their remembered experiences, the birth story is a nice place to start.	Enhances language, abstract and critical thinking

(continued)

Table 2.1 Tips for Sharing Stories with Preschoolers (*Continued*)		
What to Do	**How**	**Why it Helps**
5. *Delve into discussing your child's emotions*	Labeling and discussing book characters' emotions helps young children to identify emotional expressions. However, to truly understand emotions, they may need to start with their own. Discuss causes and consequences of preschoolers' emotions, especially negative emotions, in stories of their own experiences.	Helps children's emotion under-standing and theory of mind; self-regulation
6. *Use media thoughtfully*	Whenever possible, watch children's movies and educational TV programs *with* your preschooler rather than letting them watch solo. If the program is prerecorded, you can pause to ask a question, make a comment, and check your preschooler's understanding of the plot and the characters' motivations and feelings, similar to the way you would talk about a book or a story of personal experience. If you can't coview an entire movie or program, check in periodically with your preschooler. She might even be more eager to tell you about a show you haven't been watching than one she knows you've already seen, similar to the phenomenon that preschoolers will give more detail about an event they experienced without you.	Encourages vocabulary learning; story compre-hension; engagement
7. *Parent-Tested Tips on Media and Preschoolers (by parent and media expert Rachel Barr):*	a. Restrict preschoolers' screentime by allowing them to watch only one program or show in the morning before school, preferably after they have gotten dressed and eaten breakfast. Then screentime is over for the day. Because screentime near bedtime is linked to sleep	Maximizes benefits while limiting harmful effects of screentime

(continued)

Table 2.1 Tips for Sharing Stories with Preschoolers *(Continued)*		
What to Do	**How**	**Why it Helps**
	difficulties, scheduling screentime for early in the day (and out of the bedroom) helps your child's development in more ways than one.	
	b. NEVER put a TV set into your child's bedroom. Screentime becomes very difficult to control, both in terms of quantity and quality, once a TV set is in the bedroom.	
	c. Encourage older siblings to narrate and clarify what is going on in a show they are watching with a younger sibling. That way you are fostering coviewing even when you are not able to do so with your preschooler.	
	d. Think of your preschooler's screentime in terms of a media diet: there are some programs that you will allow every day (i.e., those with proven benefits such as *Blue's Clues*, *Arthur*, and *Clifford*) whereas others are "sometimes" shows, or treats allowed only occasionally (entertainment TV such as *Sponge Bob*). It's just as important to promote positive habits of *what* to watch as *how much* media to consume.	

Table 2.2 Developmental Snapshot of a Preschooler[31]		
Domain	**What Happens and When**	**Why It Matters for Story Sharing**
Language Development	*Words and sentences*: Children at this age are learning about five new words a day. By age 6, they will know around 10,000 words. Preschoolers are starting to use verb tenses for the past and future, although not always correctly. *My cookie breaked.* Think of these errors as a sign of progress. *Time, causality, and emotion language:* Preschoolers are starting to use language for time, especially *before* and *after*; *yesterday* and *tomorrow*, although not always correctly. They are also starting to use causal language such as *because* and *so*, and even to express hypotheticals in their speech—what almost happened but didn't. (*The horse nearly kicked me.*) Finally, preschoolers surge dramatically in their talk about their own and others' emotions.	Children can now handle books with longer and more complex text. Books still need to be geared to the child and to the moment, and vivid pictures still help to keep a preschooler engaged in the storyline. By the end of the preschool period, you can have more of a collaborative dialogue about shared experiences with your preschooler—it will feel more like a true conversation.

(continued)

Table 2.2 Developmental Snapshot of a Preschooler (*Continued*)		
Domain	**What Happens and When**	**Why It Matters for Story Sharing**
	Narratives: Preschoolers can tell a relatively coherent story about a personal experience, a book, or a movie. Stories often lack conflict, however, and end abruptly with no resolution ("The End").	Because they are now better at ordering events and using causal links, preschoolers can also talk about their experiences more successfully with people who weren't present at the original event: teachers, grandparents, friends. They will still need help filling in critical gaps about *when, where, how,* and *why.*
Cognitive Development	*Metacognition:* Children start to reflect on their thoughts and feelings. A related development is their ability by around age 4 to think about what other people are thinking and feeling—their theory of mind. Along with this awareness comes, at times, the ability to empathize with others.	Metacognition makes it easier and more interesting to discuss book characters' and real people's thoughts, feelings, and motivations for actions, and to compare these mental states with your child's thoughts and feelings. Children can also discuss why they or others can or cannot remember an experience, and why they may have different perspectives.

(*continued*)

Table 2.2 Developmental Snapshot of a Preschooler (*Continued*)		
Domain	**What Happens and When**	**Why It Matters for Story Sharing**
	Understanding of time: Children are beginning to master the conventions of time in their culture, starting with their knowledge of their daily routines and its variations, and concepts of morning, afternoon, and night. They can order two events in time if they occurred fairly close together (days or weeks but not months). Preschoolers' concepts of time are linked to but not synonymous with their language for time—sometimes they will use a word for time before they have fully grasped the concept, and sometimes they master the concept before the language.	Children can understand more of the time conventions presented in books, but will still need lots of help. A better understanding of time helps children to order narratives chronologically, which in turn makes their stories more understandable to others. Preschoolers' developing understanding of time also makes it easier for you to refer to events farther back in time.
Self-Concept Development	*Mental time travel:* Older preschoolers develop a sense of self that exists over time. They can now transport their thoughts into the past and future more flexibly.	Children can now understand events in the past or future as having happened to a continuing "me." They are better able to connect something that happened in the recent past with the current or future state of affairs.

(*continued*)

Table 2.2 Developmental Snapshot of a Preschooler (*Continued*)		
Domain	**What Happens and When**	**Why It Matters for Story Sharing**
Social and Emotional Development	*Self-knowledge:* Preschoolers are developing a stable sense of their likes and dislikes, as well as their budding personalities. *I like to do a good job at everything I do; I don't like to go down slides headfirst.* *Expanding social worlds:* Most children of this age attend some sort of early childhood education. They are going on far more outings in the larger world, with and without their parents. *Developing friendships:* Preschoolers are developing real friendships with a few other children, and they are able to play cooperatively with a wider range of children.	Your child now understands far more about the world than they did as toddlers. They will be even more interested in the other worlds that they can experience in books. Your child also has many more unshared experiences to discuss with you: events at school, grandparents' houses, and friends' houses.

(*continued*)

Table 2.2 Developmental Snapshot of a Preschooler (*Continued*)		
Domain	**What Happens and When**	**Why It Matters for Story Sharing**
	Complex play: Preschool children are entering a time of peak pretend play, in which they can easily engage in "as if" thinking (e.g., pretending a block is a car). They are beginning to coordinate lengthy and complex plays with other children.	Children's stories of personal experience may include a liberal mix of fantasy and reality. This blending doesn't mean that preschoolers don't understand the difference between the two—they do—but they seem to prefer to spice up everyday life.
Physical Development	*Activity levels:* Preschoolers are still active but have a longer attention span than toddlers. *Brain development:* The most dramatic changes are in frontal lobe functioning at around age 4, which shows in increased self-control, ability to inhibit responses, and to hold more in mind at one time.	Preschoolers' longer attention spans and improved self-control enable you to read longer books with them, stopping less often to ask questions, with a lengthier discussion at the end of the reading. You can also have more detailed conversations about the past, perhaps even while sitting down!

3

Sharing Stories with Your School-Age Child

Ages 5–8

As the wise little boy Nullah in the movie Australia *said, "One thing I know. Why we tell stories is the most important of all. That's how you keep them people belonging. Always."*

Your children need stories more than ever as they give you that last hug goodbye on the first day of school. In fact, as they leave behind the relaxed atmosphere of preschool, with its story time, dress-up corner, and imaginative play, they will need at least as many stories from you as before, if not more. The stories they need have changed, and they are now using stories for different purposes (see Table 3.2, "Developmental Snapshot of a School-Age Child").

Stories continue to matter for how children build their vocabulary and learn to tell better stories. At this stage, you are probably still reading picture books, but you may also be starting to read chapter books with your child. Children learn new words from complex picture books as well as chapter books that they wouldn't otherwise hear in everyday conversation. For instance, when I turned to a page in the first book of the popular Deltora Quest series, *The Forests of Silence*,[1] I found the words "content," "timid," and "dodged." How often have you told your 8-year-old son that he looks content, or praised your 6-year-old daughter for dodging around a player on the soccer field?

Books with a storyline become increasingly important as models for children to base their own stories on. Storybooks also help children understand what they will soon be reading on their own. From these books, children absorb storytelling formulas. The classic "high-point" storyline that I introduced in Chapter 2, for example, contains a beginning that orients the listener to the characters and to the "when" and "where" of the story.[2] Then typically the main character faces some sort of problem. The plot advances as the hero engages in various struggles to solve that problem. The action then reaches a high point or crisis. Finally, the problem is resolved in some way and the character experiences a change, either in his external situation, in her internal reactions, or both.

To get a firm sense of this classic story structure, all you need to do is think of the ever-popular story by Maurice Sendak, *Where the Wild Things Are*.[3] Sendak introduces Max and his mother in the first few pages of the story. Max soon faces a problem: his mother sends him to his room without his dinner because he has been naughty. Max escapes this problem by traveling to a magical world of strange creatures that he visits in his private boat. After a wild rumpus of dancing, singing, and cavorting, the creatures make him the King of All Wild Things, and they beg him to stay with them forever and ever. The high point in this story is clear. Max suddenly feels lonely and yells "Now stop!" to make the imaginary world disappear. The crisis resolves when Max's mother gives him his dinner and he realizes that she is the creature who loves him best of all.

By the time they enter school, many children have been exposed to quite a few storybooks containing a classic storyline. By age 6, many middle-class children have experienced over 1,000 hours of storybook reading with adults, compared to some low-income children who have logged only 25 hours of storybook reading.[4] Yet picture books are abbreviated versions of storylines compared to a chapter book or novel. Novels contain many more conflicts, complicating actions, lesser and more dramatic high points and low points, internal reactions and resolutions. Think of Dostoevsky's *Crime and Punishment*[5] and you get the idea. Somehow children have to move from the 9-sentence story of *Where the Wild Things Are* to the 533-page *Crime and Punishment* between now and the end of high school. Children entering school already possess the building blocks of classic story structure, but now they need to experience longer, more detailed, and more emotionally complex storylines in order to achieve a mature understanding of narrative.

The tension at this age is that the stories children encounter as they begin to read on their own are far below their *narrative level*: the stories they can understand and tell on their own. Compare the advanced vocabulary from the single page of *Deltora Quest* (*content, timid, dodged*) with that on a page from an excellent series of early reading books about dragons:[6] *"Please open the door, Rascal." So the little dragon put his tail in the lock and opened the door.*

The main way that most children extend their vocabulary and story skills at this age is still through the stories that family members and teachers read and tell to them. Some parents unintentionally pull back on their efforts to provide high-quality stories for children at this age as they focus instead on the demanding task of helping their children learn to read. And learning to read *is* a critical task at this age: The end of the second year of formal schooling (around age 8) is a turning point in children's reading, such that children who are reading well at this age progress dramatically in their learning, whereas children who are still struggling to read at this age are likely to experience continued academic problems, which can then lead to behavioral problems. One reason that some children "take off" in their reading by age 7 or 8, leaving others behind, has to do with the strength of their oral language skills.[7] Children with strong vocabularies and understanding of story structure zoom ahead in their reading for understanding after they master basic decoding skills. Thus, neglecting children's oral language and story development during the years they are learning to read could do them a great disservice later on, as I will discuss in more detail in Chapter 4. This "language gap" could end up having a more profound effect on boys than it does on girls, because by the time they enter school, boys are already lagging behind girls in their narrative development.[8]

Another reason that stories matter for children of this age is to help them build a coherent and positive idea of who they are. In the preschool years, children have strong opinions about their likes and dislikes,[9] but they do not yet have a realistic understanding of their strengths and limitations in comparison to other kids their age, and especially how they appear to others (see "Developmental Snapshot"). For instance, a preschooler might claim to be "the bestest runner in the world!" In contrast, an 8-year-old can and will tell you in minute detail who is the fastest runner in her class, who's the slowest, exactly where she fits into the rankings, and whether or not she's satisfied with her performance. The years from 5 to 8 are formative in shaping that growing understanding of self.[10] By age 8, most children are keenly aware of their competence in a number of different areas, such as athletic, academic, and social spheres. They also have an overall appreciation of self, or self-esteem, that ranges from quite negative to highly positive.

One way that children learn to understand and feel good about themselves is through the stories that parents tell with them about past personal experiences. Colleague Amy Bird and I found that 5- and 6-year-old children understood their strengths and challenges better when their mothers discussed negative events with them in a deeper and more explanatory way.[11] In other words, the children who consistently saw themselves as either high or low in achievement, risk-taking, friendliness, and well-being had mothers who discussed how and why they reacted to negative events in their lives. Our research suggests that the way parents discussed positive events in their children's lives was also important, but mainly for children's self-esteem, not their self-understanding.

The findings for self-esteem were clear. Parents who included a greater number of positive descriptions of the child in their conversations about positive *and* negative events had children with higher self-esteem.[12] These findings are straightforward and easy to remember: the more positive you are in describing your child's past experiences, the more positive they will feel about themselves. However, to truly understand oneself is a more complicated endeavor that requires deeper explanations about why she might have reacted in a certain way to negative experiences. Exploring the unpleasant side of life is particularly important for your child's understanding of who he is. After all, we almost all react in a similar way to positive experiences with the emotion of joy or happiness. The way we react to negative experiences is much more telling about our personalities (see Box 3.1). Do we see negative experiences as a challenge to be confronted and solved, or as a threat to our very being?

Box 3.1 Temperament* and Story Sharing

Children's responses to negative events are fairly consistent from as early as infancy and toddlerhood.[13] Some children react to a negative experience, such as a toy breaking, with destruction or withdrawal. Other children initially experience frustration and anger, but are able to persist in the face of failure and disappointment. The difference between these two approaches to setbacks is crucial to a child's happiness and to their success in school. Some children, for example, might even make something new out of the broken parts of the toy. Children who are able to inhibit their first impulse, which might be to throw the toy across the room, and to focus instead on long-term goals have the temperamental gift of "effortful control." Effortful control is a type of self-control. Although children high in self-control may still react to an event initially with a negative emotion, they use the energy from that negative emotion to turn the event to their advantage. Children who can persist at a task in kindergarten, even if it is boring or unpleasant, progress faster in their reading, academics, and socioemotional development than children who do not show as much self-control.[14]

A child's temperament is inborn to some degree and is a force with which to be reckoned, but it is not unchangeable. The way that you react to and interpret your children's reactions to negative experiences can help them move from frustration, anger, and withdrawal to a more adaptive response to failure. In my research with colleagues Amy Bird and Gail Tripp, we found that 5- and 6-year-old children whose parents helped them understand the causes and consequences of their negative emotions were higher in effortful control,

(*continued*)

Box 3.1 (*Continued*)

which means that they were better at turning frustrating or sad experiences into challenges and opportunities.[15] We are continuing to explore whether these emotional conversations with parents are helping children develop higher levels of effortful control over time, or if it's simply easier for parents to talk openly about emotions with children who already show high levels of self-control.

In the final section of this chapter I will tell you in more detail some ways to strengthen your school-age child's language and narrative skills, as well as their self-concept, through story sharing. But in order to share stories effectively, you first need to get a sense of your child's own story capacities at this age.

THE STORIES SCHOOL-AGE CHILDREN UNDERSTAND AND TELL: FROM BOOKS AND FROM PERSONAL EXPERIENCES

Stories from Books

At all ages in our society, it's easier to retell a story from a book or a movie than it is to create and tell a truly fictional story. Children's retellings at this age of stories they've heard are particularly revealing of their level of narrative development. Between ages 5 and 8, children become much better at introducing characters and including all of the major parts of the story (beginning, middle, high point, and ending) in their retells.[16] Here is an example from my research with colleagues Sebastian Suggate, Jennifer Long, and Elizabeth Schaughency of the changes in children's retellings of storybooks from 5 to 8. We first read to the children the charming New Zealand picture book, *Hemi and the Shortie Pyjamas* by Joan de Hamel.[17] In the story, Hemi is a young boy who returns from school one day to discover a note on the table from his mother saying that his younger sister Rata has broken her arm and is at the hospital; Hemi rides his bike to the hospital with

Rata's favorite shortie pyjamas and her stuffed bunny. At the hospital, his plans appear to be foiled when a stern nurse will not let him in to see Rata. So Hemi dresses up in Rata's shortie pyjamas and, pretending to be a patient, cajoles an orderly (Bob) to wheel him up to Rata's room. He gives Rata her pet bunny, and soon after they are all allowed to go home. After reading children the book, we put it away and asked children to tell us the story they had just heard.

Contrast 5-year-old Liam's retell:

Hemi came home at from school and he found a message on the table saying "Hemi, your sister fell off the swing and I'm taking her to hospital. Dad will be home at six, so go and play next door." Hemi got the sister's rabbit and her short pyjamas off the (clothes) line and then went to the hospital and gave her, her bunny and that's all that I can remember.

With 8-year-old Zachary's:

I'll start from the start. When he came home it was very quiet. The radio was not on. Then he went to the, and his mum wasn't in the kitchen. Ah, what else? And um he looked at the table and it said um, I forgot, and then he went um on his bike to the hospital. He asked the nurse, um where he was, where he, were the um children's award (ward) were and um, then he went to get, then he asked where the toilet (bathroom) was. He got changed into the um shortie pyjamas. Then he went to Bob, ah, then um Bob took him a ride in the wheelchair into the children's w...award (ward) and then he ran out of the wheelchair and he went to his sister. Then, um, Rata's other (unintelligible word) um her her her bunny. And they all went home. The end!

Both boys' retellings of the story are of high quality for their age. Both boys show evidence of metacognition in their story retelling (*That's all I can remember; Ah, what else? I forgot*). Young Liam's story is fairly complete and contains elements of a good narrative such as the use of dialogue, and he mentions by name some of the main characters

(*Hemi, Dad*). However, older Zachary's story is more sophisticated when he tells us how he's going to tell his story (*I'll start from the start*) and in providing a setting for the story (*it was very quiet*). Zachary also includes more of the complex events from the story, such as how Hemi got to the hospital, as well as the critical event of how he tricked the hospital staff in order to get up to Rata's room. He also gives his story a real ending (*And they all went home*), a technique that is typically only seen in the stories of older children. However, you will notice that neither boy gives much detail about the characters' emotions and motivations, a development that is more pronounced in the preteen years.

All of these changes in storytelling skill reflect the changes in children's thinking that are occurring at this age (see "Developmental Snapshot"). Researchers since psychologist Jean Piaget, and philosophers since Aristotle, have remarked that children's ability to reason matures dramatically from age 5 to 7.[18] School-age children are noticeably better at understanding cause and effect than they were as preschoolers, whether they are hearing a story or telling their personal experiences.[19] Because children now understand better why key events took place in a story, it is easier for them to get (and remember) the point of the story. These skills are not completely new; rather, they have been developing since early childhood, when children infer connections between events in real life (if I knock over the glass, the milk will spill) and in stories. "Why is Hemi sad?" "Because he has no pet to show," answered 4-year-old Andrew about the prequel to *Hemi and the Shortie Pyjamas*, called *Hemi's Pet*. What *is* different about a 7- or 8-year-old compared to a 4- or 5-year-old is that the older children are able to connect multiple story events together in a complex chain of cause and effect. One reason they are able to hold in mind more complex sequences is that increased memory capacity allows them to hold more events in mind simultaneously. Their oral language skills have also developed such that they are better at telling more of what they know.[20] These basic advances in children's thinking and language in turn allow them to draw deeper and more meaningful inferences across story events and from stories to life and vice-versa.

Stories from Personal Experiences

By the time children enter school at age 5 or 6, their storytelling skills for personal experiences are fairly well established. They are starting to tell stories about their experiences with little or no prompting. These stories usually come with some sort of beginning and a plot with some details, but it can still be hard to tell when different story events occurred, and often children wrap up the story prematurely with no real ending, similar to their story retellings. It's not until age 8 or 9 that children consistently tell well-formed stories of personal events.[21] In the following story, Anna at 5 tells a researcher about her first sleepover:

> Researcher: *Can you tell me about when you had a friend over to stay?*
>
> Anna: *it was fun. That wasn't a long time ago (laughs).*
>
> Researcher: *And what happened?*
>
> Anna: *I only had one (friend over), called Emily. We got to stay up late.*
>
> Researcher: *And what else happened?*
>
> Anna: *We got to eat lollies (candy) and watch a video and I got really sleepy.*
>
> Researcher: *Can you tell me some more about when you had a friend over to stay?*
>
> Anna: *Um, that's all we did. In the night we played, of course.*
>
> Researcher: *And what else happened?*
>
> Anna: *We got to colour in pictures and that's all. When she came. And then the day after we just got to play and have morning tea and then go to ballet.*
>
> Researcher: *Mmmhmm.*
>
> Anna: *'Cause Sunday. We're not meant to go on Sundays but we just have to. We had to.*
>
> Researcher: *Can you tell me some more about when your friend came to stay?*
>
> Anna: *That was all.*

Notice that Anna includes many of the major elements of a good story in her narrative: the time at which the event took place (*not a long time ago*) and the timing of some of the actions within the event (*in the night we played; the day after we just got to play and have morning tea and then go to ballet*) the people who were present (*Emily*), some things that happened (*got to stay up late, eat lollies, watch a video*), and an evaluation of the event (*It was fun*). She also commented on what doesn't usually happen, such as that they don't usually go to ballet on Sundays but they had to that Sunday. This is a sophisticated storytelling technique that contrasts the actual event with what could have happened—more of the "counterfactual thinking" that began in the preschool years. Children's ability to reason about what might have been changes dramatically in the school-age years.[22] Still, Anna's narrative is confusing in places, and it is incomplete. We don't know when in the course of events she and Emily colored in pictures. We do not get any information about other family members' activities during the sleepover, nor do we hear much detail about the girls' emotions or the reactions of others. And although Anna ends the story with the last thing that happened (going to ballet), there's no real wrap-up or conclusion to the story, very similar to 5-year-old Liam's abrupt cessation to the retell of the Hemi story.

Thus, children from age 5 to 8 have relatively strong but still developing oral storytelling skills, both when retelling stories from books and from their own experiences, coupled with rudimentary reading skills. What types of stories can parents share with them during this period that will enhance their developing language and story skills, their self-concept, and their emotional understanding?

HOW TO SHARE STORIES THAT MATTER WITH YOUR SCHOOL-AGE CHILD: FROM BOOKS AND FROM PERSONAL EXPERIENCES

The Stories You Read

Many well-meaning parents stop reading storybooks and chapter books to their children as soon as their children can read by themselves. This particular parenting task is over, they reason. Now they can hand over the reading reins to the child and focus on other issues that seem more pressing, such as struggling to help children learn their times tables or to create an interesting project for the science fair.

Because children's reading abilities at this age are still far below their storytelling and story understanding abilities, however, they need to continue hearing the more complex stories from picture books and chapter books that they can't yet read independently. Solo reading is effortful and frustrating for most children at this age because they are focused on the mysteries of decoding, especially if they are becoming literate in English with its highly irregular letter-sound mappings. Beginning reading does not provide children with the solace of stories. *So keep reading to your children for as long as you both enjoy it, even after they can read on their own* (see Table 3.1 for tips).

For example, my son Dylan at age 8 was a fine reader. His independent reading ranged from typical "hook" books for boys such as the series of *Captain Underpants* and *The Diary of a Wimpy Kid* to the more challenging *Deltora Quest* books. Even though he was capable of reading chapter books on his own, he still enjoyed the comforting ritual of nighttime reading that we had engaged in together since he was a toddler. For our shared reading, together we would choose a book out of a selection that I knew was beyond what he could or wished to read on his own. One nighttime favorite was *Eragon* by Christopher Paolini,[23] on a recommendation from his older brother as the "best series that I've ever read. It's even better than Harry Potter!" Neither of us read the book on our own so that it remained our shared experience. I remember these reading sessions as one of my favorite moments in an often frenetic day. I cuddled up with my 8-year-old after his pyjamas were on and teeth brushed and read him tales of a far-away land with sapphire-blue dragons. We immediately felt closer to each other, and all the minor irritations of the day melted away. Moreover, Dylan got to hear words like "traverse," "prosperous," and "foul." Occasionally I stopped to briefly define a word that I thought would improve his understanding of the story. "Do you know what *misfortune* means, Dylan?" "No." "It's when bad stuff happens to you, like getting sick or losing your money." But often I did not interrupt the flow of the story if I thought he could judge the meaning of the word from the context. Or I would ask him a question about a story event that just happened, or at the end of the chapter I asked him what he thought would happen next. These questions worked best if he knew that I genuinely didn't know the answer, or that there could be more than one "correct" answer. He had been at school all day and didn't need another test question. With my tired end-of-day attention span on the text, usually it wasn't too hard to ask a genuine question. "What was the butcher's name again, you know the guy who was mean to Eragon at the beginning? I can't keep track of all of these names."

These reading rituals with older children continue to serve many of the same purposes that they did in early childhood. Children learn new words from books; they are exposed to complex chains of events, emotions, and motivations; and it's a wonderful chance for you to feel closer to your child at the same time that it reveals to you their level of story understanding.

I would like to emphasize that Rich Reading with older children is mainly for developing their vocabulary, their story comprehension, and for comfort, however, not for speeding along children's decoding skill. Most likely you will have had an interaction with your 5- to 8-year-old child earlier in the day when he read to you as part of his homework. Your role in this interaction is to support his independent reading efforts, offering clues when he needs help with a word, and praising him extensively.[24]

Your role in the nighttime reading ritual is diametrically opposed to your role in early reading instruction. Learning to read is arduous. Usually the storyline, slim at best, gets lost amid the sounds of the words. Now your child needs a chance to lie back and absorb the beauty of a richer story. She's been working hard at examining the trees; now she needs a chance to view the forest. So don't go overboard by asking her questions every few sentences as I recommended that you do when she was a toddler or preschooler. Your main goal now is to tell a good story. Be sure to pause between sentences and to vary your volume and use emphasis. Adopt different voices for the characters if it feels natural and if your child enjoys the drama.

Sharing Stories from Personal Experiences

I also encourage you to continue sharing stories of past experiences with your older child (see Table 3.1). Unlike story reading, however, parents usually need little encouragement to continue telling stories of past experiences with children of this age. Because children are now adept at telling their own personal experiences, they will often bring them up on their own. Your job is to grab these golden moments and together to create a fully fleshed story based on your child's memory. As with Rich Reading at this age, with Rich Reminiscing it's okay to ask your child fewer questions about the event, although it's still best if the questions that you do ask are open-ended. And, as with book-reading at this age, it's best if your questions are genuine: most of them should be questions to which there's more than one answer, or those to which you honestly don't know the answer. Because 5- to 8-year-old children can still use some help with the beginning and the ending of the story, however, your questions could help them fill in these gaps. Throw in a few metacognitive comments about the process of remembering; your child will understand and respond. A few well-placed genuine questions instead should keep them going. "Now what did we do after you went on the waterslide at that amusement park? I'm trying to remember." Or, if you get stuck, rely on the old stand-by "What was your favorite part of that vacation?" and then really *listen* to his response.

The most important Rich Reminiscing strategy with children of this age, however, is to try to get your child to offer up their own perspective on the experience. You'll know you have succeeded if your child starts asking you the questions! In the following example, 5-year-old Charlie and his mother tell a story about a visit to a glacier. Charlie is a somewhat reluctant storyteller at first, but his mother soon draws him in using humor and an anecdote about his little sister Jessica. Notice how once she gets Charlie talking, she continues the conversation not so much by repeating what Charlie says or with direct praise, as she did when Charlie was younger, but with a related question or comment that follows in on the same topic (*It would have been really cold, wouldn't it? Cause the, you climbed up on one glacier, didn't you?*). It is clear that she has succeeded when Charlie turns the tables and asks her, "When you were coming down, did you hear that big bit fall?" and then goes on to tell his mother about parts of his experience to which she wasn't privy (seeing a lizard). His mother accepts his version of the story. Notice that Charlie doesn't respond well to what he perceives as the test question of "Did we see helicopters?" because he knows very well that his mother remembers this part. He responds much better to the question "Would you like to do that? (walk up the glacier some day)" because his mother is asking for his perspective, and there's no right or wrong answer.

Mother: *Okay, now we're gonna talk about our holiday, when we went to the glaciers? Do you remember the glaciers? (Charlie nods his head yes) Do you remember what they're called? One was called? (Pause) It was an animal's name, wasn't it? (Charlie nods his head yes) What was that called?*

Charlie: *Forgot.*

Mother: *Was it, Tiger glacier? (Charlie shakes his head no) Was it, Possum glacier? (Charlie shakes his head no) What was it? Fox?*

Charlie: *Fox glacier.*

Mother: *Oh, Fox glacier. And the other one was called? Franz___? (Pause) D'you remember? Franz Josef, wasn't it? And which was the first one we went to?*

Charlie: *Franz Josef.*

Mother: *It was. And who didn't want to walk into it?*

Charlie: *Jessica.*

Mother: *(laughs) How come? (Pause) Was she being silly? (Pause) And what did she do with her shoes?*

Charlie: *Took them off.*

Mother: *And then what did she do?*

Charlie: *Aah.*

Mother: *Put them back on again and then took them off, put them back on again took one off, didn't she?*

Charlie: *I'm glad she didn't go up the ice with them on.*

Mother: *It would have been really cold, wouldn't it? Cause the, you climbed up on one glacier, didn't ya? (Charlie nods his head yes) Was it that one?*

Charlie: *Franz Josef's one.*

Mother: *Mmhmm. Did you climb up the steps, didn't ya?*

Charlie: *I couldn't cause my one was really slippery.*

Mother: *Oh okay. And was it really cold, the ice? Cause I never touched it.*

Charlie: *Yeah, oh, I didn't wanna go the whole up the stairs because, um that road could have pulled down the ice.*

Mother: *Mmm, that's true, that's true, it was a bit scary, wasn't it?*

Charlie: *And the ice could have fell.*

Mother: *Did we see some ice fall off? On that, at Franz Josef or was that at Fox?*

Charlie: *Wasn't it at Fox? I think it was at Fox.*

Mother: *It was, wasn't it? It was pretty amazing, it just made a big noise, didn't it, and fell into the water.*

Charlie: *When you were coming down, did you hear that big bit fall?*

Mother: *Mmm, but I didn't see it. Cause we couldn't, we were away from wh-, we were in the trees then, weren't we? And um, which one was hardest to walk into? Which one took us the longest to walk into?*

Charlie: *Not the one that, the lizard was, but I think it was the other one, wasn't it?*

Mother: *Did we see a lizard?*

Charlie: *Yeah, I saw one.*

Mother: *Oh, I didn't see a lizard.*

Charlie: *I'm not tricking.*

Mother: *No, I didn't see a lizard.*

Charlie: *Then when I lifted that one up, Jessica didn't really see them but I did.*

Mother: *Oh okay, I didn't see a lizard.*

Charlie: *Went you, but you went away to that pond.*

Mother: *Oh okay, I know where you mean. Oh okay, I missed that. (Pause) So, did we see any helicopters or anything? Lots.*

Charlie: *Why can't you remember?*

Mother: *I can remember, but I just want you to tell me what you saw. What else do you remember about the glaciers, anything?*

Charlie: *What was the other one called we went to?*

Mother: *Franz Josef was the first one and Fox glacier was the second one.*

Charlie: *Oh.*

Mother: *And we saw some people walking up on the glacier too, didn't we? Would you like to do that?*

Charlie: *Would I have to walk down from the helicopter?*

Mother: *Oh some people, land in the helicopter, some people on them up there, but those people had walked up from the bottom.*

Charlie: *Did they, did they walk up there, maybe if they want a ride in the helicopter, did they walk up there for that?*

Mother: *No, you can either go by the helicopter or else you can go with a guide and walk up on the glacier.*

It may feel more difficult in some ways to continue having conversations about shared events with your 5- to 8-year-old child. Your child feels that you are testing his memory when he knows very well that you can remember the event yourself. That's why you need to frame these conversations as reminiscing about shared experiences rather than as tests of memory. Asking for your child's perspective is one way of reframing the conversation in this collaborative way. It is during these conversations about shared perspectives that you can reinforce a sense of family belonging.

Talking about Unshared Experiences

Conversations about unshared events take on increasing importance as your child grows older and has more experiences apart from you. In the following, 5-year-old Tia tells her mother about going to see the fragrant mudpools at Rotorua with her dad. (I'm confident you can figure out the meaning of the Māori word *patero* from the context.)

Tia: *Oh, Mum, there was this smelly water that we went to last time (sniffs) and it was so pateroey.*

Mother: *Smelled like a patero?*

Tia: *Yeah and it was, it smelled like two, two poos and half a poo.*

Mother: *(laughs) At Rotorua? Where were you when it smelled like that?*

Tia: *Um at the hot waters.*

Mother: *At the mud pools.*

Tia: *Yeah.*

Mother: *What were they like?*

Tia: *Oh, they were ssooo pateroey! But I didn't, I did not cover*
   my, I did not cover my nose cause it wasn't that pateroey, but it
   did smell like two poos and half a poo.

Mother: *Two and a half poos?*

Tia: *Yeah, two and half poo.*

Mother: *So what did the mud pools look like?*

Tia: *Um well, they were just hot and brown and steamy.*

Mother: *They make a noise?*

Tia: *They went bthrbthrbhr.*

Mother: *So they sounded like patero as well?*

Tia: *Yeah.*

Mother: *Goodness gracious.*

Tia: *They went ch ch chr chr.*

Notice how Tia's mother gently guides her to tell the all-important *where* and *what*, and in this case, some of the sights, smells, and sounds of Rotorua as well. Her questions are genuine because she was not present, and Tia appears to enjoy describing the requested information in vivid detail.

A major change in family storytelling at this age, however, is that it's time to move beyond your child's remembered experiences for some of your story sharing time. Children are now well capable of telling stories about the experiences they remember, but we all have amnesia for events that occurred before about age 3.[25] Between ages 5 and 8, children are still in the process of forgetting their earliest experiences. The farthest back they can remember is typically to about age 2. Thus, the only way that children can know about important events that occurred before they were 2 or 3 is for family members to tell them about these experiences. Children are also starting to become less self-centered at this age, so they will also be interested in hearing stories about *your* childhood, and maybe even some of the family stories that you know about their grandparents, aunts, and uncles. In the following, 5-year-old Anna's mother shares with her a story about learning to play the violin, an instrument that Anna is about to start learning herself. Note the way Anna's mother maintains Anna's interest by inviting her to contribute, and by drawing parallels with Anna's life. She also weaves information about other family members (Aunt Becky) and friends (Rosie) into the story as a way of introducing Anna to the family's love of music.

Mother: *Okay, I'm allowed to tell you about something now. Something special that happened to me. And it was when I when I started, when I went to my first violin lessons. Do you know how old mummy was? (Anna shakes head no) I was six. And how old are you?*

Anna: *Five.*

Mother: *Ohh, so I was bigger than you when I started having my violin lessons. But I was lucky, because someone went along to violin lessons with me.*

Anna: *Who was it?*

Mother: *It was Aunt Becky. And she was seven. And we did it together so we could help each other. Who's gonna help you learn?*

Anna: *Mum.*

Mother: *Mum. Mum's gonna help you. And we went along, to a school to learn to play the violin. And it was not St Bridget's school.*

Anna: *No.*

Mother: *It was George Street school and we went on Saturday mornings. And we had two little violins. But our violins were bigger than your one. They're probably the same size as Natalie's one at school. Yeah?*

Anna: *You could take your violin to school to teach me when it's only my teaching lessons up in the school.*

Mother: *When Nick's at school.*

Anna: *Yep.*

Mother: *He can have some lessons. You can take your violin on Friday if you like.*

Anna: *And mum, can you take your violin?*

Mother: *Oh, I don't know about that. Oh, well I might have to practice first. You can take yours. So who's got the littlest violin, do you think? (Anna points to herself.) You have. And you can just borrow a violin, and as you grow bigger, you borrow a bigger one and a bigger one, until you need a grown-up one. Like*

> *mummy's got. So that's what happened when I started to learn*
> *the violin.*

Anna: *Why, why Rosie's mum has got a small one is because she*
        might is because her one is because, Rosie's big sister might lose
        her one or Rosie might lose her one.

Mother: *So they've got a spare. I think Rosie started on the little*
          one, but now she's got a longer arm, hasn't she?

Anna: *Mm. She, Rosie did start on the little one.*

Mother: *Did she?*

The rules for story sharing change somewhat when you tell these stories about your own experiences, because your child has no direct memory of the events. You are now clearly the storyteller and your child is the listener. However, that doesn't mean that you have the right to monologue. The best stories at this age are still interactive and build on your child's interests, as when Anna's mother allows Anna to steer the conversation toward a discussion of her friend Rosie's violin. Think of these stories of your childhood experiences as a way of connecting to your child and to your child's experiences. These family stories will arise naturally as your child begins to have experiences that are similar to the experiences you recall having as a child.

Alongside these stories of your own experiences, keep telling stories of your child's earliest experiences, including repeat performances of your child's birth story. A natural time to tell the birth story is in the days leading up to your child's birthday each year. As I write this chapter, it is the eve of Dylan's 9th birthday, and his birth story has already come up several times in the past few days. We don't tell the whole story in its entirety each time, of course. It's more of a conversation in which we tell him about a new part each time it comes up: That when he was born he had dark hair that stuck straight up, and that right after he came out he snuggled up on his dad's chest and started sucking his thumb so loudly that Casey (a native Texan) said that he sounded like he was eating ribs.

These stories are also a way to foster desired behavior in your child, whether it's a love of music or empathy toward younger siblings. I have no doubt that one reason our older son Ben is such good friends with his younger brother is that we told, retold, and still tell stories of what a helpful, empathetic, and caring 4-year-old he was when his younger brother came on the scene. "When your little brother was born, you told us that you wanted to unwrap him like a present to see if he was a little brother or a sister. And you came into the hospital room and unwrapped his blanket and then you said 'I have a baby brother!' and the grin on your face was as wide as can be. And you said that the happiest day of your life was the day your brother was born."

One nice way to ensure that you have good material for future family stories when your children are older is to keep a diary of the funny, cute, and sweet things that they say when they are young. I have kept a memory journal like this for each of my children. At first it was hard at the end of a long day of teaching, mothering, and housekeeping to jot down a few of the incidents of the day. Once I got into the habit, though, I was able to write down many of the best ones. I know as a researcher of memory that even though you think you will remember that adorable saying forever, it evaporates in a few days, supplanted by the next one, if you don't write it down. And now I am so glad that I did. The kids' memory books have served several uses beyond being a source of future family stories. At the time, the journals helped me to reflect on how my children were growing and changing, and these reflections endeared them to me during the difficult early years of sleepless nights, toilet training, and tantrums. And now that my boys are older, they often beg me to see their memory books and even to keep recording things that they say. As 8- and 12-year-olds, while they were supposed to be cleaning their room, I overheard them reading their books out loud to each other. When Ben read aloud the anecdote above about the day Dylan was born, Dylan asked Ben, "And is it still the happiest day of your life?" Thankfully, Ben replied, "Yes." So the story has strengthened Dylan's bond to Ben as much as it solidified Ben's to Dylan.

Table 3.1 Tips for Sharing Stories with School-Age Children		
What to Do	**How**	**Why it Helps**
1. *Keep sharing books with your children while they are learning to read, and even after they can read on their own*	Choose books together that are more advanced than your child's current reading level. Complex picture books can still be challenging and satisfying for children of this age. Define words occasionally, and ask a few questions, but mostly savor the story and the special time together. Your child may not let you read to her for much longer.	Advances vocabulary learning and story comprehension beyond what your child can read on his own. Stories continue to comfort older children too.
2. *Keep sharing stories of past experiences of all types with your children*	Stories of shared experiences that children of this age enjoy are about family vacations, funny mishaps like the time the garbage bag exploded on their big brother, or even sad events such as the death of a beloved family pet. Ask fewer questions than you did when they were preschoolers, instead offering your memory or perspective on an event when they get stuck. A few apt questions, however, can help build your child's storytelling skills.	Promotes storytelling skill, self-understanding, and self-esteem. Talking about shared and unshared experiences can strengthen your relationship with your child and help them learn to cope with difficult events.
	Once children start school, they will want to tell you about their triumphs and tribulations. Instead of the old standby, "What did you do at school today?,"	

(continued)

Table 3.1 Tips for Sharing Stories with School-Age Children *(Continued)*		
What to Do	**How**	**Why it Helps**
	ask "What was the best/ funniest/silliest/smelliest/ worst thing that happened to you today?" When discussing negative events, help your child understand his emotional reactions and the consequences of his emotions. For both positive and negative experiences, highlight positive aspects of your child's behavior and personality as a way of enhancing self-esteem.	
3. *Expand your storytelling to include tales of when you were young, alongside your stories of your child's earliest experiences*	Even though you are the author of these stories, leave spaces for your child to ask questions, and follow in on the aspects in which your child seems most interested. Draw parallels between your experiences and your child's. In future retellings, let your child take over in telling the story of his or her life (and even parts of your life).	Promotes self-understanding, sense of family belonging
4. Parent-tested tip: *Start a journal of your child's sayings*	Write down the cute, sweet, deep, and funny things that your school-age child says. These sayings will serve as a memory bank of future family stories about your child.	Highlights how much you value your child as an individual and as a member of your family

Table 3.2 Developmental Snapshot of a School-Age Child[26]		
Domain	**What Happens and When**	**Why It Matters for Story Sharing**
Language and Reading Development	Children's *vocabulary* increases at the incredible rate of 20 new words daily, even faster than in early childhood. By age 8–9, children have a vocabulary of around 20,000 words. Mastery of *grammar* in spoken language is nearly complete by age 6, although some errors persist (for example, in irregular verb forms such as "He *bet* me to the car" instead of "He *beat* me to the car").	The dramatic increase in children's vocabulary, grammar, and story structure enhances their understanding of the stories they hear.
	Narrative: Children are beginning to master the story structure of their culture: in Western literature, the dominant structure is high-point, in which actions lead up to a climax and are then resolved.	Once children can tell a well-formed narrative on their own, they don't need as many questions from parents to help tell their stories. Story sharing can turn into more of a collaborative process.
	Reading: The hallmark development of this period in most countries around the world is that children learn to read. By age 8, some children are reading fluently for understanding, whereas other children are still struggling to "crack the code."	Reading can help children acquire new vocabulary and more complex story structures, but at this age most of the texts they are reading are below their oral language skills, so this transfer to their own stories is probably not yet happening.

(continued)

Table 3.2 Developmental Snapshot of a School-Age Child *(Continued)*		
Domain	**What Happens and When**	**Why It Matters for Story Sharing**
Cognitive Development	Children's ability to *reason* in a logical and less self-centered or egocentric manner increases rapidly during this period. This dramatic shift in children's thinking occurs for children in cultures around the world between ages 5 and 7.	Children can now understand cause and effect in events and in the stories they read in a much more sophisticated way. Their lessening egocentrism may open the way to their interest in others' stories.
	Children's capacity for *metacognition,* or thinking about thinking, also increases during this period. They are much better at reflecting on their own and others' thinking, learning, and remembering. They can use strategies to help them to learn and remember and new material, such as reciting a phone number to keep it in their head until they can make the call, or better yet, writing it down.	Children's metacognitive skills mean that they are better at remembering how to remember, and that they are less likely to appropriate someone else's experience as their own in their stories.
Self-Concept Development	*Self-knowledge:* A firmer and more differentiated self-concept emerges by the end of this period. Children develop a sense of overall self-worth	

(continued)

Table 3.2 Developmental Snapshot of a School-Age Child (*Continued*)		
Domain	**What Happens and When**	**Why It Matters for Story Sharing**
	(*self-esteem*) as well as a deeper understanding of their strengths and limitations. Some traits and behaviors become more central than others to their sense of who they are. For some kids, it's more important to their self-worth to excel in sports than in academics.	Children's self-concept is made up of an accumulation of their experiences, coupled with their own and others' evaluations of those experiences. The way these stories are told is thus crucial to children's self-views.
Social and Emotional Development	*Friendships and social networks*: Children's social networks expand exponentially once they enter school. They are developing more enduring friendships, even best friends.	Children have a vastly greater number of unshared experiences for you to discuss with them, some of which involve some thorny emotions of guilt, loyalty, betrayal, pride, and shame. They will be especially interested in conversations about past conflicts with their friends. You can discuss these disagreements and explore the surrounding emotions.

(continued)

Table 3.2 Developmental Snapshot of a School-Age Child (*Continued*)

Domain	What Happens and When	Why It Matters for Story Sharing
	Complex emotions: At age 5–6, children first start using terms for complex emotions such as pride and shame, and they can understand that parents feel proud or ashamed of them. By age 7–8, they start to feel proud or ashamed of themselves, independent of parents' reactions.	You can also discuss the good times they have had with their friends as a way of deepening those bonds.
Physical Development	*Brain development:* A time of continuing to make new connections and strengthening previous connections through pruning of synapses. Children become much faster at thinking and processing new information as more of their neuronal connections become myelinated, or covered in a fatty sheath that aids transmission.	Children's greater attention span and speed of thinking may allow them to take in more complex events and stories and later to narrate them in greater detail. This efficiency may also help you to have a more collaborative conversation with them, with more statements and fewer questions, and shorter pauses after questions.

4

Sharing Stories with Your Preteen

Ages 8–12

My very first lessons in the art of telling stories took place in the kitchen… my mother and three or four of her friends… told stories… with effortless art and technique. They were natural-born storytellers in the oral tradition.

~Paule Marshall

What most parents notice about their preteens is that they no longer seem to be changing in dramatic ways. Sure, preteens are still growing and developing, but the changes are not as noticeable as they were at younger ages. Children at this age are steadily getting bigger, stronger, faster, and more skilled—whether that skill is at swimming, piano, soccer, reading, gymnastics, math, making friends—or storytelling. It's an idyllic period of consolidation, a time of small changes in each aspect of development, a welcome lull before the storm of adolescence (see Table 4.2, "Developmental Snapshot of a Preteen" at the end of this chapter). It may surprise you, though, to learn that preteens are still learning new words at a rapid pace, especially if they are strong readers. In fact, from age 8 to 10, most preteens actually *double* their vocabularies! Even if your children are fantastic independent readers at this age, however, they are not too old to benefit from your stories.

Especially important from the preteen years are the stories that only you can tell them—the stories about *your* childhood. If told in a compelling way and at an apt moment, preteens can use these stories to help them cope with events in their own lives. Preteens also still need a great deal of help making sense of the events in their own lives through the stories you create and read with them. If they get the right kind of help from you in understanding life events and emotions, then they will better navigate those squally teenage waters with a stronger sense of self and better coping skills.

THE STORIES PRETEENS READ, UNDERSTAND, AND TELL: FROM BOOKS AND FROM PERSONAL EXPERIENCES

The Stories They Read

A welcome change in children's story worlds at the beginning of the preteen years is the rapid expansion of books and stories in which they're interested. No longer do they want to watch the same video or read the same favorite book over and over again, ad nauseam. Instead they want repetition with variation, which they satisfy by reading series of books. Their appetite for new stories of all types is strong and healthy. They need action, adventure, drama, and strong characters in their stories, and at the start of this period they are still relatively open to a variety of genres. However, toward the end of the preteen years, their reading diet narrows, often along gendered lines.[1] Some girls start to restrict themselves to realistic fiction or to girls' fantasy and mystery narratives (such as the *Twilight* and *Sisters 8* series) and boys to science fiction, fantasy, or nonfiction (*Eragon* and *Artemis Fowl* series). Boys tend to be more visually oriented in their reading; they like graphic novels and comics more than girls do. Toward the end of this period, boys' reading material may include lengthy and detailed manuals on their current passion: whether it's baseball, *Yu-Gi-Oh!*, or *Warhammer*. Of course, these gender preferences may not apply to your daughter or son (see Chapter 6). And boys and girls alike enjoy "cross-over" books such as *Deltora Quest, Harry Potter, The Lightning Thief,* and *The Diary of a Wimpy Kid.*

The preteen years are the age when some children start reading for pleasure. Why do some children reach this point and others never do? Although it seems obvious that children will only find reading pleasurable if they are good at it, not all good readers like to read for entertainment. Some children, perfectly fine readers, read only when required at school or to gain information. Reading is only a means to an end, not an end in itself. Understandably, children who have difficulty reading choose other pursuits in their free time. For these children, reading is associated with struggle, failure, frustration, and disappointment. For many reasons, boys are overrepresented in this group of unwilling and unable readers.

Other children, and some of them are boys, turn to reading with a vengeance. These children literally seem hungry for books; they devour them like candy. Is it possible to binge on books? Is it unhealthy? Like anything else done to excess, if it is taking them away from other healthy pursuits such as interacting with family or friends, or playing outside, there is such a thing as too much reading. My older son Ben was a voracious reader from the age of 6. He was one of those kids who would walk around reading if allowed. We joked in our family about needing a reading reduction program for Ben, in contrast to the reading enhancement programs so often touted by the schools. Perhaps not coincidentally, he was also one of the lucky cohort that got to read the Harry Potter series AS IT WAS RELEASED. I am convinced that these children will grow up to have an extra-special love of reading. Some of Ben's best reading memories now are of getting the latest Harry Potter book for his birthday each July, bequeathed by his Aunt Jennifer, a fellow fan, and tucking himself up in bed or on the couch to read it in as much of one go as possible, stopping only for bathroom, food, and sleep breaks (enforced by his parents!).

For these intense readers, the preteen years are usually the peak of their insatiable consumption. According to a survey of over 18,000 primary school children in the United States, most children start school interested in reading for entertainment and for learning, but then for most children their interest in reading declines steadily over the primary school years.[2] For above-average readers, the decline in reading for pleasure occurs later, at the end of primary school, but it still occurs. As these top readers enter their teenage years, their interest in reading wanes as they dive headfirst into the world of peers and other, more social interests. I don't know of any longitudinal research into adulthood on this point, but my hunch is that these children will emerge from the teenage years as lifelong readers.

Other children don't start out as intense readers but they ultimately end up there. My younger son Dylan appears to be following this path. From age 5 to 8, he was a good reader, above average for his age when tested at school, but he stoutly refused to read on his own for pleasure. At age 8, he told me, "I only read when people tell me to." He loved having me read **to** him, however, and he dutifully read everything he was assigned for school, but in his free time he preferred to be with friends, play sports, draw, or build with Legos. At age 9, however, he underwent a dramatic transformation. He still liked for his dad and me to read to him on occasion, at night in bed for comfort, but he started reading on his own with a vengeance. For the first time, he would go off on his own during the day or especially at night in his bed and curl up with a book. Perhaps he simply hadn't found his genre. What really got him reading for pleasure were the *Diary of a Wimpy Kid* series and the *Horrible History* series by Terry Deary. Fortunately there are many volumes with great names like *The Terrible Tudors* and *The Measly Middle Ages*, and there are also spinoff series now such as *Murderous Maths* and *Horrible Science*. Terry Deary is a genius for bringing history to life—"history with the gory bits left in." The books contain a mix of narrative, fascinatingly repulsive facts, and black-and-white cartoons lampooning famous scenes in history. They are a godsend for those kids who prefer nonfiction, many of whom are boys. At the same time, Dylan also started reading the ever-popular *Goosebumps* books. One day he announced, "I like history and scary stories." And at age 10, in the car on the way to the library to get yet another book in the Percy Jackson series, he told me spontaneously, "Mum, I've discovered the joy of reading."

Clearly, part of what drove Dylan to read for fun was finding his genre or genres. However, the other main event in Dylan's life at this time was that his dad and I separated. I can't help but think that Dylan's turn to reading at this juncture was not a coincidence, but that he was seeking out in his history books a world order, a meaning out of life's seemingly random bad events. Robert Emery, a leading researcher on the effects of divorce on children, talks of a similar shift for his daughter Maggie, who was 7 at the time her parents separated. Emery painfully relates how Maggie "dived into a book" the night he and his first wife told her about their separation, and that "she never stopped reading...I am awed by Maggie's love and knowledge of literature. But even today, I cannot help but feel guilt about her passion for books. Was her passion born of the pain I inflicted that night?"[3]

There's very little research on how, when, and why some children start reading for pleasure, and especially for solace, but I think there should be more research on this fascinating and important topic, especially for children faced with difficult life events. There *is* a growing body of research, however, on children's ability to identify with story characters and to predict characters' actions based on their understanding of the character's thoughts, beliefs, intentions, and motivations. Not surprisingly, preteens with a better **theory of mind***, or understanding of others' thoughts and emotions, also have better knowledge of reading processes, such as how to improve their comprehension of what they read.[4]

By the time they have been reading for 3 to 4 years, most children have switched from "learning to read" to "reading to learn."[5] However, some children who appeared to be good readers in the first few years of school hit a wall at this point as the vocabulary in texts becomes more difficult. These children are sometimes perfectly fluent readers but they have trouble understanding what they read. Reading expert Jean Chall called this the "4th grade slump." Because these children have difficulty comprehending what they read, they stall out—they are simply unable to advance to the "reading to learn" phase. All of the current evidence points to smaller vocabularies and difficulties in language comprehension as a major cause of this problem. Fortunately, if you have been sharing stories with your child, both from books and from personal experiences, then your child is likely to have good or excellent vocabulary and language comprehension skills. She is unlikely to be one of the 34% of children experiencing reading difficulties. However, if your child is one of those experiencing a 4th grade slump, and you have ruled out a formal diagnosis of reading disability, then there is still plenty of time to help him to read for understanding with the tips I will share with you below. You will want to work on it now so that the 4th grade slump doesn't turn into the "8th grade cliff" as school texts become even denser. And even if your child is an excellent reader at this age, she or he will still benefit from hearing stories from books and from experiences. Literacy expert Sebastian Suggate and colleagues conducted a study with German 9-year-olds in which the children either read a story on their own, or a researcher read or told them the same story aloud. The children learned more new words from the stories they heard aloud than the stories they read on their own.

Although good readers at this age understand and remember the "facts" of the story, as well as what the characters are thinking and feeling, even good readers still have difficulty grasping subtler story elements: understanding characters' motivations for their actions, discerning the main point or problem in the story, and predicting what might happen next in the story based on the characters' traits and previous actions.[6] These are all higher-level aspects of story comprehension that benefit from your conversations with your preteen about stories of all kinds—the stories they read, the stories they see (see Box 4.1), the stories about their own and their family's experiences.

Box 4.1 The Stories They See: Preteens and Media Use

A large US survey of preteens' media habits from 1997 to 2003 found that the most frequent media genre is still TV watching, and educational programming for preteens is sorely lacking.[7] For example, the website http://www.commonsensemedia. org lists many educational TV programs for young children, and even a few for 5- to 8-year-olds, but absolutely none for preteens or teens. Most likely, if educational programs did exist for this age group, preteens would avoid them like the plague.

Parents also reported that the time their preteens spent playing videogames had increased from early childhood, albeit there are large gender differences in this change. Boys spend nearly 4 hours per week playing videogames, whereas girls spend less than an hour. Media use explodes in early adolescence from age

(*continued*)

Box 4.1 (*Continued*)

11 to 14. Unfortunately the children who spent more time watching TV and playing videogames appeared to do so at the expense of studying, reading, sleeping, and nonmedia play. Because the link between videogame play and later attention problems in middle childhood and adolescence is very similar to that between TV watching and attention difficulties in early childhood, these increases in media time are worrying.[8] The AAP guidelines for preteens are to limit their exposure to all screens to no more than 2 hours per day, total, and to be as careful as possible in controlling the content of the media with which they engage.

I know from personal experience that it is extremely difficult to pull your preteen away from computer and videogames. Do your best to limit gaming and to substitute reading, talking, art, music, inside and outside play, and sleeping. Parents I know have tried various techniques such as screen-free days and "creative" computer days in which only creative work can be done on the computer (drawing, painting, writing, film-making) instead of gaming or YouTube watching.

At one point I optimistically hoped that role-playing videogames (RPGs), in which characters choose actions and those actions shape their life course, might result in some narrative benefits for preteens and adolescents. Very little research has been devoted to this possibility, but one Austrian study surveyed preteens' well-being as a function of their gaming preferences.[9] Not surprisingly, preteens who play fantasy RPGs such as *World of Warcraft* are more likely to experience depression, withdrawal, loneliness, and anxiety; preteens who play first-person shooter games (e.g., *Counterstrike*) are more likely to show aggressive and delinquent behavior. A longitudinal study with US preteens reinforces the finding that playing videogames early in the preteen period is linked to more aggressive behavior in adolescence, especially for boys. For girls, heavy videogame play was linked to lower academic achievement later on. These risks of videogame play do not appear to extend to time spent on the computer. Perhaps because computers can also be used for educational and informational purposes, girls and minority

(*continued*)

children who spend more time on the computer during the preteen years show gains in their academic achievement.

Also on a more positive note, the Austrian preteens who
reported discussing their Internet and videogame use with parents experienced fewer problems overall. Again, we can't nail
down the direction of this effect—it could simply be that talking to your parents about your Internet use is a sign of a good
relationship—but I don't think it hurts to have open, honest discussions with your preteen about the concerns you have about
their videogame play, and to negotiate media rules together.

THE STORIES THEY TELL (AND WRITE)

Children's storytelling also consolidates during the preteen years, but it
is not changing in dramatic or obvious ways. They now possess all the
basic skills for telling a good story. They can introduce a topic and stay
on that topic—most of the time. They are starting to introduce the listener to the time or the place for the story, although typically not to both
time and place in the same narrative. They can narrate the main actions
in the story, including a high point and some sort of ending. Preteens'
stories are not terribly exciting or insightful, but they definitely get the
job done! Their stories contain enough detail to be convincing, but are
not so detailed that the listener yawns off in the middle.

By the end of the preteen years (age 11–12), children are telling pretty good stories about single events: they are complete yet
concise; they contain a beginning, middle, and end; they are fairly
coherent to a listener in terms of the timeline of the event due to
children's accurate use of time and causality markers such as "First"
"Last," and "Because" "So" "Until"; and they are evaluated appropriately ("And that was quite sad"). Here is an example of the solid, ser-
viceable stories of older preteens: When asked to tell a story about
an important event in her life, 11-year-old Emma decided to talk
about her rat dying.

Emma: *My rat dying. Yeah, that was really sad. 'Cause umm, he*
        got cancer, and his stomach sort of had a hole in it, and it bursts

*inside out, sort of. And umm, and we didn't notice it until he
rolled over, and umm his limbs, he started, coz it cuts off your
limbs and stuff inside, like, so he started limping, so we had to
take him into the vet. 'Cause our family friend noticed it. So we
had to take him to the vet and get him put down. And then umm,
I buried him in the back garden. Yeah, that was quite sad.*

In the preteen years, children are starting to use language in different ways for different purposes. For instance, their written stories are
more complex in all ways—containing more diverse vocabulary and
complex grammatical forms—than their spoken stories. Yet it is not
until adolescence that they develop a more complete understanding
of genre and the different ways to express oneself through oral and
written language.[10]

Just as children of this age in their visual art are starting to adopt
the conventions of their culture, preteens are also adopting the artistic
conventions of their culture in their oral storytelling.[11] For instance,
in Japan where the aesthetic is more minimalist, Japanese children tell
sparer and more concise stories than their European American coun-
terparts. Younger Japanese children use abundant amounts of onomatopoeia in their stories (saying "bzzz bzzz" for a bee, for instance),
a technique that Japanese adults use liberally in the stories they tell to
children of that age. Japanese preteens and adults, however, decrease
their use of onomatopoeia in favor of more mature types of evaluations, such as commenting on characters' mental states, but their total
number of evaluations is low in comparison to stories from European
American children and adults.

Many cultures with a rich oral storytelling tradition use repetition
as a literary device in their stories. Repetition serves two functions:
first, it emphasizes a point or action in the story. Second, repetition
with variation is a highly effective mnemonic or memory technique.
Think of Homer's epic poem *The Odyssey* as a historical example in
European culture. In the following brief excerpt, note the repetition
of the phrases "thrice a day" and "sucks down":

Beneath it mighty Charybdis *sucks down* black water, for
thrice a day she spouts it forth, and *thrice a day* she *sucks it
down* in terrible wise. (Book XII)

Even in contemporary New Zealand culture, Māori mothers use relatively high rates of repetition in their stories of shared experiences with their children compared to European mothers.[12] In contemporary European cultures, with their longer history of literate traditions, the emphasis is more on the provision of new information than repeated information, and the dominant story form is one with a high-point structure. Preteens in European cultures excel at this form, at least when narrating single events (see "Developmental Snapshot"). The only ways in which their stories about single events continue to improve after this point are in their consistent provision of the time and place of a narrative (sometimes they are still vague about either the time or the setting of the original experience), but especially in the sophistication of their resolution of the narrative, including explicit links to other, related events. At this age, they are very good at providing a high point—they clearly know that stories must have a point to be interesting—but their resolutions can lack depth and subtlety. In this example, 11-year-old Jesse talks about breaking his arm. Jesse provides the listener with some setting information (*who, where*), and he elaborates on the high point (or rather low point in this case), but he does not tell us how the event was resolved.

> Jesse: *Umm well my dad's a policeman. And we were just going to a umm police picnic, where there's a little Santa and he gives out presents. And we all got gun, got little umm water guns. And we were pretending that umm, we were playing like a gun game, and I climbed up onto the garage. And I needed to get down, so there was either jump down onto the driveway or the garden. I was like, thought oh ok so umm, I'll just land, I'll just try land as safely as I could. So I jumped onto the driveway, and landed awkwardly. So yeah.*
>
> Researcher: *Yeah, is there anything else you remember about that?*
>
> Jesse: *Umm I was crying, And my I think mum came down, someone came down, and took me back up, and went to the hospital. On the way down, I asked my mum does the hospital smell bad? (researcher laughs) That's one thing I remember asking her.*

This limitation in preteens' storytelling most likely reflects deeper cognitive limitations. In order to provide a sophisticated resolution to a story, one must take a larger view on the event and be able to place it in perspective with other events in one's own and others' lives. This perspective is precisely what preteens lack. Although they are excellent at organizing and relating the details and emotions of a single event in their lives, they are not yet able to integrate multiple life events into a coherent story of their lives. In one study, Danish 9- to 15-year-olds wrote a story about a single event (a family vacation), and also the story of their lives.[13] Even the youngest children in the study could write a fairly coherent account of the vacation event. The younger preteens were not yet able, however, to write a coherent story about their whole lives. When faced with this request, they most often wrote about disconnected single events. For instance, here is one 9-year-old's life story: *I got lost from my mum and dad on the beach. And they had to ask other people to help search for me. And then they finally found me down on the beach, and then we had to go home.* By age 11–12, however, the children included multiple events in their life stories, and these events were at least somewhat chronologically ordered. Most preteens are not yet able to synthesize events that might have a similar theme or point. It is possible that some cultures encourage these associations across events and topics at an earlier age than in European cultures, with its emphasis on telling a complete story about a single event. This emphasis begins early in the culture of Western schooling, when teachers encourage children at "circle time" to tell a longer story about a single event instead of stringing multiple events together with little detail about each one.[14]

Other research on children's life stories helps us understand what is missing in the younger preteens' stories. When researchers asked 8- and 12-year-old German children to tell the story of their whole life in 15 minutes (lest some of the younger children started to go into excruciating detail, no doubt), the 12-year-olds gave more information about time and exact dates in their life stories compared to the 8-year-olds, showcasing their growing understanding of calendar time. Their stories were easier to understand because they conformed more to our conventional notions of time. The 12-year-olds were also better at stating how certain events had shaped their personalities

(*After age 10, I became a shy person because the separation of my parents made me distrust others*).[15]

Although most preteens are not yet connecting across events in deeper ways by identifying themes or consequences for their personalities, they are showing precursors to this ability. They are starting to chunk events in their lives into "life periods." So, when we asked 8- to 12-year-olds to tell the story of their life as if it were a story in a book, the older preteens were beginning to group events into chapters that were organized in conventional ways—"stuff that happened when I was in preschool, then primary school" or "those things happened when I lived in Dunedin, and that stuff happened when I lived in Auckland." As adults, when thinking of our life as a whole, we rely heavily on these life periods as an organizing device to help us order events and to remember individual events within each period. We can switch flexibly from one way of organizing to another—say from organizing life events with respect to places we've lived in contrast to schools we've attended or jobs we have held (e.g., I had the job at the architect's office while I was pregnant with my first child). Preteens show that they are developing an overview of all the events in their life by starting to organize them into life periods. This ability to group events together along different dimensions may be an important step toward drawing sophisticated connections across events in terms of their emotional content or their meaning for one's life.

Preteens' growing ability to chunk events into chronological periods may also reflect their growing understanding of the conventions of time. In modern society, time is marked in multiple ways simultaneously: in terms of calendar years, one's chronological age, and, for children, one's grade or year in school. Children must master the conventions of each scale separately (i.e., each calendar year consists of 12 months, and each month consists of a specified number of days), but they must also learn to coordinate these time scales alongside each other. "In 2010 I turned 9 years old and I was in 3rd grade for the first half of the year; then I was in 4th grade for the rest of 2010." Preteens improve from age 8 to 12 at coordinating these long-term time cycles.[16]

Preteens are also still developing the ability of insight into the meaning of events for their lives. Insight into life's events is, of course, a skill that is still developing into adulthood. Preteens show glimmers of insight, however, and *can* have quite a sophisticated perspective at times on isolated events, but usually not until they are about 11 or 12. Colleague Yan Chen and I found that preteen girls showed consistently higher levels of insight into life events than did boys, but all preteens were pretty limited in their level of insight.[17] For instance, when we asked one preteen how his parents' divorce had changed his life, he replied only: "Now I have two houses and two backyards."

There are obvious parallels at this age between children's reading development and their storytelling of personal events. It is at this age that they begin to connect personal events to each other. They are beginning to draw meaning from life events, a vital skill that continues to develop into adulthood. What we don't know yet, but which would be fascinating to research, is whether children who read more are gaining self-understanding, and whether those who are better at drawing meaning from life events are transferring those skills to benefit their reading comprehension. As adults, we read books and watch films in part to experience another world, but we attempt to learn something about ourselves in the process. (In *Sophie's Choice*, Sophie ended up choosing which of her two children would live— *What would I do in that same situation?*) Experiencing fictional worlds can help clarify our own life philosophies, our motivations, our values.

This ability to learn from stories and to apply them to our own lives goes back to our earliest experiences with books. Recall how I advocated linking the world of books and real life in the toddler and preschool chapters? It is in the preteen years that the hard work you did when your children were younger will really start to pay off. But don't stop now. The preteen years are crucial for helping your child to understand what's happening in books as well as in their own lives. Here's how:

HOW TO SHARE STORIES THAT MATTER WITH YOUR PRETEEN

The Stories You Read

I want to acknowledge first that there's very little hard data on how parents can stimulate reading interest with preteens. Let's allow common sense to prevail. Try to find books that your child will like, especially new series to pique their interest. Model reading for pleasure. Create cozy rituals to foster reading for entertainment (see Table 4.1 for tips). Go to the library regularly and help your child find the books he would really like to read. If you're feeling creative, help your children create story worlds at home, on your own or with their friends, by dressing up as their favorite book characters and acting out storylines. My younger sister and I practically lived full-time in story worlds during this age period, recruiting as many children from the neighborhood as we could to help out. Our firm favorite was to act out the *Little House* series (Jennifer was cute with curly dark brown hair, so she always got to be Laura. I was always the tallest in the neighborhood, girl or boy, so I was stuck being Ma or Pa, or on a lucky day, older sister Mary.) On days when there weren't any other children about, we became Ella and Sarah, two sisters from the *All of a Kind Family* series about a Jewish American family living on the lower East Side of New York at the turn of the 20th century. Both story worlds were far from our 1970s suburban Texas existence, which was no doubt most of the appeal. Our parents aided and abetted us in creating these story worlds: my mother by sourcing and sometimes sewing up pioneer dresses and bonnets, and by reading the *Little House* books to us at night, and my father by building us a fabulous "homestead" playhouse in the back yard as the stage for our extended dramas on the prairie.

Continue to read to your preteen if he or she will let you. Unless he is reading at a very advanced level independently, the vocabulary he is exposed to in books is still going to lag behind his own vocabulary levels, at least at the beginning of the preteen years. And even if she is reading at an advanced level, you can still use shared reading as a time to expand her reading diet and to strengthen your bond. Try to choose a book for shared reading that is beyond his current reading level if you can. It needs to be one that you both want to hear; otherwise you will find reading aloud to be a chore and your preteen will sense your lack of enthusiasm. It is at this age that you might be able to sneak in some of your old favorites that you remember reading as a child. The *Ramona* series, *The Moffats*, and *Family Sabbatical* were some of my childhood favorites that I managed to read to my children during the preteen phase. These are books that they would never have read on their own, either because they seemed too old-fashioned or too "girly," but for whatever reason (perhaps they were humoring me), they listened happily when I read them aloud. Ben was 12 when I read aloud *Family Sabbatical* at the start of our own family sabbatical to Texas and South America, and an entry I made in his memory book at the time was, "Wow, I'm 12 years old and I'm still listening to my mum read to me."

If your child does not want you to read at bedtime because she thinks it's too babyish, or because he has his own reading that he wants to do then, find a time during the early evening or on the weekend when you can read together from your shared book. Shared reading in the living room is a satisfying substitute for watching TV together. Reading expert Jim Trelease lists some wonderful read-aloud books for all ages.[18] As with your younger children, save this special book for your shared reading time; don't sneak a peek at the coming attractions. It should be an experience of shared anticipation. To adapt Rich Reading for preteens, before you begin your reading session, DO recap briefly where you are in the story and what happened previously. During the reading itself, though, don't ask a lot of questions or engage in lengthy discussions unless you think there's a word or a plot twist that your child might not understand. At this age, children need to be absorbing the story as it unfolds so that they can appreciate the larger story structure. At the end of the reading session, DO speculate with your child about what might be coming up in the next chapter or two. These requests for predictions and inferences are just as good at stretching your preteen's thinking as they were for your preschooler.

If you have a reluctant listener on your hands, I think it's okay to let them draw alongside you, or play with their Bratz dolls or Lego as you read. If they are listening at all to the story, you will notice them pause their play at crucial moments in the narrative. Sometimes they will abandon their toys altogether and come curl up next to you as the story magic takes over. My reasoning is that a story half heard is better than no story at all!

Stories about Personal Experiences

Even though your preteen is now perfectly capable of telling an under-standable story about a personal experience, he or she will still need your help in fleshing out the story and in understanding emotions and motivations (see Table 4.1 for tips). Most important, they will need help in understanding the meaning of the event for their own lives, especially if the event is a negative one. One way that we know this is through a host of experimental studies of a technique called "expres-sive writing," pioneered by psychologist James Pennebaker, in which participants write for 15–20 minutes a day on 3 to 4 consecutive days about a traumatic or negative experience in their lives. When adults engage in expressive writing about negative events, they experience psychological and physical benefits: several months later, in com-parison to adults who wrote about nonemotional experiences, they are less depressed, less anxious, and even have better immune func-tioning.[19] But does expressive writing work for children? Apparently not for preteens. When researchers asked preteens to write about emotional or nonemotional experiences, all children experienced decreased depression and anxiety from diary writing. However, writ-ing about emotional experiences showed no benefits over and above writing about nonemotional experiences. And those children who used more emotional words in their writing about emotional experi-ences were actually more depressed and anxious two months later.[20] It's possible that focusing on negative emotions without being able to resolve them actually made some children feel worse as a result of the diary writing exercise. Preteens still need a great deal of help making sense of experiences, especially negative experiences.

Although the research on parent-preteen storytelling is still sparse, there is every indication that parents are vitally important for helping preteens make sense of the events of their lives. Psychologist Robyn Fivush and colleagues found that when families have collaborative conversations together about events in which preteens' perspectives are confirmed and validated, preteens experience a greater sense of well-being in terms of higher self-esteem and self-competence.[21] When talking about negative or stressful events, it's important for parents to flesh out the *who, where, what,* and *when* of the event for their preteen children. The idea is to create order out of chaos because preteens are not yet able to accomplish this coherence on their own. It's especially important when discussing negative experiences that parents talk specifically about the negative emotions involved and why (*We were sad because Grandma died*) rather than simply offering general expressions of negative emotion (*It was really hard on all of us*). When parents repeatedly dwelt on negative emotions surrounding stressful events without resolving or explaining them for their preteens, their preteens experienced higher levels of depression, anxiety, and behavior problems. This finding fits with other research that preteens with asthma, a chronic stressor, showed better well-being when mothers explained in more detail *why* their children might feel the way they did about their asthma.

The work in this same group of families on their conversations during dinnertime underscores the important role of fathers. During dinnertime conversations, mothers are more likely to talk about remote events than are fathers, who are more likely to focus on events of the day. Children's well-being is highest when both types of events are discussed—that is, when mothers provide more information about remote events, and evaluate children's contributions to their stories, and when fathers request more information about their children's day. A picture is emerging in which both mothers and fathers play vital but different roles in family storytelling with preteens. Mothers are doing more of the work in filling in the family history for their preteens, in line with their role in many families as the "kin-keepers,"[22] whereas both mothers and fathers are important for getting preteens to talk about their everyday experiences, both positive and negative. There's no reason, however, why fathers can't also tell stories of family history with their children.

When using Rich Reminiscing with preteens about positive happenings, such as participating in a wedding, winning a soccer game, or going on a family vacation, it's still best for your child's self-esteem to focus on the positive aspects of those experiences. How did your child help get the winning goal by passing the ball to the striker at just the right time? How did your child feel when he finally got to the head of the line for Space Mountain? Positive talk about positive events appears to be particularly important for younger preteens' self-esteem (8- to 10-year-olds). When Yan Chen and I asked parents to talk with their 8- to 10-year-olds about family vacations, parents who evaluated their children more positively and who talked less about their children's negative emotions had children with higher self-esteem.[23]

In this conversation about a family vacation between 9-year-old Sarah and her mother, notice how her mother keeps the talk extremely positive, and ends on a positive note.

> Mother: *We're going to talk about the one (holiday) we just went to in January for the Colgate Games, where did we go then?*
>
> Sarah: *Ah we went to Nelson.*
>
> Mother: *That's right, what did we go there for?*
>
> Sarah: *Um, we went there for this um, Colgate Games and we went, and my friend was there, and we went there there and they're got all the clubs and that that were going there and only the, ah, only the people that get high scores get to go to Nelson, and yeah.*
>
> Mother: *Okay so who, who, who, how did you get there do you remember?*
>
> Sarah: *Um went there by ah um car.*
>
> Mother: *And how cool was that?*
>
> Sarah: *Not cool at all.*
>
> Mother: *(laughs) Where did you sit in the car?*
>
> Sarah: *I sat in the back all the time.*
>
> Mother: *Did yah? Did I not let you in the front?*
>
> Sarah: *No.*
>
> Mother: *Ah well.*
>
> Sarah: *Never.*
>
> Mother: *And where did we stay? Do you remember?*
>
> Sarah: *We stayed at the Ophir Lodge.*
>
> Mother: *Ahh good, I didn't even remember that. And what was the best thing about staying there?*
>
> Sarah: *Well it had a toilet in there.*
>
> Mother: *For Mia (little sister).*
>
> Sarah: *(laughs) Well that there were comfortable beds in there and that the best thing about the house was because that they*

had nice comfy beds and they had nice um, they had nice photos on the tv.

Mother: What about um where, where it was really close to? What was the best—

Sarah: Ah very close to the beach.

Mother: Yes, how cool was the beach?

Sarah: Ah cool and it wasn't, and I found like a million shells....

Mother: Mmmm.

Sarah: That you don't normally find in Dunedin.

Mother: That's right, how many did we collect that night, that you did that?

Sarah: Fifty?

Mother: At least.

Sarah: Mmm maybe more.

Mother: That was nice wasn't it?

Sarah: Yeah. And my friend was there...

Mother: Yeah.

Sarah: Katie that played the poet game with me, she's been my friend for ages, and she does her skates with me, and Lou (little brother) went to their pool.

Mother: Yeah that's right, at their motel unit didn't they?

Sarah: Yeah they have a pool.

Mother: How much time did you and Katie spend in the pool?

Sarah: Fifty hours probably.

Mother: And what about the games, what did you think about the athletics?

Sarah: Ah it was fun, there was a day that it was really rainy and then I was scared I was going to slip but I was on grass, but then I didn't slip and that's good on the relay, and I got, got like about one for coming, one little flag thing.

Mother: Ah yeah the pennant, pennant or something they call it.

Sarah: Yeah yeah I got one of those coming third, and then I got this little ribbons for coming like second, I mean not second um for fourth and fifth.

Mother: Yeah that's right.

Sarah: *And I got another one for fourth and then I got a little red one for to say welcome, a little thing like that.*

Mother: *Yeah that's right.* [intervening talk about little brother] *Mmm ah it was a great trip wasn't it?*

Sarah: *Yip*

Mother: *It was the best trip ever.*

Sarah: *Yip*

Mother: *(laughs) That's cool, Sarah.*

This pattern of children having higher self-esteem when parents focus on positive aspects of positive events, such as family vacations, is identical to findings with younger children.[24]

For families with older preteens (11- to 12-year-olds), however, the picture looked quite different. When talking about positive events like a family vacation, older preteens had higher self-esteem when their parents started to talk about some of the *negative* aspects of positive events and their children's *negative* emotions. Even at this older age, it's still best to keep the talk positive on the whole, and to end on a positive note.

Mother: *Mmm, yes, it was very cramped. Unfortunately at Glenlake Lodge they had misunderstood what we needed and booked us into a cabin and because it was the busy holiday season we ended up but having no choice but to stay there. Never mind, we coped, and it was fun because we cooked dinner in the main part of the restaurant and it was good to watch the helicopter taking off.*

The message is that the degree to which you can bring up negative aspects of positive events depends on the age and developmental level of your preteen. As they get closer to adolescence, preteens get better at acknowledging and accepting that most experiences are a mixed bag of emotions. Your child may be exceptionally mature and be able to handle talk about negative aspects of positive events at age 9 or 10, but for most children, it's better to wait until age 11 or 12 to start acknowledging the downside of supposedly positive events. And whatever the age of your child, as I will tell you in more detail in the adolescent chapter, it's still best to end the conversation on a positive note (*and it was fun because we cooked dinner in the* *main part of the restaurant*). Because preteen girls in particular are already becoming prone to **rumination***, or obsessive, unproductive thinking about negative events, it is vital at this age that you model positive resolutions when discussing positive AND negative experiences.

In terms of specific ways to use Rich Reminiscing with your preteen about shared experiences, it's especially important now for you to confirm her perspectives, particularly her perspectives on her own emotions, and to make sure that the conversation is balanced, with your child telling at least half of the story. You will still need to ask a few open-ended questions here and there, but your questions are less important at this age because preteens are perfectly capable of providing their version of the event. The goal is to create a coordinated story about a past event in which both you and your preteen are contributing to the story in a collaborative way. It's okay to negate or negotiate the facts of the event, but be willing to back down if you might be in the wrong. Around Mother's Day I was reminiscing with Dylan (aged 10) about past Mother's Days, and I incorrectly recalled that it was his big brother Ben who made a card for me one year and attached a bag of herbal tea so that I could have a relaxing moment. I also recalled that Ben had made the cup of tea for me later that day. Dylan ever so politely corrected me that he was the one who had given me the card with the tea bag, and that he knew because he remembered making it in Mrs. Gray's class at school, and that after he gave it to me we snuggled in bed together for my Mother's Day "lie-in" while I read a book of mythology to him. I acknowledged that he was absolutely right about giving me the card with the tea bag, and I apologized for attributing it to Ben. Dylan said that he wasn't the one who had made me the cup of tea, though, so we left the discussion with the possibility that maybe Ben really did do that bit. The point is that preteens have pretty amazing memory skills, so if you have even the slightest doubt about your own memory, it might pay to trust their version of the experience.

Stories from Your Childhood

Although you've probably told your younger children some stories of your own childhood, it is in the preteen period when they start getting really interested in hearing about what you were like as a child.[25] Before this age, they're mostly too focused on their own affairs, and it's too hard for them to imagine you as a child for the story to be vivid enough to interest them. With their increased cognitive and perspective-taking skills at this age, it's now easier for them to imagine a little Mom or Dad doing the silly, brave, dangerous, or generous things in your stories.

In writing this book, I have become more aware of how often and when I tell my children stories about my own childhood. These stories come up naturally throughout the day in response to some related incident or issue. I'd say that every day I tell at least one or two brief stories about my own childhood to my children. In one study, families told a story every 5 minutes, or about 6 stories per meal![26] Most of these stories were about events of the day, but one-third were about events from the family's past, including parents' stories of their own childhood. Slowly but surely, we are passing down the stories of our lives to our children—and all the lessons that we think we have learned. To this day, every time I carry a stick for any reason, I think of my father's admonition "Never run with a stick" and the accompanying story he told about his older brother Felix running with a stick of bamboo, falling, and poking a hole through his lip. "He had a scar there for the rest of his life."

This story would fall into the class of morality tales, and we all know there are many: "Put that Nerf gun down. Don't ever point a gun at someone's face. Remember the story about how Dad once shot Uncle Barry with a dart gun and it permanently damaged his eye? Uncle Barry never forgave Dad for that, and Dad still feels bad about what he did to his little brother. You don't want to do something to Dylan that you will regret for the rest of your life...." (and probably on for a bit too long). These morality tales can and should be brief.

The more interesting stories about your childhood, and the ones your children most want to hear, are those that are directly relevant to their situation but aren't of the preachy variety. These stories serve several purposes: First, they show that you are listening to your child's current concerns and that you empathize with what he or she is going through at the moment. Second, these stories reinforce to your child that he's not alone, that others have experienced similar problems. When Dylan hurt his achilles tendon playing basketball, I told him the story of how I hurt my achilles tendon while riding with my dad in a child seat on a bicycle. I was too big for it and my feet dangled down and one got caught in the spokes. I still remember the feel of my heel getting caught and trying to cry out as my dad "pumped" the bicycle to make it go even faster, and how horrible he felt when he realized what had happened. I had to go to the emergency room because they were afraid the tendon was torn, but it wasn't, and I remembered my mom making me a vanilla milkshake after I was safely home in bed, how good it tasted and how secure I felt. Dylan, age 9, listened raptly with wide eyes and asked a few questions like who was Achilles and why did he have a tendon named after him. Then Dylan went on to tell a story of one of his recent injuries, when he fell by a stove, put his hand out to stop himself, and got a nasty burn. You know your story worked if your child produces one of his own on the same theme. Psychologists Carole Peterson and Allyssa McCabe have used this technique of "giving a story to get a story" to great success with children from ages 4 to 9.[27]

These stories from your childhood work best if they stay small and are inserted into the normal stream of conversation: they must be highly relevant to your child's current situation, they need to be relatively short but dramatic, and you should try to draw an explicit link to your child's life (*So that's how I hurt my achilles tendon when I was just a bit younger than you are now, and everything turned out fine in the end*). Pretend you are making a pitch for a movie idea and you have only 2 minutes, because that's about the maximum time you have to tell a story during a conversation with a child and have her stay interested—this length is of course different if you prepare your child for a longer, more drawn-out story, perhaps at the dinner table or at bedtime. As always, talk animatedly, but not too quickly, and be sure to answer any questions that come up during or after the story, even if they take you on a tangent away from your point of the story (the history of Achilles). If it's a story your child has heard before, be prepared for him to contribute to the telling, and confirm, correct, and expand on those contributions to create a collaborative storytelling time.

This is the prime age for helping children create visual representations of their life stories, for interviewing grandparents about their experiences and about family history, and for scrapbooking or digital storytelling of family holidays or fun times with friends. Mapping a family tree can be a fun activity for some kids in this age group, and there are even websites to help you do this with scanned photos if available. If your child is part of one or more blended families, then your family tree may quickly grow into a "family forest."[28] Seeing all of the ways that they are connected to important people in their lives will help preteens to see themselves as part of a larger web of relationships. These activities won't appeal to every preteen, though, so use your judgment. But do it now for those children who show an interest, because in a few years your teenager may think you are a complete nerd for even suggesting such an activity.

This is also the age at which some preteens, most of them girls, get interested in diary writing. (It is possible, though, that the *Diary of a Wimpy Kid* series may be encouraging diary writing among preteen boys too.) I have mixed feelings about diary writing for young girls in particular. Because of what we now know about the possible perils of focusing on negative emotions without help in resolving those negative emotions, in spoken or in written form, I worry that diary writing may encourage rumination at a young age. However, if your daughter or son wants to keep a diary, I don't think you should stop them. And you definitely should not read what he or she has written! That violation of privacy would not set the stage well for your future relationship with your teenager.

Always remember: You are creating a memory bank of stories for your child to draw on in the teenage and young adult years when they will need stories desperately to guide them in difficult life decisions. So choose, and tell, your stories wisely.

Table 4.1 Tips for Sharing Stories with Preteens		
What to Do	**How**	**Why it Helps**
1. *Read books with your preteens as long as they will let you*	One parent-tested tip is to choose a book for your shared reading time that neither of you reads on your own. It's best if you can choose a book that is slightly beyond your child's current reading level, as long as the book is interesting to both of you. If your preteen prefers to read his or her own book at bedtime, then read your shared book during the day—and allow your child to play with toys during the reading session if he or she wishes. Continue to define a word here and there, or to ask a genuine question, "Now what was the name of that guy who stole the dragon's egg?" but save most of your discussion for before the reading session (to replay the most recent events) or after (to go over any plot twists or especially character motivations that your child may have missed).	Advances vocabulary learning, aids story comprehension, creates comfort and solace.

(continued)

Table 4.1 Tips for Sharing Stories with Preteens (*Continued*)		
What to Do	**How**	**Why it Helps**
2. *Share stories of all kinds of experiences with your preteens*	Preteens will still enjoy stories about family vacations, holidays, and times that things went horribly wrong in a funny way. Help your preteen to make connections across events. For instance, you can contrast the earlier camping trip when the tent leaked with the later camping trip when it didn't rain a drop. Or you can compare the sadness that your child felt when her dog died with the sadness you felt when your grandmother died. **Be sure to allow your child to tell at least half of the story**. Supply a bit of the story yourself and then wait for your preteen to fill in the next bit. Follow your child's lead by adapting the next bit you tell to match onto the aspect she just narrated. If your child doesn't mention emotions, you can supply your own emotional perspective and then ask for his. *Do not ever assume* that your child shares your emotional perspective on an event. Keep conversations mostly positive, especially with younger preteens.	Enhances storytelling skill, self-understanding, emotion understanding, well-being, and self-esteem.

(*continued*)

Table 4.1 Tips for Sharing Stories with Preteens (*Continued*)

What to Do	How	Why it Helps
3. *Help fill in the first chapters of your child's life by telling stories about when your child was very young*	It's a comforting ritual for you to keep telling your child's birth story, usually on each birthday, being sure to let your child contribute to the story from previous versions. Weave in other stories of his or her early childhood as they come up naturally in conversation. For instance, when your child wins an art award at school, you can tell the story of the first art competition that he won when he was 3 years old. Take care! Because your child can't remember these experiences, you are authoring them for your child. Highlight positive aspects and attributes of your child in your stories.	Promotes self-understanding and a sense of belonging.
4. *Tell stories of your own past and your families' past*	Preteens love to hear these stories as long as they are apt and appropriately timed. When he is having trouble with a friend, you could tell the story of a fight you had with a friend and how it was resolved. Make explicit connections to similar situations in her life.	Helps preteens gain insight into life events; establishes connections across generations.

(*continued*)

Table 4.1 Tips for Sharing Stories with Preteens (*Continued*)		
What to Do	**How**	**Why it Helps**
	When telling stories of your families' past, provide as much detail as you can, although you won't always have firsthand memories of these events. Even providing children with a few details about their ancestors is a way of linking them to their family histories. "Your great-great-grandmother Nellie used to win prizes for her cakes. She lived on a farm in Texas and made 20 cakes a week and sold them at the market to earn extra money for her family. You're a bit like Great Great Grandma Nellie because you make really good cakes too."	
5. *Parent-Tested Tip*: Start a *book-of-the-month* ritual	I began this practice when my children were young. On the first day of every month (payday), I take them to the university bookshop and we all select a "book of the month." The atmosphere is quiet and calm, so we usually spend several hours browsing and then finally selecting our	Engenders a love of books and of reading; if you choose the right bookstore, it exposes your child to high-quality books. If money is tight, take him to a nice used

(*continued*)

Table 4.1 Tips for Sharing Stories with Preteens (*Continued*)		
What to Do	**How**	**Why it Helps**
	books. Then we head home for some more cozy reading time with a cup of hot chocolate for them and a cup of tea for me.	bookstore, or arrange a bookswap party with her friends.
6. *Parent-Tested Tip:* Create a "Story of My Life" timeline with your child	You can decorate your timeline with accompanying photos of significant events. Or scrapbook special family events such as holidays, birthdays, and family vacations.	Helps children order important events in their lives; highlights memories of special family events
7. *Media Tip:* Watch movies with your preteen	It's still a good idea to watch movies with your preteen, asking questions at key points if not too distracting, or discussing the movie afterward to make sure they understand the plot and the characters' goals, emotions, and motivations for their actions. Children of this age no longer need as much assistance in understanding the basic plot of most movies, but they still need some help figuring out characters' motivations and complex resolutions.	Helps children's understanding of longer and more complex storylines

Table 4.2 Developmental Snapshot of a Preteen[29]		
Domain	**What Happens and When**	**Why It Matters for Story Sharing**
Language and Reading Development	Continued increase in *vocabulary*: By age 10–11, children have a vocabulary of around 40,000 words. This doubling of vocabulary from 8 to 10 occurs in part because children are now able to learn new words from books.	Vocabulary growth leads to advances in preteens' oral and written storytelling.
	By age 10, most preteens (around 2/3) are fluent *readers* who can understand what they read. Preteens are starting to become more efficient and strategic when reading for understanding—they are starting to know when they haven't understood what they are reading and to go back and reread. Some preteens are also avid *writers* of fiction, nonfiction, or autobiography.	Children's reading of more difficult books may also expose them to more complex story structures that could transfer to their oral and written storytelling. Reading complex story lines might help increase the level of detail and precision in storytelling and story writing. Creating stories in written format allows for more complex and detailed plots and character development than is possible in most oral stories.

(*continued*)

Table 4.2 Developmental Snapshot of a Preteen (*Continued*)		
Domain	**What Happens and When**	**Why It Matters for Story Sharing**
Cognitive Development	*Speed of processing* information increases rapidly during the preteen years, especially from 8 to 12 years.	Processing speed might help children tell longer, more complicated stories entailing greater memory demands.
	Children advance in their understanding of the *conventions of time* (clocks, calendars). This growth is especially evident in their ability to coordinate multiple time scales, such as knowing that they turned 10 during 4th grade, which was during the 2009–2010 school year.	Conventional time knowledge helps children date the time of events, which is relevant for their ability to order events in their life in relation to each other.
	Increases in *metacognition and perspective-taking*: Children move from understanding that others have different perspectives to being able to view a situation from another's perspective. Toward the end of the preteen years, they may even be able to view situations from a 3rd-party perspective, coordinating both perspectives from a neutral vantage point.	Preteens' ability to take more sophisticated perspectives in stories might help in tailoring information to their audience. *I thought that she thought that ... You remember it this way, but I remember it that way.*

(*continued*)

Table 4.2 Developmental Snapshot of a Preteen (*Continued*)		
Domain	**What Happens and When**	**Why It Matters for Story Sharing**
Self-Concept Development	*Self-esteem* continues to rise until age 11 or 12, when there is a dip in self-esteem for both boys and girls. Boys recover their childhood levels of self-esteem and more by high school, but girls do not reach and exceed their childhood levels of self-esteem again until they are young adults.	Shared storytelling needs to stay mostly positive, and end on a positive note, because children's self-esteem is extremely fragile at this point.
	Self-concept continues to differentiate according to athletic, appearance, behavioral, academic, and friendship realms. One advance in this period is the growing ability to coordinate multiple selves (*Who I am at home with my parents* vs. *Who I am at school with my friends*).	Gains in self-understanding may help children know why they acted a certain way in one situation and another way in a different situation (e.g., they might act kind and forgiving with a friend but not with a brother or sister).
Social and Emotional Development	Deepening of *friendships*—children have fewer but closer friendships, often same-sex at this age. Friendships are now based on mutual trust, sharing of interests, and cooperation. Toward the end of the preteen years, friendships are based on intimacy and loyalty.	Reminiscing with peers begins in earnest at the end of the preteen years.

(*continued*)

Table 4.2 Developmental Snapshot of a Preteen (*Continued*)		
Domain	**What Happens and When**	**Why It Matters for Story Sharing**
	Preteens can understand *mixed emotions* as well as fuller understanding of *complex emotions* such as pride, guilt, and shame.	Preteens' sophisticated appreciation that emotional perspectives on an event can change over time allows more complex story sharing.
	Coping skills: Major advances in coping include being able to use self-talk to calm oneself; reframing a problem; generating multiple solutions to a problem and choosing one solution over others. Gender differences in coping start to appear by age 10–11, with girls more likely to ruminate on negative events, and boys more likely to problem-solve or use distraction.	Story sharing, especially about personal experiences, is one way to help children learn to cope with negative experiences in positive ways, and to model problem-solving and resolution rather than rumination.
Physical Development	Rapid increases in all aspects of *executive functioning* (inhibition, speed, memory capacity) occur in the preteen years from ages 9 to 12.	Longer attention spans enable children to read longer books and to concentrate for longer stretches of time.

(continued)

Domain	What Happens and When	Why It Matters for Story Sharing
	Brain development: Pruning of connections creates more efficient cortical networks. Girls experience cortical thinning in the frontal lobes at 9.5 years, whereas boys don't start until 10.5 years, possibly reflecting/leading to gender differences in executive functioning.	Executive functioning helps children monitor their understanding of what they read. It might also help them organize their oral stories and to select events and literary devices appropriately to use in their oral and written stories.

Table 4.2 Developmental Snapshot of a Preteen (*Continued*)

5

Sharing Stories with Your Adolescent

Ages 12–18

Man is eminently a storyteller. His search for a purpose, a cause, an ideal, a mission and the like is largely a search for a plot and a pattern in the development of his life story—a story that is basically without meaning or pattern.

~Paul Auster

What do all parents of adolescents[1] know but developmental psychologists rarely acknowledge? Most young adolescents go through a period when it's very hard to engage them in conversation, any conversation, much less storytelling. Your wildest efforts are met with monosyllables, even grunts. I have actually heard myself saying more than once to my teenage son, "Was that a yes or a no?" Previously vivacious, talkative, and engaged children appear to go absolutely silent. Study after study identifies early adolescence as the most negative and contentious phase of parent-child relationships.[2]

Fortunately, this desert of silence is an illusion. Most adolescents still want and need desperately to talk to the adults in their lives. In fact, although the time adolescents spend with family members decreases dramatically from age 10 to 18, you may be surprised to learn that the time they spend *talking* with their parents stays constant over that period. For girls, the time they spend talking with their mothers even increases in late adolescence. They simply don't want to talk on your agenda and your timetable. If you are setting the topic and the time to talk, most often you will be met with the impenetrable wall of silence, or at best one- and two-word responses: "Fine," "Yeah," "No," and "It's okay, Mom." "It's AG, Dad." ("All good," for those of you not yet initiated into textspeak).

The good thing is that the solution is one you have already learned in the earlier chapters of this book. But now these principles are as important, if not more important, than they were for your toddler or preschooler. In some ways, it's helpful if you think of your teen as going through another toddler phase: (1) They are asserting their independence, which is why you get into power struggles with them; and (2) There is a definite gap between the intensity of their emotions and their cognitive capabilities to control and focus those emotions, especially in early adolescence. So, in keeping with the "teenager as toddler" theory, here's what you must do in order to successfully share stories with them.

1. **Follow your teenager's interests.** Try to let him set the topic and the course of the conversation. See Chapter 7 for some practical tips on the best times to talk and the activities that will help conversations spring up naturally with teenagers.

2. When you do ask them questions about their experiences, **try to make your questions open-ended.** *How was that for you when Evie told you she didn't want to be friends anymore?*

3. **Respond by repeating, rephrasing, and adding to what your teenager says** to make sure you understand, and so that she knows you are listening. You should be listening, REALLY listening, more than you are talking almost anytime you have a conversation with your teen. *I see what you mean. Sounds like Evie has some other problems in her life right now.*

All of these techniques, however, need to be delivered in an adult voice so that your teen doesn't feel patronized. And waiting for the optimum time and place to talk is now even more essential than when your child was younger. You MUST be willing to drop everything, and I do mean everything, when your teenager is ready to talk, even if that moment is—and it probably will be—at 11:00 on a night before an important meeting at work. Realize that you may not have another chance for a month!

Try not to think of your adolescent as being self-centered and stubborn. Just as it is vital to think of your toddler's temper tantrums as a product of the gap between their cognitive and self-control capabilities and their strong desires, it's best to think of your adolescent's silence and grumpiness as a product of the dramatic changes they are going through physically, cognitively, socially, and emotionally (see Table 5.2, "Developmental Snapshot of an Adolescent" at the end of this chapter). No wonder they are so self-focused. They will not always be this way. In a few months or at most a few years, your sunny, talkative child will reemerge in an adult body.

Bear in mind too that adolescents are also developing conversational skills with their siblings, friends, and romantic partners, not just with you. One of my friends overheard the following conversation between her 14-year-old son James and his friend Steve about Steve's new girlfriend:

James: *So, have you kissed her yet?*
Steve: *Kissed her? That's the least of my worries. I'm just trying to keep the conversation going.*

Why does it matter that you continue to share stories with your adolescent, especially when it is such a Sisyphean task? Your adolescent still needs your guidance through stories, more than he ever did before. The stakes are high: They are negotiating one of the most difficult passages of their lives. They are forming identities that they will carry with them into all of their future relationships—with friends, romantic partners, neighbors, workmates, children—and into their careers. Your stories can help them to create a self that is resilient, caring, optimistic, and communicative.

Some parents of teenagers seem to think that their main task is to encourage their adolescents to become autonomous beings. And independence IS a crucial task of adolescence. It is equally important, however, for adolescents to maintain connections with family while creating new connections with friends and community members. Although by late adolescence, teenagers actually spend more time with friends and romantic partners than with parents, their parents remain important to them throughout their lives if their relationship is strong. In fact, one of the best predictors of adolescents possessing a strong sense of self AND forming healthy relationships outside the family is the strength and health of their relationships with family members.[3] Sharing stories with your adolescents will help them to accomplish both types of connections: with family and with friends.

THE STORIES ADOLESCENTS READ, UNDERSTAND, AND TELL: FROM BOOKS AND FROM PERSONAL EXPERIENCES

The Stories Adolescents Read

Most adolescents are fully independent readers.[4] That doesn't mean, however, that they are spending much of their free time reading for pleasure. The time adolescents report reading books for pleasure decreases steadily through the teenage years, displaced by listening to music, watching TV, playing computer and videogames, and sports.[5] For many adolescents, even those who are excellent readers and who read avidly prior to adolescence, reading has diminished in importance in their lives. My personal belief is that this hiatus in reading is not something we should bemoan. It is a temporary product of all the other developments in their busy lives: social, athletic, musical, academic, and cultural pursuits. As long as they were keen readers before this age, it is a pursuit to which they will return later in life.

One reason for the hiatus in leisure reading is that they are now reading more for school, both fiction and nonfiction, and that reading is assigned to them. There is simply less time to read for pleasure. And in terms of life balance, if they are spending several hours a day with books for school, it may be better for them to spend their precious few leisure hours socializing with friends and in musical, artistic, or sporting activities than doing more reading. Perhaps it's best to think of this stage of reading in terms of improvements in quality, not quantity. They should be deepening their insight into the material they do read, even if they are reading less often for pleasure. It's great if you can keep them interested in doing at least some reading outside school by keeping a book "going" on the bedside table, and stealing larger chunks of reading time when at the beach on summer vacation or on a rainy Sunday afternoon. But it is unrealistic to expect adolescents to spend hours reading every day for pleasure, and it may even keep them from accomplishing important developmental tasks in the social, physical, community, and cultural arenas of their busy lives. In fact, one study even revealed a long-term link between time spent reading in early adolescence and depression.[6] However, if your teen is not reading at all for pleasure, or if the time he used to spend reading books is instead being replaced by time spent with screen media, then see my tips below (Box 5.1) for increasing leisure reading and putting the brakes on gaming and TV watching. In adolescence, it's all about balance: between family and friends, between schoolwork and entertainment, between spending time alone and with others.

Box 5.1 The Stories Adolescents See and Enact: Teenagers and Media Consumption

---

Most computer and videogames that adolescents play, even role-playing games, are not narratives per se (e.g., Runescape, Minecraft, Sims). Stuff happens, or stuff is collected, but it's not encapsulated in story form. The few videogames that are narrative in form tend to be of two types: first-person shooters, such as *Halo* and *Mass Effect*, or fantasy narratives such as *Skyrim* and *Oblivion*. All are violent to a greater or lesser extent. And the narrative format of the games does make them highly engaging—some would say addictive—for teens. I overheard my son Ben (15) and his friends referring to the "storyline" of *Mass Effect 2*, which has won top gaming awards. I asked Ben later what he meant by storyline, and he replied: *The storyline is what makes it interesting to play. So you can have a game with great graphics and everything, but if it has a sh*& storyline, you don't want to play it. It's just boring. The storyline is what keeps you going.*

Unfortunately, adolescents' greater cognitive capabilities do not appear to protect them from the effects of videogame violence. All of the research I reviewed in the preteen chapter on

(continued)

Box 5.1 (*Continued*)

the effects of violent videogames applies equally to adolescents in terms of the links between long hours of gaming and problems with aggression, withdrawal, and depression. Experimental studies, in which adolescents play different types of videogames in a lab and then dish out varying doses of hostility to a confederate, also support a causal connection between videogame violence and aggression for boys and girls. The effects are not huge, probably because there are many other reasons for adolescents' aggressive behavior besides violent videogames, but they are robust across many different types of studies: correlational, longitudinal, and experimental.[7] This risk may be greater for adolescent boys due to the sheer greater amount of time they spend playing videogames,[8] although when girls are heavy gamers, the risks are the same. Why, you may ask, are violent videogames scapegoated, when most parents don't bat an eye when a teenager spends hours reading the fantasy battle scenes in *Eragon* and *A Game of Thrones*? I think this is a very good question, but right now it is an unanswered one. As parents, and as researchers, we need to know whether reading violent material in books and watching them on movies is equally harmful for adolescents as enacting them in videogames. Research has not yet tested the impact of the delivery system of violence on adolescents.

Social networking is yet another screen phenomenon that has taken firm hold in our teenagers' lives. Teenage boys and girls both report spending time every day on social networking, although girls outstrip boys in the length of time they spend on these sites (probably because the boys have turned to gaming instead!).[9] The evidence is still unclear as to whether social networking is largely a positive or negative influence in teens' lives. Some research shows that social networking can enhance teens' written communication and technical skills and strengthen their friendships. Potentially, social networking could provide a safe forum for teens to create and safely explore alternate ideal identities. On the negative side, however, other research shows that social networking can be a forum for cyber-bullying and that it can even lead to social withdrawal and "Facebook depression" as teens compare the seemingly more exciting, fun-packed virtual

(*continued*)

> **Box 5.1** *(Continued)*
>
> lives of others with the banality of their own real lives. The AAP recommends sticking to the age guidelines for social networking sites (minimum age of 13) and actively supervising your teen's use of these sites. My own rule for social networking is that until they are 16, the boys must stay online "friends" with me if they want to have a Facebook account so that I can keep track of inappropriate content and potential cyber-bullying or "trolling."

The Stories Adolescents Tell (and Write)

Becoming a teenager is a critical age in personal storytelling development. The critical development is insight. Before age 14 or 15, very few teenagers have true insight into life's events. They can tell you that their lives have changed, sometimes in dramatic ways, but it's very difficult for them to say what these changes *mean* for who they are, and how events in their past have shaped the person they are becoming.[10] Recall that preteens are able to narrate and make some sense of single events in their lives, but they aren't very good yet at deep interpretation of events, or at connecting across events in their lives. This ability to compare and contrast events—and to group similar events across one's life—may be a precursor to drawing meaning from those events.[11] Recall that in the preteen years, girls have a slight edge in insight over boys. By mid-adolescence and beyond, girls tell richer and more emotional stories of their lives compared to boys. Throughout adolescence, boys may still need help from parents in understanding and interpreting life events and emotional experiences.[12]

Contrast Anna's and Charlie's stories of events they selected as "life-changing" at age 12. Both stories are about a grandmother's death, but Anna reaches a deeper level of insight into understanding the way her grandmother's death shaped her life, by deepening the connection with the woman who became her step-grandmother. Charlie, in contrast, offers only a simple emotional perspective on the death: "sad."

<u>Charlie's Life-Changing Event at Age 12</u>

Charlie: *When Nana died last year, umm we were on holiday in Nelson. And we started coming back home and when we got to*

Christchurch we got a call that said she'd died. And mmm that's
probably it.

Researcher: *And how did this event change your life?*

Charlie: *Umm, like sad.*

Anna's Life-Changing Event at Age 12

Anna: *Well my nana died the year my brother was born. Like*
before he was born so that changed my life. Oh when I was four
or something my grandad, maybe I was three, my grandad mar-
ried my nana, who died, um married her friend. Like they were
really good friends. He married her, and um yea. I really like her.

Researcher: *And how did this event change your life?*

Anna: *Because if they didn't get married well, I, I'd still know her*
probably but not as well. And she's really nice.

At age 16, Anna and Charlie selected different events to discuss as life-changing. Anna's was starting high school (which occurs at age 12 in New Zealand) and Charlie's event was starting to play rugby competitively at age 13. Anna is once again insightful, even eloquent at times, about how entering high school has changed her view of herself and her relationships. Charlie is getting closer to drawing meaning from life experiences too as he discusses how his love of rugby shaped his friendships and even his choice of which high school to attend, a traditional all-boys' school.

Anna's Life-Changing Event at Age 16

Anna: *Going to high school. Um, I got way more confident in*
like, my brain, and and like what I could do with everything.
Like everything I enjoy I just became way more confident and
I was actually good at it. And I think when I got to high school
I became closer with my brother because we were already quite
close in age but like when you get older the age gap kind of
shrinks. So it wasn't really high school that did that, 'cos we're
at different high schools but more the fact that I was high school
age I suppose. And that's really nice.

Researcher: *And how did this event change your life?*

Anna: *Um, I'm not as self-conscious now. And, I'm just happier,*
I don't know really. And it's nice that I'm closer with my brother,

'cause we've always been quite close but closer. It's good. And like his friends are my friends and he's friends with all the people I'm friends with so it's like we're just this massive group of people that are really cool.

Charlie's Life-Changing Event at Age 16

Charlie: *Starting playing rugby in Year 8 (7th grade). It was one of the hardest years to start... 'cause people were different sizes and stuff... and I didn't really like it first year... but... yeah, I made heaps of new friends. (11-second pause) Stuff like that.*

Researcher: *Mmmhmm... anything else you can remember about it?*

Charlie: *Played for Kaikorai [rugby club]... and I remember going away to like... (11-second pause) Invercargill and stuff.*

Researcher: *Okay... and can you tell me how this changed your life?*

Charlie: *Because friends now and stuff are based around rugby... met heaps of new people and stuff... and... sort of chose to go to Kings High 'cause I like rugby.*

We were not able to see Tia at age 12 because she was living overseas at the time, but at age 16 her life-changing experience was the move to Australia. Clearly she has reflected on this experience at length, and is able to integrate multiple points of view on the experience, including her own burgeoning thoughts on her Māori identity. Her perspective is more sophisticated than either Anna's or Charlie's, no doubt in part because of the more difficult and complex life events with which she has had to grapple.

Tia's Life-Changing Event at Age 16

Tia: *Moving to Australia. Well I think I was nine, May actually, yeah we just moved. I remember when Mum told us and we sort of cried for ages but then like it was actually really good for us because I think it was good to not be the Māori kid for a while, like we just got to be another kid.*

Researcher: *Yeah.*

Tia: *And I think that was really good for learning yourself, like we didn't have any prejudice or anything so that was good. Yeah*

we got a lot of opportunities that we wouldn't have had if we
hadn't moved and we got to be with Joe who's my stepdad. He
looks after us. We sort of, I don't know, we kind of went up in the
financial scale of things as well. We were pretty poor in Brighton
like with my Dad so that was quite important as well because we
sort of learnt. Like 'cause we'd always learnt not to expect things
so we were really happy when we got them and then Australia is
really materialistic and so we sort of we were behind in that but
we didn't care and so that was also important because we didn't,
yeah. It was just cool.

Researcher: *And how did this event change your life?*

Tia: *Well we just got all those experiences and I was introduced*
to music. I probably wouldn't have been otherwise because we
wouldn't have afforded it which is a really big thing for me. And
the whole Māori thing and yeah.

(Earlier in the interview, Tia clarified that she wasn't really intro-
duced to Māori culture until she got to her current high school,
because "like my father is my link with the Māori culture and he
didn't really teach us anything. Like we said a karakia (prayer)
before (meals) but we didn't know what it meant or anything.")

Sometime between age 14 and 16, teenagers become capable of integrating events into a life story. If you think about what a story of
one's life involves, this is an extremely complex task. The building
blocks are the ability to first understand and tell a story of a single
life event, to choose which events to include in the life story, to be
able to make connections to other similar events, and to pull all of
these events together into a coherent whole. The storyteller must also
take the interests of the listener into account. Obviously, to attempt
to include every happening in a life story would be meaningless (and
extremely tiresome for the listener). Writer and psychologist Harriet
Lerner said, "Telling a true story about personal experience is not just
a matter of being oneself, or even of finding oneself. It is also a matter
of choosing oneself."

Some adolescents (most of them girls) are now serious keepers
of a private diary as a way of coping with life events.[13] Many adolescents, boys and girls, write about their daily experiences—from

mundane to major—on social networking sites, blogs, or via instant messaging with friends. In contrast to the preteen years, when writing about negative experiences seemed to increase depression and anxiety, experimental research reveals that writing about a negative event can now help teenagers to cope and flourish. When teens were asked to write about a negative experience for 20 minutes a day for three consecutive days, their levels of distress decreased and their positive outlook increased up to 6 weeks later compared to teens who wrote about a neutral experience.[14] Note that the expressive writing technique involves only three brief writing sessions: Expressive writing does not mean ruminating endlessly on a negative event, which is known to lead to depression. Teens benefited even more from expressive writing when they blogged about their problems rather than wrote about them in a more traditional format, perhaps because in the blogging condition they received anonymous feedback from peers.[15]

Life story development does not end in mid-adolescence: far from it. Even after teenagers are able to filter events, integrate them, and tell a relatively coherent story about their lives, they will continue to deepen their understanding of life events into late adolescence and adulthood. Teenagers make a quantum leap in insight into life events between ages 16 and 18, and it may be even later that young people find a "theme" or "thread" that runs through their life to give it purpose.[16] As parents, I don't think that we can or should hand our teenagers a theme for their lives—they have to figure this out for themselves—but through story sharing we can help them develop the skills of thinking about life events that will enable them to select their own theme for their life. Writer Paul Auster noted the importance of a life theme for self-understanding: "We construct a narrative for ourselves, and that's the thread that we follow from one day to the next. People who disintegrate as personalities are the ones who lose that thread."

Even into midlife, we continue to gain wisdom in understanding the impact of events on our lives.[17] Personal storytelling is by no means fully developed by adolescence, but it seems to have reached a critical mass at around age 15 or 16, when teenagers are able to tell the stories of their lives-in-the-making.

SHARING STORIES WITH YOUR ADOLESCENT

Sharing Stories from Books

Given the fact that adolescents spend less time reading for pleasure than they did as preteens, the opportunities for sharing books with your adolescent using Rich Reading techniques are more limited (see Table 5.1 for tips). Rich Reminiscing about family stories and conversations about personal experiences now plays a much larger role in your story sharing compared to stories from books. There is very little, if any, hard research on how parents can continue to enrich their teenager's reading development, so here I will share with you some parent-tested tips for encouraging a love of literature and a deeper understanding of written stories with your adolescent.

One way is simply to read alongside your teenager, whether that means going to a bookstore together and sampling the wares, or lying end-to-end on the couch on a Sunday afternoon reading your own books. One of my happiest memories—ever—is of a golden afternoon in a bookstore cafe with Ben, aged 13. We were each reading our own books while having cake and a cup of tea for me, a hot chocolate for Ben. Occasionally you can share a bit from your book, or ask a casual question about the book your teenager is reading. Later that day at dinner or before bed, you can try to engage in a more extended discussion about the storyline, the character motivations, and the merits of the book. If your teenager is reading the book for pleasure, though, make sure that you don't turn your conversation into anything that might resemble a classroom discussion or it will be a very short exchange indeed.

If you can manage to read a book *with* your teen, all the better. One of the most heartwarming sights I have ever seen was a diminutive mother and her hulking teenage son reading each other a novel in an airport waiting area. They each held one side of the book, first the mother reading quietly and then the son loudly reading out the dialogue of one of the characters, popping peanuts in his mouth in between passages.

This tip may seem obvious, but when your teenager has a reading assignment or a book report, try to read the assigned book at the same time so that you can discuss it with him or her. I didn't quite manage this with Ben's book report on *The Life of Pi*, but I did read enough to know that the tiger was more than it appeared, so we were able to discuss symbols, allegories, and different levels of meaning in a story. Thankfully, his dad, aunt, and teenage cousins had all read the book in full so they were able to add their interpretations. As long as you are *discussing* interpretations, and having a true exchange of ideas, not letting your teenager lift your ideas by writing them down verbatim in their report, then this extra help from family adds to adolescents' experiences with mature themes—and you are in a much better position than their teachers to help teenagers link these themes to their own lives, especially to their early childhood experiences. Remember that integrating across life events, and by extension from literature to life, is the critical task that adolescents are accomplishing in their narrative development in these years.

Relate their understanding of literature to their level of personal insight at the same ages. From age 12 to 14, young adolescents are at best only achieving vague insight into their own experiences, much less someone else's. Insights are coming fast and thick in mid-adolescence, but insight into one's experiences continues to develop throughout adolescence (and I would argue throughout the lifetime).[18] What we don't know yet is whether reading fiction helps adolescents gain insight into their own experiences, or vice versa. Most likely, both directions are occurring: from life to literature and from literature to life. Reading a book on the right topic at the right time can be life-changing. How many young adolescent girls have found solace and insight in Judy Blume's book, *Are You There, God? It's Me, Margaret.*

Even for avid adolescent readers, boys' and girls' genre preferences can differ, and girls report enjoying reading more than boys.[19] Anna and Charlie exemplified these gender differences by age 16: Anna reported that her favorite books when reading for pleasure were realistic fiction and "chick lit," whereas Charlie reported a strong preference for funny novels and books about sports, as well as a leaning toward cartoons, comics, and magazines. Tia showed more diversity than either Anna or Charlie in her stated preferences for autobiography, biography, classic novels, poetry, fantasy, and nonfiction as well as funny novels and romance. The type of reading material boys and girls gravitate toward may affect how easily they can draw parallels from art to life. It seems much easier for one to benefit from realistic fiction than fantasy or comics in terms of applications to life. Sure, the themes in a fantasy work such as *Eragon* are timeless and universal—loss of the father; tests of strength and courage; realizing your own strengths and limitations—but abstracting these themes and applying them to your own life may be harder via a work of fantasy than realistic fiction. (And all the battle scenes may well distract teenage boys in particular from pulling out these themes in the first place.)

At age 14, Ben spontaneously proffered one Sunday morning, after tucking himself back in bed with some hot buttered toast and a new book, "I just love reading fantasy." When I asked him why, whether it was to escape from real life or to figure out something about his own life, he responded straight away, "To escape!" Of course, realistic fiction can also serve an escapist function.

Sharing Stories from Personal Experiences: Theirs, Yours, and Your Family's

In the late preteen and early adolescent years, it is still possible to have a fairly lengthy and in-depth conversation with your child about shared and unshared experiences, about their early lives, and about family history. Savor these conversations. You may experience a mild to severe drought in family story sharing with your teen until mid-adolescence. Before age 12 or so, you still have the luxury of using Rich Reminiscing techniques to enhance the *quality* of the conversations you have (see Table 5.1 for tips). In our research, we are finding that the way parents talk about positive and negative experiences with their 11- and 12-year-olds can be a protective factor against depression and low self-esteem in mid-adolescence. In mid- and late adolescence, teens with a more positive take on the stories they tell about positive and negative events in their lives also report higher levels of self-esteem.[20]

Specifically, when discussing negative events, parents of happy, well-adjusted young adolescents like Anna and Charlie (recall that we were not able to see Tia at age 12) discussed but did not dwell repeatedly on the negative emotions surrounding the event, either the child's or others' emotions. In the following conversation about Anna's "melt-down" at a tennis tournament, Anna's mother helps her construct an orderly narrative of a highly stressful day. Her mother quickly and squarely confronts the problem, and asks Anna how she felt at various points during the event, encouraging her to compare and contrast events and emotions. The emphasis, however, is on what Anna learned from the experience, with a clear message of "perseverance in the face of adversity" that Anna had already learned, possibly from previous conversations about the day. Anna's mother reminds her of all of the support she received from the other coaches and the kids in resolving the meltdown and carrying on. The pair ends the conversation by discussing a more positive tennis tournament later on, with Anna's mother ending on the high note, "You played really well."

Mother: *How did you feel at the start of the tournament?*

Anna: *It was alright, I was kind of nervous.*

Mother: *It was your biggest tournament ever, wasn't it?*

Anna: *Yeah. And then I played someone and I lost but I knew I'd lose so it didn't matter. And then I played someone else and I thought I'd win but I didn't and I was sad.*

Mother: *So that was the difference?*

Anna: *Yeah, and then I didn't win any of the others and then I won the last one.*

Mother: *And it's not easy to talk about those really bad things is it? But do you want to say what happened in the middle? It's like a meltdown. Really, wasn't it? Yeah kind of. And there were tears.*

Anna: *Yeah*

Mother: *There were tears because it just wasn't a good day at all, was it?*

Anna: *No, not really.*

Mother: *And you didn't want to do it.*

Anna: *No.*

Mother: *And did your mum say that's okay Anna, you don't have to do it?*

Anna: *No (laughs).*

Mother: *What did mum say?*

Anna: *She said, what did you say?*

Mother: *That you had to finish the match.*

Anna: *You have to finish and so I did and then I got a present 'cause I kept going.*

Mother: *It's really important we thought to have acknowledged the fact that you kept going on it was really…*

Anna: *Persevering.*

Mother: *Perseverance in the face of extreme difficulty. It was a really great thing to do. And also Anna you got lots of encouragement from the other coaches…*

Anna: *Yeah.*

Mother: *And the other kids in fact, even when you were having a wee meltdown.*

Anna: *Yeah.*

Mother: *Okay so um yeah that was really hard and we didn't know that you were going to react like that and cry in the tennis tournament and not want to do it did we?*

Anna: *No, not particularly.*

Mother: *Not particularly, it was a bit scrappy. There were some little girls there and they were just a bit scrappy and it wasn't even proper tennis pretty much.*

Anna: *No.*

Mother: *You just didn't really like that, I guess. So…*

Anna: *The under 17s was better because I didn't expect as much.*

Mother: *That's a really good point, yeah. It was better in lots and lots of ways yeah and ah the tennis was actually better…*

Anna: *And*

Mother: *…they were all the bigger girls the tennis was better.*

Anna: *I was the youngest by about two years.*

Mother: *Absolutely the youngest. And you nearly won one set and you did win another set in the under 17s so even though you came last…*

Anna: *But*

Mother: *…you played really well.*

When discussing positive events with their young adolescents, the specific technique that parents of well-adjusted teens used was to link conversations about shared positive events with other positive events, past, present, or future. In discussing a trip to Australia, Anna's mother brought up a similar family trip to an amusement park in New Zealand when Anna was 8. When discussing the potentially mixed emotions surrounding a visit to an amusement park, where it rained for the only week in the past year, Anna and her mother acknowledge the negative but focus mainly on the positive aspects of the experience. Note the synchrony and balance between the two in this conversation, which is by now collaborative reminiscing of the highest order.

Anna: *We went to Australia and we went for a week and it rained. It was the first time it rained in a hundred and, ah no 315 days.*

Mother: *Yeah.*

Anna: *And it was the week we went to Dreamworld (amusement park). And it rained really hard.*

Mother: *It was freezing, wasn't it?*

Anna: *Yeah, a lot of the rides were closed.*

Mother: *Yeah.*

Anna: *Like the roller coaster, but it was okay because there wasn't as many people there and I got to hold a koala and that was fun. And we saw my cousins and I haven't seen them since I was eight. And we went shopping and I got some jandals (sandals) and clothes and went to Australia Zoo and I think it was the week before Steve Irwin died.*

Mother: *It was really close, yeah.*

Anna: *Yeah.*

Mother: *That was pretty sad.*

Anna: *And the big guy came up with the big head.*

Mother: *Yeah.*

Anna: *With Steve Irwin, that was quite funny. And the wombats were really cool.*

Mother: *Yes, they were.*

Anna: *And Molly (Anna's older cousin) went after the sheep. And that was funny.*

Mother: *Mmm. She had to go to Australia Zoo and admire the sheep.*

Anna: *Yeah, um and were they turtles or tortoises?*

Mother: *Ah that was a Galapagos tortoise I guess, that really big one.*

Anna: *They were all really cool. Wallabies, wasn't it, and the cassowaries, they were cool, I liked them.*

Mother: *And you actually bought a toy cassowary.*

Anna: *But it was actually an emu but we call it a cassowary.*

Mother: *Because we can.*

Anna: *Yeah just because. And I went into the airport on the way home and Dad had it on his shoulder and he was making parrot noises, and that was funny.*

Mother: *People thought that was pretty cute and funny didn't they?*

Anna: *Yeah. And ah the kookaburras are funny.*

Mother: *Just the birds around the house were funny weren't they?*

Anna: *Yeah.*

Mother: *We liked that. Pelican and*

Anna: *Ah the pelicans are really cool.*

Mother: *And those cockatoos.*

Anna: *And we went to Bribie Island?*

Mother: *Yes.*

Anna: *And we swam in the sea*

Mother: *It was warm.*

Anna: *Yeah.*

Mother: *It didn't rain there that day.*

Anna: *No it didn't rain that day, it was . . .*

Mother: *It was our nice day.*

Anna: *Saturday, the day before we went home.*

Mother: *Yeah.*

Although this message of focusing (mostly) on the positive may seem a bit Pollyanna-ish, it fits with research on the extremely important role of positive thinking in mental health, and of the dangers of **ruminating*** on negative experiences without resolving them. Every raincloud in Dreamworld *does* have a silver lining. By early adolescence, children are starting to experience a dip in mood and self-esteem, so for parents to dwell repeatedly on their negative emotions at this vulnerable age might do more harm than good.[21] As you did with your older preteen, you can still talk about the negative aspects of positive experiences, but be sure to focus mostly on the good things that happened and that are to come in your adolescent's life. Boys in particular may need some extra help in understanding and interpreting negative events and emotions into adolescence.

In mid-adolescence (ages 14–16), parents in our research studies, even those with well-adjusted teens, tell us that they are lucky simply to have A conversation, ANY conversation with their teen! Quantity becomes more important than quality at this age. If you're not even able to have a conversation, the quality of the conversation becomes a moot point. But keep the talk going in both directions to whatever degree possible using the techniques below, because there will come a time in late adolescence (or beyond for some) when you will be able to have a truly collaborative conversation again with your child, now nearly a young adult.

At age 16, Charlie audiotaped conversations with his mother and father on separate occasions about positive and negative experiences in his life. Both conversations were harmonious, funny, and collaborative. Here I include Charlie's conversation with his dad because fathers are such a rare treasure in research on child development:

Charlie's Positive Event: Going Water-skiing

Dad: *We were out at Lake Waihola and the weather was really was really calm and really flat which is really good for water-skiing, and Charlie...*

Charlie: *Yep.*

Dad: *Um, what did you do?*

Charlie: *Got up on a single ski for the first time.*

Dad: *And how many goes did it take ya?*

Charlie: *Oh a couple.*

Dad: *Only a couple ___?*

Charlie: *A couple of hard falls and...*

Dad: *I'd been having a go for a couple of times and I just totally faced planted...*

Charlie: *Yeah. (laughing)*

Dad: *Hurt myself and then you got up and um just did it really, after a couple of goes...*

Charlie: *Had a few a few falls though first yeah.*

Dad: *But yeah you just did it really really well so...*

Charlie: *Yeah it was a good exper...*

Dad: *So it was awesome...*

Charlie: *Good yeah*

Charlie's Negative Event: Failing the Driver's Licence Test

Dad: *And the second thing is the negative um when Charlie um went for his written part of his driver's licence.*

Charlie: *Learner's yep.*

Dad: *Um in June last year. And you were a bit gutted (upset) the first um time because you missed out on your ah written for the first time didn't you ___... ?*

Charlie: *Yeah I couldn't ride ___ scoot around (laugh).*

Dad: *You had a we had brought a scooter for him and um he um was keen to get his driver's licence, his licence his learner's licence so he could ride his scooter and he'd been practicing quite hard and what yeah...*

Charlie: *Yeah failed.*

Dad: *___...*

Charlie: *Yeah failed failed by like a couple of questions.*

Dad: *What was the um you had a practice...*

Charlie: *They questioned about tyres or something blowing out.*

Dad: *Yeah one was and ___ like ___...*

Charlie: *Something about trailer weights or something.*

Dad: *Yeah.*

Charlie: *Unnecessary questions really.*

Dad: *So they were quite bizarre sort of questions ___ and you hadn't swatted (studied) for them and you were a bit gutted...*

Charlie: *Yeah.*

Dad: *And then how long did you have to wait before you could re-sit it again?*

Charlie: *Oh you could have done it on the day but I waited probably another couple of weeks was it?*

Dad: *Yeah but they ___...*

Charlie: *___ few more study days.*

Dad: *And then the second time you passed it didn't ya no worries?*

Charlie: *Yep got them all right.*

Dad: *So that was a sort of a negative but yeah...*

Charlie: *Yeah.*

Dad: *But it turned out to be all good.*
Charlie: *Yep.*

The conversations are brief, but they get the job done, and the affection and trust between Charlie and his dad are obvious. The techniques that work when talking to teens are exactly the same as those you have used all along, but with a different balance: a few open-ended questions to get the talk flowing (*What was the, you had a practice?*), followed by lots of confirmation (*Yeah*) and positive words (*You just did it really, really well*). Listen carefully to what your teen has to say, and follow in on those topics. Note how Charlie's dad pulls around the conversation on the negative event of failing the driver's license test to the positive outcome of passing easily the second time around.

In late adolescence, parents' discussions with teens about their experiences can become deeper, more intimate, and more challenging. In one study, older teenagers were able to discuss sad and important events with their mothers, and they revealed their vulnerabilities in the process. Older teens achieve better resolution of those vulnerabilities when their mothers continue to ask open-ended questions about those experiences. By this age, teenagers can handle and perhaps even benefit from their mothers' challenges of their actions, reactions, and interpretations of their experiences.[22] In the following, 17-year-old Tia has a spirited conversation with her mother about not getting the part of Yum Yum in her school's production of *The Mikado*. Her mother does not hesitate to challenge Tia's views about the girl who did get the part. She calls a "biatch a biatch," so to speak, and then she helps Tia to reframe her view of the experience.

Tia: *Ok so The Mikado and*

Mother: *Which is a production that Tia's in for school at the moment*

Tia: *Yes, and I didn't get the main role because I did the second when I was asked to sing the fifth of a chord and the fifth when I was to sing the second, that's what let me down.*

Mother: *Is that what they said?*

Tia: *Yip*

Mother: *Did they?*

Tia: *Yeah, so yeah um so that that—*

Mother: *Ooooo you still feel hard about it!*

Tia: *No, I really really aarrrgh! (frustrated noise)*

Mother: *And you got a little bit out of character 'cause someone else got the main role*

Tia: *Oh yip well*

Mother: *or the part that you wanted.*

Tia: *But the but the this the main thing that annoyed me about it was that there are other people that can do it better than her and I just really am not arrrgh!*

Mother: *And you're still struggling with the poor girl.*

Tia: *No, I'm—*

Mother: *And you're still struggling to be charitable towards the fact that someone else got it and they may well be deserving of that.*

Tia: *No, but she's not!*

Mother: *(intake of breath) Tia, that's very—*

Tia: *She has no she has no charisma.*

Mother: *very unkind.*

Tia: *And she can't, she doesn't have, like she has problems with her life which mean that she won't be able to—*

Mother: *Well this just might be what she needs.*

Tia: *I don't think so, and like even is just what what really really ground my gear (upset me) was that Miss Tate (teacher) was all like um the main thing is chemistry and uh the two main roles love each other well well she doesn't love him but he absolutely loves her, and the other main thing was supposed to be acting and she's useless—*

Mother: *Tia, that's very unkind.*

Tia: *And the third main thing is supposed to be singing and she got it because of singing and she's not that good.*

Mother: *(gasp)*

Tia: *She just got the harmony*

Mother: *You're being so nasty!*

Tia: *I know, but that's how I feel and then the reserve is for acting and singing*

Mother: *You be nice to her.*

Tia: *I like the reserve but if if singing is the most important then why isn't she the reserve?*

Mother: *Oh, you bitter bitter bitter woman.*

Tia: *Obviously I've thought about it.*

Mother: *So you've thought about it now you have to think kindly about it.*

Tia: *(laughs) I can't.*

Mother: *Well you do, 'cause you'll let yourself down if you be a—*

Tia: *Biatch.*

Mother: *Biatch, yes.*

Tia: *Yeah.*

Mother: *You don't want to be like that.*

Tia: *(sigh)*

Mother: *Oh my goodness, yes well—*

Tia: *Yes, so why that wasn't that like me because....*

Mother: *Because you were being a*

Tia: *usually*

Mother: *a biatch.*

Tia: *Well I think I just, I'm also I'm quite a jealous person so the jealousness got in front of the kindness I'm really really bloomin' jealous.*

Mother: *Jealous or envious?*

Tia: *Jealous! What is the difference?*

Mother: *But you've had such a wonderful time in France and the universe is sharing the love, you can't have every good thing.*

Tia: *You sound like a crazy hippy mum.*

Mother: *I am a crazy hippy mum.*

Tia: *No, you're not.*

Mother: *I was born in the 60s, in the early 60s,*

Tia: *Mum—*

Mother: *with peace, love and mung beans, so*

Tia: *Yip*

Mother: *You have to let other people shine sometimes too, deary sweet*

Tia: *Ohhh*

Mother: *deary sweet*

Tia: *a tear*

Mother: *(laughs) Get over it!*

Tia: *Not likely.*

Mother: *You've done very very very very well—*

Tia: *I'm better than her!*

Mother: *Well she might turn out to be very very good.*

Tia: *Grrrr*

Mother: *Or she might break her face and they ask you to do it on the night.*

Tia: *(laughs)*

Mother: *So you just need to learn all the parts and be prepared like a Girl Guide (laughs)*

Tia: *(laughs) Ok*

Mother: *and enjoy being in the chorus and have lots of fun.*

Tia: *Ok.*

Talking about Your Adolescent's Own Experiences, from Now and from Long Ago

Although adolescents are now pretty good at understanding their emotions, they still need help understanding the meaning and the impact of their experiences, despite the vibes they give off indicating otherwise. If the preteen years were a time of consolidation, think of adolescence as a time of making connections—between their own earlier experiences and who they are now; between your experiences and theirs; between your family history and their own lives—past, present, and future. You can help your adolescent make these connections by bringing up her early childhood experiences whenever you see a link to her current experiences. In this way, you are helping her to create continuity in her life and in her identity. When talking to your adolescent about his more recent experiences, continue to use the Rich Reminiscing techniques of letting your teen set the topic if possible, asking a few well-placed *open-ended questions*, and responding by *confirming*, or *repeating/rephrasing* what your adolescent just said to let him know you are listening. The focus will be much less on "what happened" and much more about how your teen and everyone else felt, reacted, and interpreted the event, and especially how the event ended or was resolved.

Be respectful of your teen's point of view. Don't be offended if she rejects your interpretation of her experiences. When she disagrees, try to draw her out about what her interpretation is and her reasons for her preferred interpretation. TRY TO SEE THINGS FROM YOUR

ADOLESCENT'S PERSPECTIVE if you want him or her to do the same for you. Just as it is important for your adolescent to see the sunny side of life, it is also important for YOU to view your adolescent in a positive light, and to portray him accordingly in your stories about him, and with him. Parents who portrayed their adolescents in an optimistic way in storytelling demonstrated better parenting skills with their adolescents two years later.[23]

Sharing Stories from Your Childhood and from Your Family's History

When sharing family stories with your teens, intergenerational stories about your own childhood and about their grandparents' lives become very important in shaping their identities.[24] If your teens have close contact with their grandparents, either face-to-face or virtually, enlist their help in enriching your teens' databank of family stories (see Chapter 7 for tips for grandparents on story sharing). For these stories to have maximum effect, once again, the topic and timing are everything. The right story told at the right moment could have a lasting, even lifelong effect on your adolescent—so be ready, and choose with great care the stories that you share. Teens want to hear these stories, and they remember them in vivid detail at times, even if they were only told once.

When we asked Anna, Charlie, and Tia to share with us the stories their mothers and fathers had told them about their own childhood, they did so readily. In line with other research on family stories, Anna's story from her mother's childhood is more elaborate than her father's childhood story, whereas Charlie's story about his dad's childhood is more detailed and more meaningful to him than his mother's childhood tale.[25] Tia related a story about her stepfather, with whom she has become extremely close in the years they have been together as a family.

<u>Anna's Family Story about Her Mother</u>

Anna: *When my mum was seventeen she lived in America for a year she went on AFS (exchange), so she told me lots about that especially now because I'm going on an exchange as well..... so it's like she's done that too. Yeah. But she didn't have to speak another language, so ... She's told me lots about it, and um, also she keeps in touch with her host family and like send each other*

Christmas presents and stuff so it's like her host family is still a part of her life and like clearly her own mother died. I want to find out even if she hadn't told me.

Researcher: *Yeah, and so why do you think she told you about this?*

Anna: *Um, I don't know, the stories are just really cool with what she's done and also if we're watching a movie or something that's set in America and something weird happens it's like really American high school she'll tell us stories about what it was like when she was at high school in America and how it's actually like that when you're over there.*

Charlie's Family Story about His Dad

Charlie: *My dad... when he used to play rugby for... Kaikorai... his dad... my granddad was a coach for him and stuff... and... and he's told me he wasn't very good, and... he played on the wing, but he wasn't very good... didn't get much game time even though his dad was a coach... but yeah.*

Researcher: *Okay... and how do you know that story about your dad?*

Charlie: *Just from him telling me it a few times.*

Researcher: *Okay... so why do you think he would have told you about it?*

Charlie: *Just sort of like a motivation story... just... yeah.*

Tia's Family Story about Her Step-Dad

Tia: *Yeah, he was pretty cool though actually. He used to go to Kings High and you know, Kings and Queens* (girls' high school) *are really close so he'd jump over the fence and he'd like to run down the hallway to see how far they could get down the hall 'cause it was like one big stretch and they used to try and get into the Principal's office and once they actually got there, that's him and his friend Jed, who's really cool as well, and they got into the office and they didn't know what to do. It was just like oh...*

When the researcher asked Tia why she thought her stepdad had told her this story, she replied,   *"Oh it's good for old people to reminisce. I don't know, he likes to tell us how cool he was."*

Clearly these teenagers do take an interest in their parents' and step-parents' lives, especially if they can find some connection between their parents' lives and their own. Anna wanted to find out about her mother's high school exchange experiences as she prepares to embark on her own, and Charlie appears to like the idea that his dad used to play rugby too, even though his dad admits he was not very good.

All of these stories, however, even Tia's stepdad's tale of high school mischief, are relatively mild. What about sharing stories of your own adolescent experiences of which you are now less than proud? Tales of petty theft, vandalism, experimenting with drugs, unsafe sex, and risky driving? I'm of the mindset that you should never lie to your adolescent when he or she asks you a direct question about your own teenage experiences. Your lie will eventually be discovered, at potentially great cost to your relationship with your teen. There are certainly some stories you can choose not to tell, however, at least not until they are young adults or even parents themselves. And you can end the story with the lesson you learned and that you hope your adolescent will learn from unsavory aspects of your past. In a fascinating study about how parents should talk to their adolescents about their own marijuana use, or abstinence, in their teenage years, most parents and all the teenagers interviewed valued honesty in disclosing former marijuana use.[26] Parents and teenagers diverged a bit in the message that they thought should accompany the disclosure, though. Most of the teenagers interviewed felt that a response to their question that encouraged safe experimentation (see the Drug Free America website at www.dfaf.org for ideas) was better than a response that acknowledged parents' own former experimentation but advocated total abstinence for their own teenagers. Researchers don't yet know how these different parental responses affect adolescents' *actual* marijuana use. We do know, though, that adolescents young and old are more likely to take on their parents' advice and lessons through storytelling when parents act in a warm, yet firm and structured way with their teenagers—when they give their teenagers some independence but always with limits: a style you may have heard referred to as "authoritative" (not to be confused with authoritarian) or positive parenting.[27] Young adults have stronger identities and are better able to draw positive resolutions to their most negative experiences when they experienced positive parenting as adolescents.[28]

Table 5.1 Tips for Sharing Stories with Teens

What to Do	How	Why It Helps
1. *Read alongside your teenager whenever possible*	Read your own book while he is reading his, and read the books assigned to her in school. Ask teens questions about their leisure reading, but keep it light and casual. For their classroom reading, you can help them delve into deeper interpretations. Whenever possible, link the book world to their own world and vice versa.	Models a lifelong love of reading; helps teenagers draw connections and develop interpretations. You are the best person to help your teen link his or her life to literature.
2. *Keep the conversations going as much as possible about your teenager's experiences*	Let your teenager set the time and topic of conversation. Offer interpretations but don't force them—it's his life, after all, and you will not have been present for many of the experiences you will discuss with your teen. When discussing shared experiences with teens, whether negative or positive, be sure to end on a positive note.	Helps teens develop insights into their life experiences, some of which will be painful ones.
3. *Let the family stories fly thick and fast*	Tell stories about your teen's early childhood, your own childhood, and your parents' lives at any time that seems apt and at any point that your teen is prepared to listen.	Teens with a better grounding in family history experience greater well-being. Family stories may help them strengthen their identities and to cope with difficult situations.

(continued)

Table 5.1 Tips for Sharing Stories with Teens (*Continued*)		
What to Do	**How**	**Why It Helps**
4. *Parent-tested tip*: Create a family tree, enlisting the help of grandparents and great-grandparents.	Ben (13): "Mom, do we have a family tree? They're cool." Some teens may now be interested in creating a family tree. Make your own tree or use an existing website or program. Try to accompany factual information (births, deaths, marriages) with family stories whenever possible. Getting out the old family photos and scanning them is a great way to get started and to put faces to all the old-fashioned names. Better yet, help your teen record interviews with the older members about their family stories of each of the family members in their living memory.	Increases your teen's knowledge of family history and gives him or her a sense of connectedness and belonging.
5. *Media tips:* DO NOT allow teenagers to have a computer, TV, or gaming console in their bedrooms. DO NOT leave the TV on in the background when no one is watching.	Adolescents spend less time reading when they live in houses in which the TV is on constantly and when they are allowed to have a TV in their rooms.[29] Confiscate all portable screens (including cell phones) at bedtime if your teen is in the habit of texting, viewing, and gaming into the night.	Helps adolescents develop healthy sleep habits; protects them from heavy media use that could affect their well-being and academic achievement; promotes reading and interacting over gaming.

Table 5.2 Developmental Snapshot of an Adolescent[30]		
Domain	**What Happens and When**	**Why It Matters for Story Sharing**
Language and Reading Development	Young adolescents now have *vocabularies* of over 40,000 words, many of which are for abstract terms. One way that adolescents' vocabularies continue to expand is in the words they encounter primarily in school—such as *acknowledge* and *hypothesis*—their academic vocabulary. Another way vocabulary continues to develop is in the *depth* of word meaning, including multiple meanings and nuances. Most adolescents are now fully independent *readers,* but reading comprehension difficulties can arise as school texts become more difficult, and as adolescents are expected to read a much greater volume of material in a shorter period of time.	Most middle- and high-school curricula do not explicitly emphasize vocabulary learning, which is essential for reading comprehension and academic success. The conversations and stories you share with your adolescent can still help to broaden and deepen their vocabularies.
Cognitive Development	Adolescents' *theory of mind* continues to develop as they construct reasons for others' actions and emotions based on what they think others may be thinking and feeling. Adolescents are increasingly in charge of their own thinking: deciding what to reflect on, when, where, and for how long.	Ongoing improvements in thinking and reasoning are linked to adolescents' understanding of their own reasons and motivations for actions in telling the stories of their own lives, as well as to increases in reading comprehension.

(continued)

Domain	What Happens and When	Why It Matters for Story Sharing
Table 5.2 Developmental Snapshot of an Adolescent (*Continued*)		
	Reasoning: Adolescents are also able to take a longer-term view of events that extends farther back in the past and forward into the future. They are able to construct connections between the distant past and the present.	Gaining a longer-term view helps adolescents link events in their own lives from the past (even into the family's distant past) to the present and into the future.
Self-Concept and Identity	*Self-Concept:* Adolescents develop a more nuanced view of who they are in general, as well as with different people and in different situations. They also develop an even stronger sense of their strengths and limitations. Adolescents are slowly forming *identities* with respect to their values, political ideas, religious commitments, and aspirational selves. Mid-adolescence is a watershed in identity development.	Self-understanding is crucial for forming a coherent and meaningful life story. In hearing and telling stories about their lives, adolescents are also gaining self-understanding.
Social and Emotional Development	*Friendships* and *romantic relationships* increase dramatically in importance for both boys and girls at puberty, but relationships with parents remain important throughout adolescence (and beyond).	Early adolescence may be a critical time for parents to help children cope with negative events and with complex relationships by exploring emotions, solutions, and resolutions through story sharing.

(continued)

Table 5.2 Developmental Snapshot of an Adolescent (*Continued*)		
Domain	**What Happens and When**	**Why It Matters for Story Sharing**
	Dramatic changes occur in *well-being* in early adolescence. Both boys and girls experience a dip in mood in early adolescence, but girls' rate of depression increases dramatically by age 13, whereas boys' levels of depression stay low or decrease. *Coping:* In adolescence, girls are much more likely than boys to respond to stressful events by ruminating on problems (internally or with friends) rather than taking action. Rumination can prevent effective problem-solving and leads to depression.	
Physical Development	*Brain development:* A rapid increase in the brain's gray matter occurs at puberty, followed by ongoing pruning of connections and increases in white matter, which speeds transmission. By mid- to late adolescence, the result of these brain changes is more efficient and selective processing of information—*executive functioning*—particularly in terms of the ability to inhibit responses and in planning, monitoring, and selecting appropriate strategies.	Both reading comprehension and life story coherence should benefit from more efficient and selective processing. Pruning of neuronal connections depends on an adolescent's experiences: If an adolescent reads and converses in deeper and more challenging ways, those experiences will shape his or her ongoing brain development.

6

All Kinds of Children, All Kinds of Families

I wouldn't trade anything for my story now.

~ Maya Angelou

Just as every child and parent is different, so is every family. Here are some ways to tailor your story sharing to your own child and family.

SHARING STORIES WITH BOYS AND GIRLS

Like it or not, one of the ways that parents' story sharing differs is by virtue of whether they are sharing stories of personal experience with their daughters or with their sons. (In contrast, very few if any differences emerge when parents are reading books to their sons and daughters.) In some studies, researchers have found that parents tell richer and more detailed stories about past events with their daughters than with their sons. Parents delve into a more in-depth discussion of emotions with their daughters compared to sons, especially when discussing sadness. These different ways that parents talk to girls and boys are found across different English-speaking cultures but they are not as evident in Asian cultures, in which there is less talk overall about past events and past emotions.[1] Nor are these differences in the way parents talk to girls and boys as apparent in more egalitarian cultures, such as New Zealand, in comparison to more traditional communities in the United States. My doctoral supervisor Robyn Fivush and I first noted these differences in parents' stories about the past with their daughters and sons in Atlanta, Georgia, in the 1990s. In a few studies, young girls are already more advanced than boys in their understanding of mind and emotions, so it could be that parents are responding to these differences in emotional development when they talk in different ways to boys and girls.[2]

As a parent of a son, however, you can certainly choose to do things otherwise (see Table 6.1 for tips). Just because parents on the whole talk in less detailed ways with their sons about their past experiences does not mean that you have to follow the crowd. My colleagues and I found that when we trained parents of toddler sons to talk in more detailed ways about their past experiences, parents were easily able to do so, and boys benefited as much—or even more— from these enriched conversation styles as girls in their language and narrative skills, and in their understanding of mind.[3] So, by all means, if you have a son, use all the techniques for Rich Reminiscing that I've outlined in Chapters 1 through 5. In fact, if you have a son, it is even more important for you to use these conversation techniques early on, because we know that left to their own devices, many boys will lag behind girls in terms of understanding their own experiences and emotions when they are preteens and teens.[4]

Boys in particular still need help from their parents into the preteen years when talking about the causes and consequences of emotions, especially complex emotions such as guilt, shame, pride, and embarrassment. Preteen boys also benefit more from their parents' explanations of their past negative emotions compared to girls of the same age.[5] These discussions can be accomplished in all sorts of ways: Talking about boys' *own* emotions, particularly their past emotions, is probably still the most helpful, but they also need to understand other people's emotions. One obvious way to talk about others' emotions is to discuss a book character's feelings and motivations for his actions. It may not help that in the books boys are drawn to read, characters' emotions and motivations are not as complex and nuanced as the main characters in the books girls favor. Main character Percy Jackson in *The Lightning Thief* is about as complex a figure as preteen boys get in their fiction—a mysterious past, misunderstood powers, a wicked stepfather, a desire to protect his mother—perhaps not surprisingly, *The Lightning Thief* is one of the few books that crosses gender lines for this age group.

MOTHERS AND FATHERS SHARING STORIES

As far as we know at present, there are very few, if any, differences in the way that mothers and fathers read books to their young children, and young children enjoy and benefit from sharing books with both their mothers and their fathers. Mothers and fathers are also equally able to engage their children in telling detailed, rich stories about their children's personal experiences. Mothers may be slightly more willing than fathers, however, to discuss emotional aspects of negative experiences with their children from an early age. Fathers appear to pitch in more at the preteen years to discuss emotional experiences, especially when their children are experiencing difficulties.[6] In the stories that adolescents tell about their parents' childhood, their stories about their mothers are more detailed and richer emotionally, whereas their stories about their fathers are a bit sparser, indicating that fathers may not be telling their own childhood stories as elaboratively with their children and adolescents.[7]

In research with adults, men often rely on the women in the family (wives, sisters, mothers, aunts) to keep them connected, and even to keep track of their shared memories when part of a couple.[8] When the matriarch of a family dies, it is almost always one of her daughters, not a son, who carries on with the job of keeping the family connected through letter-writing, phone calls, e-mails, sending photos, and organizing reunions. Yet there is no biological reason that men cannot serve this role in the family, and in family interactions, fathers can be just as elaborative as mothers when reminiscing with their children when they take the opportunity to do so. Dads, don't wait until your preteen is experiencing problems to start sharing stories of his or her personal experiences, or your own. You are perfectly able to tell wonderful stories with your children from early in their childhood, so get in there and do it now! (See Table 6.1 for tips.)

The stories that dads share from their own childhoods are likely to have themes of adventure, achievement and hard work, mischief, and risk-taking. Mothers' stories of their own childhood with their young children are more likely to be about relationships and family routines, such as baking cookies with grandma.[9] These stories may reflect differences in mothers' and fathers' experiences during their childhood, or they may reflect their preferences for which experiences are most valuable to pass down. As far as we know, all of these family stories are treasures for children, so tell whatever stories from your childhood come naturally to you. Of course, bear in mind your child's age, interests, and trouble spots. If you have a child who is constantly getting into mischief at preschool, it may not help for Dad to tell stories of how he was always naughty in school too, unless those experiences are told as a cautionary tale or in the spirit of "And I turned out just fine, so don't worry."

SHARING STORIES WITH ACTIVE, DISTRACTIBLE CHILDREN

What if your child is more active and impulsive than most, even hyperactive? Parents whose children are low in persistence and self-control have a harder time engaging their children in long, detailed stories about their children's experiences, especially about the emotional aspects of their experiences.[10] All of the story sharing techniques I outlined earlier will still work with your active child; however, you might need to have an extra dose of patience and creativity when using them (see Table 6.1 for tips). You might also need to go down a level (from school-age to preschooler, for instance, if you have a highly active and distractible 6-year-old) to ensure that the techniques you're using are developmentally appropriate for your child. Story sharing will need to be applied in shorter, more interactive bursts and perhaps amid other activities. Make liberal use of the "talking while doing" techniques that I outline in the next chapter. And pay special attention when choosing storybooks to ensure that the book is interesting to your active child.

Even if your child is eventually diagnosed with ADHD, don't despair. Building up collaborative communication techniques, filled with praise and open-ended questions, will benefit their language skills and learning later on, as well as your relationship. Research shows that children with ADHD actually have highly detailed memories for specific past events, and anecdotally, parents and doctors working with children with ADHD have noted their relative strengths in memory for distinctive events. In one study, preteens with ADHD recalled past events in even more detail than preteens without ADHD.[11] It seems that children and adolescents with ADHD are noticing things that are happening on the periphery of events that the rest of us may miss. And in a study with college students, young adults with ADHD performed well in a long-term memory task if the task was highly structured at the time of learning.[12] The college students with ADHD had less organized personal memories than those without ADHD, however, suggesting that it is organization, not raw memory capacity, that is impaired in ADHD.

I do not yet have hard research evidence on this point, but related evidence and common-sense suggests that you can help your child with ADHD to better organize their personal memories by having detailed conversations in which you ask your child about the main components of the memory: when it happened, where, who was there, and the order of the event, as well as the emotions and feelings involved. *Every time* you engage your child with ADHD in an activity that requires cognitive and linguistic effort, you are also helping him to strengthen his **working memory***, or ability to hold information in mind for a short time, which is one of the weaknesses frequently observed in children with ADHD. If you can manage to have a lengthy and detailed conversation about a single topic or book, you may even be helping your child with ADHD to learn to stay on task.

SHARING STORIES WITH CHILDREN WHO HAVE A HARDER TIME ADJUSTING TO NEW OR DIFFICULT EXPERIENCES

You will already know if you have one of these children. They have various labels in the psychological literature: inhibited, slow-to-warm-up, or simply "difficult" children. Whether it is because of shyness or because of their strong negative reactions to events, all of these children refuse to plunge headlong into life. And, while frustrating for parents, in the long-run it can be a protective and even admirable quality. I prefer the term "strong-willed" or even "edgy" if we must label these children. They may not be easy, but life with them is never boring!

As babies, they cry loudly and frequently. They are easily startled by the slightest sound or puff of air. Once upset, they are difficult to soothe. They may not seem to want you to touch them or cuddle them. Ironically, as toddlers, they are the children who cry the longest and loudest when separated from you, and they have a hard time calming down when you return. They are easily frustrated—if they have difficulty with a puzzle, they may throw the pieces across the room rather than move on to another activity. As preschoolers, they are passionate and stubborn about everything from the clothes they wear to the food they eat, and the other children they will play with. When going to school for the first time, they are the children who find it difficult to even enter the classroom, much less have you leave them there. As preteens, they can be fairly settled, especially if they are able to stay in the same school or neighborhood, but they may not want to try new sports or activities. If a friend slights or teases her, or if a teacher is cross with him, a strong-willed child is upset for days. As teenagers, they may withdraw more than most and restrict themselves to a few select friends and activities. They may not extend themselves academically or socially.

Sound familiar? If so, all of the techniques that I outlined in previous chapters will work for your strong-willed child, but you will need to take everything slower than you do with your other more amenable, outgoing children (see Table 6.1 for tips). Be especially patient when asking questions so that she has time to formulate a response in her own time. Don't rapid-fire questions at her or she will immediately turn off and turn away. Choose thoughtfully the stories to discuss. Your strong-willed child is likely to be pickier about the events he wants to talk about and the books he will read, and more easily offended by inept interpretations of his actions and emotions. See this as a strength, not as a weakness. These children are highly sensitive creatures with strong minds of their own. Respect their choices, their feelings, and their pace in life. Research shows that if you can accommodate to their highly emotional sensibilities, then you will be able to have detailed conversations with them about their experiences, even if those experiences are negative ones.[13] No, they are not "easy" as children or as adolescents. But with love, accommodation, and patience they will bloom into sensitive, interesting adults.[14]

SHARING STORIES WITH CHILDREN WITH LANGUAGE DELAYS

Book reading is a natural technique to help children with language delays or with the diagnosis of specific language impairment (SLI). All of the question and follow-up techniques from Chapter 1 will help your preschooler or young child with language delays to develop his or her expressive language skills.[15] After all, **Dialogic Reading*** was originally developed for children with language delays. Remember that children naturally say more in response to an open-ended question than in response to a statement about the book (*What's the boy doing now?* versus *That boy is having a bath.*) Although it may seem easier on your child to ask yes/no questions (*Is the boy taking a bath?*) instead of open-ended questions, your child will benefit more from the open-ended questions. The goal is first to get your child talking, and then to encourage him to use longer and more complex sentences. Your pauses after an open-ended question are as important as the question itself: Make sure that you give your child with language delays extra time to formulate a response. And once she does give a response, be sure to follow up and expand on that response (*Yes, the boy is taking a nice warm bath. And what color is his duck?*) Be patient and be prepared to go down a level or even two to ensure that you are getting active participation in the story sharing.

Although book reading is a wonderful technique to use with children experiencing language delays, so is talking about their personal experiences. In one study, children with SLI and their mothers read books and talked about the past together.[16] Overall, the children talked more in the book-reading conversation than in the conversation about past events, probably because talking about past events is less structured and thus more difficult for children with language delays than is book-reading. Also, in contrast to the style of talk that was linked to children's storytelling during book reading, when discussing past experiences, all kinds of questions that mothers asked were helpful for the children: whether the question was open-ended, yes/no, or even a repeated question. Talking about the past may be more difficult for children with language delays because of the additional memory demands compared to book-reading, so perhaps any question is useful for getting them talking in this context. They will need more help from you to get talking in these conversations than they do during book-reading. You may need to use some of the techniques for sharing stories of personal experience with toddlers and preschoolers when drawing out narratives from older children. Using photographs of the experience during the conversation may also lessen the memory demands for your child. Because children with SLI typically are still having difficulties telling personal narratives into adolescence,[17] your persistence in helping them to tell these stories at younger ages will pay off (see Table 6.1 for tips). Exchanging personal stories is an important way for adolescents and young adults to communicate with each other and to form relationships.

SHARING STORIES WITH ADOPTED CHILDREN

What if your child is adopted? You will be able to share stories with your adopted child in nearly identical ways as if you were biologically related. Story sharing is about sharing experiences, not about sharing genes. The only differences may come about when telling your child's birth story and when telling your family stories. I am assuming here that your child knows that he or she is adopted when using the following story sharing techniques.

If you adopted your child at or near birth, you probably know some details of their birth and their days as a newborn. By all means, share those details with your child when telling his or her birth story, but expand the story to include his or her entry into your family as special and chosen. Jamie Lee Curtis's book *Tell Me Again about the Night I Was Born* is a delicate and affirming birth story of an adopted child that you could use as a springboard for discussing your own adopted child's birth story.

Share your family's history with your adopted child in just the same way as you would with your biological child (see Table 6.1 for tips). However, once again you can extend the family history by including anything you know of your child's birth parents' history. If there are significant negatives in the birth family history, I leave it up to you to decide what to include and what to leave out when your child is young. Eventually, your adopted adolescent will want to know every detail that you possess about her birth parents, no matter how negative. I believe it is your obligation to divulge those details, but you must do so in a sensitive way that is appropriate for your adolescent's ability to cope with that knowledge. Adopted adolescents have to work harder than other adolescents to carve out and create their identities, especially if his adopted family is of a different ethnicity from his own.[18] The research conducted so far on this important issue shows that sharing information gradually with your adopted child as he or she grows up is vital in their eventual acceptance of his or her identity. If they know the facts, they will be less likely to rely on idealized fantasies about their birth parents.

GRANDPARENTS TAKING PART

Everything we know about the benefits of grandparents taking an active role in their grandchildren's lives leads me to suggest that grandparents can share stories in much the same way as parents, to the extent that time and geography allow. However, there is absolutely no research on how grandparents share stories from books with their grandchildren, and there is only limited evidence on grandparents' family storytelling with their grandchildren. Psychologist Michael Pratt and colleagues report that nearly all adolescents (87%) in their research could think of a story about a time when their grandparents had taught them a value to which they now ascribed, so clearly grandparents are doing their part.[19] Young adults had stronger identities when they could remember and report direct interactions with their grandparents during childhood (for instance, a specific story or interaction with a grandparent) that helped them shape their own values.

Colleague Robyn Fivush and I proposed that grandparents can play a vital role in passing down family history, given that their own experiences and their memories of family events stretch farther back in time than do their own children's (your) memories.[20] And in my PhD student Federica Artioli's study of Italian families, young adults who grew up with their parents plus other adults (most of whom were grandparents) in their houses reported earlier memories than young adults who didn't have these experiences.[21] One young man in Michael Pratt and colleagues' research said about his grandpa's stories:

> *What he (my granddad) said to me stuck. What he said was I need to know my own limits, my abilities. Other people are going to have their opinions and worries and concerns, but being independent is taking that stuff into consideration, but then also doing what you can.*[22]

Grandparents and other adults, such as unmarried aunts and uncles, may have more time to interact with children and to share stories with them than do their own parents, who are busy running a household and holding down jobs.

If your child is fortunate enough to have a grandparent living in the same house or nearby, or one who comes on extended visits, by all means share the techniques in this book with him or her.[23] The techniques may need to be adapted slightly because grandparents won't have as many shared experiences to discuss with their grandchildren, but the basic strategies remain the same. Grandparents also have some inherent advantages to parents as story sharers. As I mentioned earlier, they typically have more free time than parents. They may also have more patience with their grandchildren (and possibly slower reaction times) than you do as a parent; longer pauses after a question mean that question is more likely to be answered. After all, most grandparents don't have to discipline their grandchildren the way you do—only spend quality time and have fun with them! Plus, as noted above, they have a huge advantage in terms of their memory bank of family stories. As long as they share these stories with grandchildren in an interactive, not didactic way, your children will benefit from their wealth of family history.

Grandparents, don't forget to share with your grandchildren the books that you enjoyed with their parents when they were young. If you have the original thumbed-over, even chewed-on copies, all the better, but these days it's possible to find many previously out-of-print books through websites like amazon.com or bookdepository.com.

I was fortunate to have one of my grandmothers live with us for long periods of time when I was a young girl. My grandmother, Adele Brossier Reese (we called her Mimi), sold her house in Coconut Grove, Florida, when she was in her 70s and then proceeded to live with each of her 5 children and 24 grandchildren for several months at a time before she died when I was seven. Mimi Reese's arrival on a plane was a big deal in our family. And her pink corset was an endless source of fascination to my young eyes. But best of all were her stories. Every evening while my mother was cooking dinner, Mimi Reese regaled my brother and sister and me with hair-raising tales of homesteading in late 19th-century Florida, in an area called Lemon City that was to become Biscayne Bay. Black panthers and Indians were the most memorable parts of these stories, some of which are now immortalized in the book *Lemon City: Pioneering on Biscayne Bay, 1850–1925* by Thelma Peters. Mimi Reese also read countless stories from books to us. I owe my fascination with family storytelling in part to Mimi Reese's influence: She was a born storyteller. I know that not every grandparent has such exciting tales to tell, but trust me that even the tamer stories from your childhood will seem quaint and engaging to your grandchildren because they are about a time and place that will seem like another world to them.

Even if you live far away from your grandchildren, you can still share stories with them (see Table 6.1 for tips). Faced with the prospect of two of her three grandchildren living overseas, my own mother carried on in the family tradition of story-sharing by taping herself reading storybooks, complete with questions, pauses, and comments tailored to her grandchildren's lives. When my children were young, she mailed the tapes to them along with the books so that they could listen to their own Mimi reading stories to them. A book parcel from Mimi was a big event in our house. Be sure to make new recordings for each new grandchild. My younger son Dylan used to listen to the tapes that my mother made for Ben. Patiently at first, and then a little more heatedly, two-year-old Dylan would correct her "I not Ben, I Dylan!" Soon after, Mimi made some brand-new tapes just for Dylan. When your children are older, the recordings are a reminder to them of their connections with extended family even when halfway across the world. And after their grandparents are gone, they will know they were loved. My dad made some story tapes for his grandkids before he died which are now reminders of him and of his love of a good story.

Video-calling via Skype or facetime is also revolutionizing the way that grandparents can interact with their grandchildren. No longer are they limited to a batch of photos once a month, or disjointed telephone calls with preschoolers who would rather be playing than talking to someone they can't even see. Today's grandparents, if they are lucky, can see their grandchildren developing day by day, week by week, even if they live half a world apart. You could even try reading a book to your grandchild on a video call. It is not as easy to interact with him or her this way as in real life, but it is definitely the next best thing.

And if your children no longer have access to their own grandparents, borrow someone else's grandparents to share *their* stories with your children. Some communities even offer tax credits to senior citizens for going into schools to read and tell stories with children.

SHARING STORIES WITH CHILDREN FROM ALL KINDS OF FAMILIES

Many families these days do not fit the stereotypical "nuclear" arrangement of biological mother and father and one or more children, and no other people living in the household. The "postnuclear" family is likely to be smaller and different in a myriad of other ways from the stereotypical configuration. Parents and children might be spread across two households. The child might live only with his biological mother or father, but not both. The child might never see her biological parents if adopted or in foster care. The child might have *more* adults in his household(s) and in his life than typical if grandparents, great-grandparents, aunts and uncles, older siblings or step-siblings, or step-parents and step-grandparents are part of the picture. These demographic changes are happening throughout North America and

Europe and in developing countries, even in cultures that were highly familial in the recent past, such as Italy.[24] In Māori culture, the term **whānau*** encompasses these extended family networks.[25] A person does not have to be biologically related to the child to form part of their whānau, nor must they live in the same house. And certainly you do not have to be biologically related to a child to share stories with him or her. You are part of the whānau if you care for and look out for the other members, and if they do the same for you.

What do these changes mean for family storytelling? We are not yet completely sure, because most research still focuses on biological parents telling stories to children, and to be honest, on biological mothers telling stories to their children. But there are some indications that growing up in an extended family setting and being around a greater number of adults could intensify the storytelling environment for a child. In New Zealand with its high rate of parental separation, my PhD student Federica Artioli found that young adults whose parents separated early in the child's life (before age 6) and then repartnered had more memories from early childhood than young adults whose parents stayed together or who separated later. We think that when more adults are involved in a child's life, whether those adults are step-parents or grandparents, the child is engaged in more interactions, and perhaps in more family storytelling. We are now looking into the possibility that parents who remarry or repartner are telling stories of the child's early experiences more often than parents who stay together. Perhaps the child's early memories are reinstated as the parent fills in the step-parent about the child's early years. In any case, the young adults who grew up with separated parents were not at a disadvantage in terms of their early memories compared to children whose parents stayed together.

The concept of whānau is integral to the practice of sharing stories. We don't share stories just within our nuclear family. We share stories of our experiences with all of those who are important in our lives. The techniques outlined in this book will work with any adult and child as long as they have a store of shared experiences to discuss. Our children can benefit from this expanded notion of family that extends beyond two generations (parent and child) and beyond biological boundaries. Children's lives can also be enriched by knowing the stories of their grandparents, aunts and uncles, step-parents, and close family friends. These extraparental stories can help them to experience different histories, and perhaps different cultures, and to compare them to their own. As adolescents, they can start to see how their family's experiences fit into their larger community, their country, and even into the global community of cultures.

SHARING STORIES WITH CHILDREN FROM ALL CULTURES

For some parents, sharing stories from books is not an especially natural or comfortable activity (see Box 6.1). Many parents from Hispanic and African American cultures, in particular, report that they do not read books with their children as often as do parents from other cultures.[26] When parents in these cultures read books with their children, many adopt a "sit-still-and-listen" policy to reinforce children's learning.[27] Unfortunately, these less interactive ways of reading books may not engender high-quality or enjoyable book-reading experiences for very young children. If you are a parent who is not as comfortable sharing books with your child, the good news is that sharing other kinds of stories with your child will reap many of the same benefits, plus a few new ones, as book-reading. Parents in all of the cultures we have studied so far report that they frequently and naturally bring up stories of their children's experiences, their own experiences, and their family's history. For instance, many of the Peruvian mothers in psychologist Gigliana Melzi's research found it easier to adopt an interactive conversational style when reminiscing about family stories than when reading picture books with their children.[28]

Box 6.1 On the Tyranny of Book-Reading

When they find out what I do for a living, grown men sometimes confess to me, in conspiratorial whispers, that they don't really enjoy reading. "In my spare time, I'm a doer, not a reader," said one male friend. And this from a highly successful professional who reads a great deal for his job! Clearly it is possible to be

(*continued*)

Box 6.1 (*Continued*)

successful at school, and in life, without reading for pleasure. Many of the benefits of reading can be gleaned through other means, such as participating in a conversation about shared activities, or watching a good movie together and discussing it afterward. When we watch a good movie, we are experiencing some of the same psychological processes as fiction of identifying with characters, feeling and understanding emotions, and following a storyline. True, the storyline is necessarily less complex than in a multilayered novel, and less cognitive effort is involved when the images are handed to us rather than created. And perhaps there are some long-term benefits in terms of persistence, effort, and identification that we can get no other way than through reading a book. But should a child or an adolescent who simply does not like reading in their leisure time, despite their parents' and teachers' best efforts, be forced to read? Should they be made to feel guilty and somehow deficient for not enjoying something that many others do enjoy? To me, this is like saying that anyone who doesn't like chocolate ice cream must have something wrong with him. Perhaps we should just accept that some people prefer vanilla, or a bowl of fresh fruit. As long as children are able to read skillfully and efficiently for information, we should relax and let them pursue the activities they truly love in their free time.

However, that doesn't mean that parents from all cultures tell family stories in the same ways. Parents from child-centered European cultures tend to tell highly detailed and interactive stories of their children's everyday experiences, replete with a focus on the child's emotions and motivations in their stories. Many European-descent parents shy away from talking about their children's past misbehavior, preferring instead to talk about positive shared experiences. Many parents from Hispanic cultures also tell detailed and interactive stories of their children's experiences and emotions, but one type of story they focus on is their children's behavior, whether appropriate or inappropriate, as a way of socializing children into proper demeanor. Chinese parents share with Hispanic parents this focus on proper behavior, with many

Chinese parents also telling stories of their own admirable behavior as a child or teenager to provide a role model of proper behavior for their children. Whether they are reading books or sharing other stories with their children, many Chinese parents talk more about behaviors and less about internal states such as emotions.[29]

These differences in topic and focus are not right or wrong. Every culture uses stories in ways that help children to grow up with the characteristics that are valued in that culture: whether it is independence and autonomy, or proper behavior, or caring about others or the land. For instance, many Māori parents tell incredibly rich, detailed birth stories with their children because the child's birth and subsequent return of the placenta to the land has marked cultural significance. In fact, the word in Māori for placenta is *whenua*, which is the same as that for land. One lovely birth ritual that many New Zealand parents have adopted is to plant the placenta under a special "birth tree" for the child as a spiritual connection to the land.

No matter what culture you are from, you can choose the stories you discuss, and the ways you talk about them, to promote the values that you wish to see in your children as they grow up. Across all cultures studied so far, however, a style in which parents discuss stories in interactive ways with their children and who talk in depth about internal states is linked to benefits for children in that culture—whether the benefits are in terms of children's language development, their memory skills, or their emotional understanding and self-knowledge. As a Taiwanese parent in one study said about the benefits of telling family stories:

> *I feel that when people talk about their experiences, these are all their best, best points, like crystals. It feels like they (children who hear these experiences) can be saved from going down the wrong paths (in life).*[30]

Even when two parents come from the same culture, each of his or her family's stories will have a unique flavor and slant. Each family history offers children and adolescents a different view of growing up, a different way of being and becoming. Anthropologist Margaret Mead saw this diversity of options as potentially confusing for young New

England adolescents a century ago, in comparison to the relative mon-oculture that Samoan adolescents faced at that time. In New Zealand[31] and around the world, children are increasingly coming from fami-lies with multiple ethnicities. A child born in New Zealand to a Thai mother and a German father, for instance, is in an enviable position to integrate cultures and family histories to create his own unique iden-tity that is a blend of all. I see this familial and cultural diversity as a wonderful opportunity for our adolescents to choose who they are, uniquely, from among the smorgasbord of selves, while at the same time affirming the common threads that tie us all together.

Table 6.1 Tips for Sharing Stories with All Kinds of Children in All Kinds of Families

What to Do	How	Why it Helps
1. *Share stories with your sons as often and as vividly as with your daughters*	Practice sharing detailed stories studded with emotions with your sons as well as with your daughters.	Helps close the gap for boys' language development and emotion understanding
2. *Fathers, don't leave all the family storytelling work to your children's mother*	We know that you are just as good at sharing stories with your child as she is, so no excuses!	Enriches storytelling for both boys and girls
3. *Parents of adopted children have extra family storytelling duties*	Adoption experts recommend that you use a "life book" with adopted children to help share even seemingly tiny bits of information about his or her life before entering your family, and to help your child structure his or her more complex life story.[32]	Strengthens identity development and self-esteem in adopted children
4. *Grandparents, share stories with your grandchildren with whatever means are available to you*	Use face-to-face story reading and storytelling, or via recordings and video calls, even letters. Remember that you know more stories than anyone about their parents when they were young!	Strengthens family connections and family history across the generations

(continued)

Table 6.1 Tips for Sharing Stories with All Kinds of Children in All Kinds of Families (*Continued*)

What to Do	How	Why it Helps
5. *Share stories with children who have special needs*	If your son or daughter is highly active, has strong emotions, or language delays, you can still share stories using similar techniques to those introduced earlier in the book. You may need to adapt the techniques by going down a level or two and by being more patient, creative, and accommodating in your story sharing. Your hard work will pay off for your child's language, self-concept, and emotional development.	Helps promote language, emotion understanding, self-esteem, and self-control for children with active and difficult temperaments
6. *If you are separated or divorced, continue to share stories with your child*	Share stories about your child's early years and of your family history (see Chapter 7 for more tips). And if you remarry, you will get extra chances to tell positive stories about your child's early years with your new partner—let your child help fill in the details so that you are telling the story together.	Enriches storytelling for children from all kinds of families

7

Practical Tips for Sharing Lasting Stories

Stories have to be told or they die, and when they die, we can't remember who we are or why we're here.
~*Sue Monk Kidd,* The Secret Life of Bees

How can we share stories that will continue to matter to our children and adolescents into adulthood? Research suggests time and time again that a helpful strategy across all ages is to invite your child or adolescent to participate in the storytelling. If they are active participants in the storytelling, they will be more likely to remember and retain the story for years to come. The best way to invite your child to participate, however, is going to differ depending on the age of your child, and the type of story you would like to share. My techniques of Rich Reading and Rich Reminiscing involve adapting to your children as they grow into more capable readers and storytellers. You wouldn't ask an adult, "You wanna play with me?" Nor would you entertain a 2-year-old with a lengthy story about your early childhood experiences. Instead, the best and most memorable storytelling occurs when parents share the story in a give-and-take manner, paying close attention to children's interest (see Box 7.1). If a 2-year-old wants to talk about what she had for a snack at the Botanic Gardens instead of about the beautiful foliage, she will stay more engaged in the conversation if you ask her to elaborate and expand on that aspect of the event.

Box 7.1   The Two Most Important Story-Sharing Tips across the Ages

---

Tip #1. ACCOMMODATE TO YOUR CHILD'S INTERESTS: Gear your story sharing to your child's or adolescent's interests. Tell and read stories *your child* wants to hear.

Tip #2. ADJUST TO YOUR CHILD'S LEVEL: Adjust your story sharing to your child's narrative level (see Chapters 1 through 5). Through your questions, either during or after the story, gently draw your child into telling or understanding a story she can't quite manage on her own. As your child gets older, be sure to let him or her tell more of the story when it is personally experienced.

If an 8-year-old wants you to tell for the 20th time the story about the time you stood up to the school bully, tell that story. Then ask him what he would do in that situation, or if anything like that has ever happened to him. Thus, in the toddler years, the give and take of story sharing needs to occur in nearly every turn of conversation. By middle childhood, most children can hear a whole story as long as you keep it exciting and allow them to ask questions along the way. The "take" can come after the story when you invite them to tell one of their own.

The best moments in book-sharing follow a similar path. With toddlers, the most effective reading style is highly interactive. Children of this age have great difficulty following a storyline, so it's best to ask open-ended questions about the pictures on every page to keep them engaged. Toddlers are mainly learning new vocabulary from books, but don't focus just on the names of objects. Toddlers are also learning action words and emotion words from books. When your children are in the preschool years, your reading style still needs to be highly interactive in most sessions, but now you can start to ask more complex questions about what's going to happen next in the story, or why a plot twist occurred. Emotion talk is vitally important at these ages, and now you can expand to include talk about complex thoughts, such as, "Why did he try to trick his mother?" You can also start to employ diverse storytelling skills by slipping in a poem or a short personal narrative in its entirety, without interruption, as long as you follow up by asking for the child's reaction.

By primary school, most children can listen to you read picture books and chapter books in fairly large chunks, but it's still a good idea to stop every once in a while to check their engagement and comprehension of story events and characters' motivations and reactions. Because you are usually reading to only one or two children, you (unlike teachers) have the luxury of relating the book to your children's own experiences. Similar to the techniques you've developed for telling stories about personal experiences, you can ask at the end of a story, "Has anything like that ever happened to you?" and "What would you do if that happened to you?" or "Do you know anyone who's like Thomas in that book?"

Finally, try to keep on reading and sharing stories even when your child grows into an adolescent. You'll need to choose cooler books, or better yet ask your adolescent to pick one, and you probably wouldn't want to read them at bedtime! Stretch out at opposite ends of the couch on a Sunday afternoon and read the latest Anthony Horowitz aloud to each other. If your adolescent refuses to let you read aloud because it's too babyish, simply read your book at the same time that he is reading his. Bring in some snacks and casually ask what's happening in his book or what he thinks about it. Would he recommend it to a friend?

In the car on the way home from a disappointing basketball game, slip in a story about a similar loss from your own adolescence. As with a toddler, you'll have to gauge your adolescent's interest carefully. You may also have to become a more skillful storyteller with your adolescent. Unlike a younger child, your adolescent won't hang on your every word unless it's well chosen and from the heart. Respond sympathetically if your adolescent follows up with her own story or asks questions, but don't force it. Let her muse and make connections at her own pace. These conversations and stories can be brief and still have an impact—and sometimes the impact is much later, so don't get discouraged if you don't get an immediate reaction. You are adding to the story bank; it's up to your adolescent to make withdrawals as needed.

STORIES FROM FAMILIES AROUND THE WORLD

After you've mastered these two basic techniques for sharing stories from books and about family events with your child, you may want to spice up your storytelling by trying out some ideas from other families and cultures. For instance, in some Native American communities, families or whole communities tell stories together, in which each member of the story circle takes turns adding to a story of shared personal experience. This is a lovely way to build a story together about a major event in your life as a family, such as a family holiday or the birth of a new sibling. With these communal stories, you could try incorporating the "build-up" style from indigenous Australian cultures in which they repeat, with variation, prior elements of the story. Before a storyteller starts to add her bit to the story, she could repeat, in her own words, some of the elements that other family members offered up previously. This technique is a fun way to make sure that everyone is listening to the story as it is being told, not just thinking about what they're going to add.[1]

This "repetition with variation" technique is also a highly effective way to develop children's memory and language skills. Think of it as an extended version of the "repeat and extend" technique that you used when your child was a toddler. Cultures with strong oral traditions display amazing mnemonic feats in their storytelling. The way they accomplish these retellings is not magic, but simply the science of memory. Repetition of what your child says with elaboration, association, alliteration—all of these strategies are highly effective memory tools as well as engaging storytelling techniques.

Other techniques are home-grown and arise naturally within families. For instance, after a talk I gave to a parents' group on the power of stories, one parent told me about a family tradition in which each night the parent and child took turns creating stories about a mouse family in which the characters shared some amazing similarities with their own family. This storytelling tradition started with the first child but was passed down to younger siblings.

Both of my children went through a phase in early childhood, from about 2-1/2 to 4, when they wanted "just one more story" after the last book was read and the lights were out. For my older son Ben, whose passion was trains and especially Thomas the Tank Engine, his dad and I took turns making up short stories that starred Thomas, Gordon, Henry, and of course the twin engines Bill and Ben. (After our younger son Dylan was born, we renamed the twin engines Dyl and Ben). The naughtier the trains were, the bigger the inevitable crash, and the more Ben enjoyed it. Of course, the story had to end a little more calmly, typically with a chastisement from Sir Tophamm Hat, in order to achieve the desired effect of getting Ben to sleep.

For my younger son Dylan, who craved routine and repetition, I created a new series set in "The Land of *Something*" in which each night a boy named Billy was magically transported to a land that contained only one substance. Before I began the story, I always let Dylan fill in the blank, be it mud, rocks, paper, or chocolate syrup. Some nights it was the "The Land of Strawberries" (his favorite fruit) in which all the houses and the furniture were made out of strawberries. Strawberry erasers, strawberry balloons, even strawberry cars. Billy always confronted some sort of difficulty in the new land, such as when he got hives from eating too many strawberry erasers, and he always decided to return to his own land in the end. These stories were brief, no more than about 10 sentences, told in a soporific tone of voice, and embarrassingly formulaic. There's no danger of this series ever hitting the bookshelves at Barnes & Noble. However, these stories did the trick. They gave my kids "one last story" that comforted them with its affirmation of their world's order and helped them drift off to sleep.

Young children are a forgiving audience, so don't be afraid to create a new storytelling tradition that is perfectly suited to your family. And who knows? Your family's favorite may turn out to be one that other families like too—see Alison Croggon's website for her night-time-series-turned-novel *Jimmy Wonderspoon* (http://www.alison-croggon.com/novels/jimmy.html).

TIMES AND PLACES FOR SHARING FAMILY STORIES

The greatest thing about family story sharing is that you're virtually unlimited in the times and places you can use it. Okay, you probably don't want to tell family stories during church, but storytelling is appropriate at almost any other time and place. There are some activities during which family stories seem to spill forth naturally and effortlessly, though, so I'll focus on those. It's often easier to share family stories while you are engaged in another activity, rather than sitting and staring at each other.

Talking While Eating

Research has established that dinnertime is a good setting for families to tell stories and to have rich conversations.[2] Personally, I find that storytelling and mealtimes are more compatible for older than younger children, but I do know families who can weave stories in at dinnertime even with toddlers and preschoolers. The good part about dinnertime as a conversational setting is that you are all in the same place, looking at each other, with nothing to do but eat and talk. The bad part about dinnertime is that it can be a high-pressure situation for picky eaters, and it comes at a tired and grumpy time of day for most toddlers and preschoolers, and even some older children and parents as well! When we spent time in South America, we found that the extended lunchtime in that culture was ideal for family conversation. Of course, one reason it works in South America is that the 2-hour lunch is part of the culture. Shops and schools are closed, and everyone is expected to be at home eating with family. You can create these more relaxed mealtimes in your own home, however, with a regular weekend brunch or lunch. Sunday is usually a good day because there are fewer scheduled activities.

Children already feel pressured to eat, sit still, behave, and have good table manners at mealtimes; you don't want them to feel pressured into hearing or contributing to family stories on top of all that. So use your judgment with this context depending on what works best for you and your family. Some families like a very structured

storytelling routine at mealtimes in which they all take a turn telling the best and worst things that happened in that day. I think this
structured approach can be good, especially in families with a wide
age range of children so that even the youngest or quietest gets a turn
to talk. It also works well if you happen to have a monologuer in your
family (child or parent), as long as you make sure that person goes
last! However, some families dislike this kind of structure and prefer
to have a free-flowing conversation.

For families with school-age children, meals are a natural time for
parents to share some of their childhood stories. Children appreciate not being the focus of attention momentarily, and perhaps it
even distracts parents from noticing table manners for a few minutes. The parent telling the story does need to make sure to leave
spaces for the children to ask questions and make comments. Pause
at the end of the story in case children want to contribute a similar
story of their own.

In some families, mealtimes do double-duty as informal planning
sessions, whether it's to brainstorm about a big event such as where to
go on a family vacation, or short-range planning such as the family's
next birthday party or how to best prepare for an upcoming com-
petition. This "future talk" is a natural time to bring up related past
events, such as other family vacations or competitions that you par-
ticipated in as a child. Focusing on the best or worst family vacation,
obstacles that you overcame, or simply the funniest moments usually
makes for good stories.

Remember to turn off the TV during mealtimes, and at other
times whenever possible. Having a TV on in the background inhibits
speech and parent-child interaction (see Chapter 1). Instead, watch
a TV program or a movie together after dinner, and talk about it as a
family post viewing.

Talking While Moving—Walking, Running, Hiking

There's something about moving that brings out the stories in all of
us. Talking while walking feels like a deep-seated and natural activity. Perhaps our hunting and gathering ancestors told stories to while
away the long hours of walking spent in search of food. I recommend

that you start walking and talking early with your child; that way you might have a chance of continuing this activity into adolescence![3]

In New Zealand, where cars and fuel are more expensive, we are a one-car family most of the time, and in South America, we were car-less. Walking has obvious financial and health benefits, but you may not have thought about how it also benefits your relationship with your kids. Again, it is the combination of moving without direct eye contact that seems to free up the tongue for conversation. For instance, one day while walking my kids to school in South America, I noticed that both boys brought up past events on their own. The first one occurred when we walked past a house that reminded 13-year-old Ben of our house in Massachusetts over 5 years earlier. He said, "Remember that time that it snowed really hard there and we had to dig tunnels on the sidewalk to get through?" Then he proceeded to talk about seeing a man out shoveling snow whose snot had frozen around his nostrils. I can't verify the accuracy of this story, but it was certainly entertaining. This story then triggered 9-year-old Dylan to recall the time that he was playing in the snow in Massachusetts at about age 3, and an errant snowball hit him square in the face. And so on, and so forth.

My sons' memories of their early childhood probably stand out more than they do for most children because we now live in a very different place, but reminiscing about them together solidifies their memories and our history as a family. These stories were short, easily accomplished in less than the 10 minutes it took to walk to school, but in that brief time we renewed our ties as a family and they arrived at school refreshed and laughing. My role in the conversation was minimal. I added a sentence here or there about how high the snow was, the year that the massive snowstorm occurred, as well as how old each child was at the time. But these stories belonged to the kids and I let them tell them.

Try to create a habit of walking together to the local park instead of driving, to school if you live close enough, or to the closest supermarket, coffee shop, or restaurant. If you're geographically blessed, walk along the beach or the waterfront or take a hike in the mountains on the weekend. You will be surprised at the way any tension between you and your family melts away and the stories start coming out naturally. Don't force it. You or your child will see something on your walk that reminds you of a time when . . . . and you'll be away.

Talking While Traveling—Trains, Planes, Automobiles, and Buses

The moving theme continues. Car rides, whether long or short, to a new place or the same old routine, are a natural spot for family storytelling. Think about it. You are all strapped in with nothing better to do than look out the window and talk. For all but the longest car rides, take away the Nintendo DS or PSP, switch off the van's DVD player, and talk to each other instead. Several studies have established that cars are a natural place for storytelling. In researcher Christine Marvin's wonderful study called "Cartalk!," she found that preschoolers talk about past and future events more often while in the car than at home or at school.[4] Using cars as a conversational setting appears to work especially well with young children and again with adolescents (as long as it is you and not your teenager who is driving). There's something about sitting beside each other without direct eye contact that helps adolescents in particular to spill out their deepest thoughts and fears. You've heard that primates interpret direct eye contact as an aggressive gesture? Well, so do teenagers!

Planes, trains, and buses all work in the same way as cars but have the added advantage that you are beside your children instead of with your back to them, and best of all, someone else is in charge of driving so that you're not distracted or stressed. Relax and have an unhurried conversation with your child about something you see out of the bus window, or about the first time your child rode on a plane. I have not found subways, however, to be conducive to story sharing. People tend to talk much less in a subway than in a bus or plane, probably because it is quieter, more crowded, and they are facing strangers, so they feel more self-conscious. Also, there's not enough waiting time in a subway to get into a good story.

Talking While Waiting

That brings us to waiting, whether at doctors' offices, airports, or in lines. These are again natural times for storytelling, because your child is a captive audience. Waiting rooms can also be a good time for shared book-reading, except that you typically get interrupted at a critical point in the story. Family stories are easier to pick up and leave off in this sense. And of course when waiting in a line at the post office, bank, or supermarket, it's much easier to tell a story than to read a book, and it serves as a great distracter too.

Talking While Working

Doing chores together with your child or adolescent is a surprisingly natural time for stories to emerge. To get the full effect of talking while working, try to find an activity that involves side-by-side or across the table positioning and that is not so strenuous or challenging that you lose the thread of the conversation. The more mindless and repetitive the activity, the better it is for sharing stories.

Ditch the dishwasher and hand-wash your dishes every night, letting one child at a time dry or put away dishes, according to their height and coordination. Even preschoolers can dry silverware safely and put it into the tray. Like walking and talking, dishwashing is a side-by-side activity that promotes talking and story sharing, and it's one of those golden opportunities for sharing a few minutes of precious talking time with adolescents. Or, with more than one child, share stories from books by taking turns as "reader," "washer," and "drier."

Gardening is another low-key, quiet activity during which story sharing can happen. There's something about digging in the earth with your hands that makes you reflect on your own childhood and share those stories with your child. Almost all children enjoy mucking about in the garden from the time they are toddlers. You may have to pay your teenager to pull weeds alongside you or to help you dig up a garden plot, but think of it as a relatively low-cost activity compared to going out to the movies or to dinner together.

If you talk while cooking or baking, you have the added opportunity of adding in a few family stories about favorite recipes from your grandmother, or your own favorite dishes that your parents cooked for you. And while shelling nuts, snapping beans, or peeling potatoes together, it feels almost impossible NOT to share a story or two.

Try talking while folding clothes with your child or when you are ironing. A colleague with grown children shared a lovely story with me about how she used to iron every Sunday night for relaxation (go figure). Her son would sit on the floor near her, taking in the soothing smell of freshly ironed clothes, and they would chat about anything and everything. Recently, her son, now in his 20s, returned home for dinner on a Sunday night. After dinner was over, he asked, "Aren't you going to do your ironing, Mum? That's why I came over tonight!"

Talking While Playing

Try talking while fishing, especially if you are in a boat together or fishing off a dock. I don't think these techniques would work with more active fishing pursuits, such as fly-fishing, unless you use small, funny stories as a distraction when tying on a new fly or helping your child untangle her line for the 20th time that day. You might be able to share a very short story or two while shooting hoops, in between baskets.[5] Talking while drawing, coloring, or painting is an excellent time to share stories. Research has confirmed that children tell longer and more complete stories about their past experiences while they are drawing a picture of those activities.[6] But you don't have to restrict yourself to drawing. You can talk about past events while doing any craft or artistic activity, such as scrapbooking, quilting, or knitting, as long as it is not too demanding on either of you. Scrapbooking is an obvious time to share stories about fun times together as a family, or proud moments savoring a child's accomplishments.

WHAT TO TALK ABOUT? WHICH STORIES TO SHARE?

Talking about Milestones and Firsts

When your child experiences a "first," whether it is learning to ride a bike, tie shoes, losing the first tooth, or starting school, family stories arise naturally. These stories may be of an older sibling's experiences or of your own. To maximize the effects of these stories, be sure to link the events with your child's own experiences, but be careful to avoid comparisons between siblings.

Talking about Happy Times—Weddings, Births, Christenings, Bar/Bat Mitzvahs, Birthdays, Holidays

Tales of Christmases or Hannukahs past—when talking together about holidays, make sure that you focus not just on the loot everyone got, but of funny or touching, distinctive things that happened. The time the tree fell off the roof of the car on the way home; the time it snowed so much on Christmas Eve no one could get out for days; in New Zealand, of having a Christmas Day barbecue on the beach. The repeated nature of rituals makes them vital for a sense of family identity and belonging, but the stories of rituals that are most tellable and memorable are about the times when something out of the ordinary happened in the course of the routine. Distinctive events are easier for children (and adults) to remember, and if your children remember the event more vividly, then it's easier for them to contribute to the storytelling and to pass the story down later to their own children.

Talking about Sad Times—Accidents, Injuries, Death, Divorce, and Disasters

Bad stuff happens in life. Beloved pets and grandparents die. People have accidents and major illnesses. Parents divorce. Houses burn to the ground. Earthquakes, tornadoes, and hurricanes destroy whole towns and the people in them. Whether it was meant to be or not, it is. Should you tell family stories with your kids about the bad stuff?

Yes. Eventually. You must talk about the bad stuff with your kids, even if those events are incomprehensible to you too. You start this process by responding to your child's questions, giving them only the information that they need and want at the time (see Box 7.2). These brief answers in direct response to your child's questions will help you start to shape your family story about the tragedy. Children's questions reveal their level of understanding of the event, their emotions, their perspectives. It is not just your story—it is the whole family's, although you as parents are the lead authors.

Negative events are highly tellable because they tend to comprise a classic goal-oriented structure to the narrative, with a clear low point (instead of high point in this case) and, we hope, a resolution. It's okay to talk about negative events as long as you are positive on the balance and as long as you resolve the event for the child. The story about the time the Christmas tree caught on fire and the presents were destroyed is fine to take on as a topic, as long as you can find some tinsel lining. When difficult or traumatic events are never discussed in a family, this silencing can leave lasting emotional scars on children.[7] Maya Angelou claims, "There is no agony like bearing an untold story inside of you." Better to bring things out in the open, as long as you are emotionally ready to have the conversation. The mother in the following example is obviously not quite ready to attempt this conversation with her 5-year-old daughter Maria about her separation from Maria's father. She offers no resolution, and Maria is left to comfort her mother, not the other way around.

> Mother: *Now let me ask you what's made you really sad?*
> Maria: *Daddy.*
> Mother: ' *Yeah, what about Daddy?*
> Maria: *Left.*
> Mother: *He left. Where did he go?*
> Maria: *Don't, now don't start crying!*
> Mother: *I'm not. So what um was so sad about that?*
> Maria: *Daddy leaving.*
> Mother: *Daddy doesn't live with us, is that, you got really upset about that?*
> Maria: *Yep. (Mother ends conversation)*[8]

In the wake of a death or disaster, family storytelling about the event is probably the farthest thing from your mind. There are phone calls to make, arrangements to organize, the physical labor of moving to a different place. Rituals. Routines. These activities keep our bodies moving so the event can sift into our consciousness slowly, sometimes reorganizing our whole way of life and the way we think about ourselves. You can't create a story to help your child when all the ramifications of the tragedy are not yet clear. Wait until you have developed a resolution of sorts before telling this story with your child.

Don't wait too long, though. Think of it as a story in the making. You are creating rough drafts of the story, but it will take a long time, if ever, to get to the final draft. And that's okay. Eventually, you will be able to find an ending for your story that involves redemption instead of simply destruction, pain, and loss.[9] And the next time your child asks "Why?" or "How?" you will have your story ready.

Finding redemption in tragedy is *not* the same as accepting that "it was meant to be" or the detestable "it was for the best." It's okay to acknowledge to your kids that some things are simply bad and that you wish they hadn't happened. But they *have* happened, so now you have to cope and help your child cope too. Good things can arise from the ashes. You certainly don't have to dwell on these tragic events. But you do have to address them, in time, when it's right for you and your child.

As painful as it may be for you, it helps your child for you to talk through what happened and help resolve it. Wakes, funerals, and memorial services, and those all-important family meals before and after, are natural occasions to talk about the loved one's escapades, triumphs, and sorrows. We are usually kind to the dead, bringing up tales of success rather than failure, and focusing on that person's best qualities. Here is a chance for you to elaborate on the child's connection with the family member by recalling funny or sweet times with your child. Be as specific as you can if you remember actual events. Instead of saying "Your Uncle Barry always used to toss you up in the air when you were a toddler and you would laugh and laugh," try "I remember one time when Uncle Barry tossed you up in the air, which you loved for him to do. You said 'More Bear, More Bear' (you called him Uncle Bear) and begged for him to keep going. He played with you all afternoon." The more vividly you can tell the story, the more likely it is to become part of your child's family history.

As you develop your family's story about a negative or traumatic event, be sure not to confuse **rumination*** about that event for reminiscing. You'll know you are ruminating instead of reminiscing when it feels like you're playing a well-worn tape in your head instead of thinking productively about how to resolve a negative event. Perhaps because of their reminiscing prowess, women are much more likely to ruminate than men from a young age. Think of rumination as reminiscing gone to seed. You need to eradicate rumination, because focusing unproductively on a negative event leads to depression. And rumination is the last thing you want to model for your preteen or teenage daughter.

The good news is that we get better with age at reflecting on negative events and resolving them through our stories. In one study, psychologist Lynne Baker-Ward and colleagues found that midlife adults
showed higher levels of resolution in their narratives of life events
compared to younger adults.[10] At least one thing gets better in middle
age! Perhaps we simply get more practice as life's trials accumulate.
For once, the research facts *do* fit with conventional wisdom. We do
get wiser the older we get.

On a lighter note, some of the best family stories are of trials and
tribulations that your family experienced together and conquered.
We heard some especially good ones when we asked families to share
their stories of family vacations with us. In the following example,
10-year-old Daniel and his parents recount their family's misadven-
tures while trying to make a plane to Singapore.

Dad: *Check-out time was 10 o'clock.*

Daniel: *Yeah, check-out time was 10 o'clock so we had to get up.
And we ran, we packed up and we got out of the hotel and we
took a taxi out and we just ran and ran and ran in the airport
and then I said, "Dad, I really need to go to the toilet."*

Dad: *You had to go to the toilet, I'm saying, "Get out of the cubi-
cle, the plane's about to take off!"*

Daniel: *And Mum was, Mum and Natasha (little sister) were
running around on the, um,*

Dad: *To gate 38*

Daniel: *Yeah, and, um, and then um*

Dad (to Mum):   *And there was clothing, underwear, falling out
of your handbag (laughing)*

Daniel: *(laughing) and, and there were nappies (diapers) every-
where and Natasha didn't need to go to the toilet or anything but
she was just standing there in mum's arms going 'uh, uh, uh'.*

Dad: *She was very young*

Daniel: *Yeah*

Dad: *And then we finally got to the gate and we were the last
ones onto the plane, sweating like pigs, and then what?*

Daniel: *And then we got onto the plane*

Dad: *And then the plane was delayed for an hour.*

Admittedly, most of these stories are only funny in retrospect, but they make some of the most lasting in your collection. They can be told and retold and even handed down across generations. There's nothing like surviving a tough time to bind people together.

Box 7.2 A Special Note on Family Stories after Separation or Divorce

---

How to piece family stories together after a separation or divorce? It's not just filling a hole as with a death—it's a rending of the fabric of the family. Literally torn in two, with the children (if they're lucky) traveling back and forth between the two halves, can family stories help heal the loss?

I believe that family stories can help make a family whole again after divorce, even if the family is to remain apart. There is no research at present on the benefits of story sharing for children of divorce. What follows are my ideas for story-sharing based on solid findings within the divorce literature and within the family story literature, bolstered by my personal experience and my friends' experiences. Here's what we know from research about when children cope better after separation/divorce:[11]

1. **Children cope better if their parents can avoid fighting in front of them** or over the phone in earshot of them, especially if the fighting is about the children. Work out your disagreements about custody and the property settlement between you privately, in a counselor's office, at mediation, or even court if necessary, but don't do it in front of the kids. Listen to their preferences, but then make the final decision together as their parents. You are **both** still their parents, **always,** even if you no longer live together.

2. **Children need to know that the separation wasn't their fault.** Parents split up for all kinds of reasons, usually more than one, and kids can't understand most of those reasons. There are many good books that take you through explaining the separation and/or divorce to children of different ages. As with other negative experiences, it's okay to confront directly

(continued)

Box 7.2 (*Continued*)

your child's questions about the separation or divorce itself. It's important to explore the negative emotions but to help resolve them for your child, especially with younger children. The main thing children need to know is that the separation didn't occur because of them.

3. **Children need to continue to have a relationship with both parents as much as this is possible.** Enough said.

Given these well-founded principles on how to help children cope after separation/divorce, what are the implications for sharing family stories with your children?

1. **Sharing new memories.** *Children benefit from sharing open-ended, elaborative conversations about the novel experiences they share with you.* The implications of this principle of family story sharing are relatively easy for divorced parents. Even in the postdivorce chaos, or especially in this chaos, it's important for BOTH parents, to whatever degree possible, to continue to have positive experiences with their children and to talk about these experiences in an open-ended and elaborative way, in which you encourage your child to give voice to their perspectives on a shared experience. These experiences could be familiar, comforting ones, but it's also important for you to begin to create new traditions and new experiences for each of your new families. If you are fortunate enough to be sharing custody, think of your child as now having two new, complete (albeit smaller) families rather than two incomplete half-families. New families need new traditions, and in talking about those new experiences you are creating a history for that new family. This process is more dramatic in the case of divorce than in new families formed in other ways, but even in nonseparated families, change is a given. New family members are born, adolescents grow up and move away, elderly grandparents move in, the whole family uproots to a new neighborhood or city—families are all and always changing. No single person defines a family. You, as the sole parent, are in charge of defining and creating the culture of your new little family. Don't wait for a step-parent to enter the picture to start this process. Your new family is a whole unto itself, with or without a new partner.

(*continued*)

Box 7.2 (*Continued*)

2. **Sharing memories from your child's early experiences.** *Children benefit from knowing whence they came.* Enacting this principle of family story sharing is going to be harder, because many stories about your child's early life will involve your former spouse or partner. You can focus mostly on your child's experiences in sharing these stories, which is what would happen anyway if you were still in a two-parent family. DO mention your former spouse if he or she was present—don't cut him or her out of the picture. Be sure to avoid any spiteful comments. Your child doesn't want to hear bad things about her other parent. The birth story may be a good place to start. Focus on your child—that's the part that's most interesting to him anyway. If—and only if—you can avoid rancor, snide comments, and sentimentality, mention your partner's role in the process. "And your dad was the one who cut your cord. And he said, 'Hello, James' to you. He was so happy." The birth story is a wonderful opportunity for you to reinforce to your child how much both parents love him or her.

3. **Sharing other family stories.** *Children benefit from knowing stories from both sides of their family's history.* If you are in a solo-parent family, follow the same principles as for two-parent families in telling stories of your own childhood as they come up naturally, being sure to make links to your child's life if you can.

Should you tell your former partner's family stories? If you were with someone long enough to have a child together, no doubt you have a whole store of family stories about the other parent. Are these family stories now yours to pass on? This is a tricky one. Again, if you can pass on these stories without rancor or revisionist history, or if the other parent is absent and you are the only conduit for your child to receive these stories, then perhaps it's okay. But most likely, the child's other parent would like to be the one in charge of passing down their family's history. It might be better for you to say something like, "You should ask Dad about the time he got in trouble with Uncle Bobby for skipping church. That's a good story." If you

(*continued*)

Box 7.2 (*Continued*)

can talk about the other side of the family in a positive way, then everything we know about children's functioning after separation/divorce is that it's good for them to know these details. And if your child is not in contact with the other parent and you are in sole charge of passing down this information, I believe you actually have an obligation to do so, just as you would if your child were adopted and you knew details about their birth family. If the facts are unsavory, you don't need to dwell on them or be judgmental (but don't gloss over them or sugarcoat them either, especially as your child grows into an adolescent). Remember that your former spouse or partner is and always will be your child's parent. Be kind! Be generous! But try not to be overly sentimental or nostalgic, because that's not good for your child either.

It's ironic that telling positive stories about your child's relationship with a departed loved one is probably easier than telling positive stories involving a living former spouse. However hard it is, though, it's vital for your child's ability to cope with the loss that you learn to tell these positive stories. Your child desperately needs to hear positive stories about their early days with both a mother and a father in the same house, especially if the separation happened so early in their lives that they have no memories of their own of this time. The more specific you can be, the better. Again, the birth story is a good place to start practicing these positive stories.

To put my own words of advice into practice, I asked my PhD student Federica to record me telling Dylan's birth story to him when he was almost 11, about two years after his dad and I had separated. Here's what came out. I will let you be the judge of whether I am able to follow my own advice!

Elaine: *So that, let's see, it was a Wednesday morning and I woke up and um and I felt things, pains in my belly and I thought, "Ooh, yay, the baby's gonna be born today." And I could just tell as soon as I woke up and I was really excited.*

Dylan: *Was it, was I already born?*

(continued)

Box 7.2 *(Continued)*

Elaine: *No no it's just you start having pains first, and that's*
          sort of to get your body ready to push the baby out—
Dylan: *Ewww.*
Elaine: *Ewww. Ok, but you start having these pains in your*
          tummy and that's when women know they're gonna have the
          baby. They're called labour pains. And, and so the plan was
          that when I went into labour we were gonna call Jamin and
          Cindy to look after Ben while you were being born because he
          was supposed to go to kindergarten that morning, and so they
          came by and they got Ben and they took him to kindergarten.
Dylan: *Mm*
Elaine: *And I said, "Maybe this afternoon you'll have a baby*
          brother or sister," because we didn't know what you were. And,
          and so the pains started getting worse, and I was still at home.
Dylan: *Mmm*
Elaine: *You getting bored?*
Dylan: *No*
Elaine: *And, and Dad was worried that I hadn't eaten anything*
          so you know how Dad likes to feed people, well he made me eat
          healthy food like kumara (sweet potato) and some other stuff
          cause he was worried I was gonna get weak while I was having
          the baby. That was good. And so I ate and then I said "Casey,
          you've really got to get me to the hospital." And um, and so
          he took me in the car and it was, I was in the backseat of the
          car 'cause I was really worried that I was gonna have the baby,
          have you in the back of the car, but I made it into the elevator at
          the hospital and we went up to the room where the doctor and
          the midwife were, and do you know what the midwife's name
          was? Have I ever told you this before?
Dylan: *Nope*
Elaine: *Mary. And you know that's funny because my mum's*
          name is Mary Nell and Dad's mum's name is Mary Ann
Dylan: *(chiming in) Mary Ann*
Elaine: *So the lady who brought you into this world was also*
          Mary and she's a really lovely lady. She's Irish.
Dylan: *Is she on Facebook?*
Elaine: *Is she on Facebook?*

(continued)

Box 7.2 (*Continued*)

Dylan: *Yeah.*

Elaine: *I'm not sure. We'll have to see. I think she lives back in Ireland now but she—*

Dylan: *Do you think she'll remember you?*

Elaine: *Oh yeah, she would definitely remember me. Yeah. Because she was my midwife for Ben and for you, so she knew us pretty well. And, and so the pains were still coming and everything and then all of a sudden it was just time for you to be born and that happened—*

Dylan: *Fast-forward.*

Elaine: *Ok, fast-forward over that part! And you know what we always say about when you were born?*

Dylan: *What?*

Elaine: *You know what it is, you've heard me say this.*

Dylan: *Butt first*

Elaine: *No, your head came out first. And what did we see when your head came out?*

Dylan: *What was it?*

Elaine: *A bunch of hair.*

Dylan: *Oh yeah.*

Elaine: *You had so much hair and um you just had hair, all, it was so long. And you had hair on your head, you had hair on your ankles, you had hair on your back, you basically had hair all over your body.*

Dylan: *How much hair on my back?*

Elaine: *Quite a bit.*

Dylan: *It's gone now.*

Elaine: *It was a special, special, yeah, it's a special hair that babies have sometimes when they're born, called lanugo, and it just, it rubs off after you're born. But yeah, you had so much hair that later on when Brent came to visit us in the hospital he said "We're gonna call this baby Reese's monkey!"*

Dylan: *Ha (laughs)*

Elaine: *And Harlene came to visit, Harlene and Mike, and Harlene said, "That's the cutest baby I've ever seen." And, but the best part was when Ben (big brother) came—*

Dylan: *Yeah.*

(continued)

Box 7.2 *(Continued)*

Elaine: *And Jamin and Cindy, and you know this part—*

Dylan: *Mmm*

Elaine: *Where, we had told him that when the baby was born that he would get to unwrap the baby like a present, and so he unwrapped you like a present and you know what he said?*

Dylan: *What?*

Elaine: *He said, "I just got a baby brother! Yay!" And he was so happy that you were a boy. He wanted a baby brother. And later on he said, "The best day of my life was the day Dylan was born." Is that cool?*

Dylan: *Yeah.*

Elaine: *You know, sometimes you guys fight now, but he does love you a lot. And he didn't want to be an only child, so he was so so glad to have a little brother. And I think he probably would've been glad too if you were a little sister, but.*

Dylan: *Yeah.*

Elaine: *He was really glad that you were a boy. And so that's the story of the day that you were born, and we were all so happy that you were so healthy and hairy and cute.*

As hard as it may be for you to recall these early days in light of how the relationship ended, it may even help you to cope as well to tell these positive stories. Instead of blocking out the past or rewriting history, you can acknowledge to yourself and to your child that there were good times together as a family. Even though those times are now past, they are a part of your life—and the first chapters of your child's life—and always will be.

8

The End of the Stories?

We are lonesome animals. We spend all our life trying to be less lonesome. One of our ancient methods is to tell a story begging the listener to say—and to feel—Yes, that's the way it is, or at least that's the way I feel it. You're not as alone as you thought.

~*John Steinbeck*

Should you ever stop sharing stories with your children? No, I don't believe you should. In fact, your role as a family story sharer actually gains importance as your children reach adulthood. When your children graduate from high school and college, start their first jobs, get married, and have children, they continue to want and need your own stories of these major transitions. They will not always want to follow your path, but your experiences, for better or worse, will help them choose their own path in life, and the kind of parents they want to be.

Your stories of your children's first years are also essential for your grandchildren. No one else in the world has the firsthand knowledge of their parents' first years as you do. As with adolescents, however, choose carefully the stories to tell your grandchildren about their parents. If you know a certain family story annoys your adult son, or illustrates a less than desirable trait, there's no need to tell it to his children. Again, show sensitivity to the way your children want to appear to their own children and the values they want to inculcate in their own families. By all means, tell your own stories too. They will be more likely to be passed on if your grandchildren hear them as lived experience rather than as secondhand knowledge from their parents.

Sometimes, despite your best efforts as a story sharer and as a parent, your child or teenager will become unhappy, even depressed. She may be lonely, have trouble making friends, or have difficulties at school. He may cut or use drugs. She may have an eating disorder. He may take crazy risks and end up in trouble with the law.

Story sharing is by no means a cure-all for the dangers of adolescence, nor is story sharing an inoculation against life's many and sundry ills. Story sharing can't make a bad teacher go away, nor can it put food on the table in times of need. Story sharing can't reverse a genetic propensity toward substance abuse or mental illness.

Yet story sharing *can* provide your child and adolescent with solace and with a means of understanding and coping with life's hardballs. Stories can give your child a way out of a problem, or perhaps a way into a solution. Story sharing can help situate a toddler, a child, a teenager in a world filled with people who care about them, past and present, and who possess both inspiring and cautionary tales. These tales may help your adolescent carve out the person he or she strives to be, whatever hand was dealt genetically or in life circumstances.

Think of story sharing as a gift that you can continue to offer your child throughout your life, a gift that costs virtually nothing but your time, memory, and creativity, a gift that your children can pass on to their children in a never-ending chain. Memory is fallible and ephemeral, yet in old age it seems that what one values most, and remembers best, are the stories.

So start sharing stories early with your children and keep them coming, back and forth, up and down the generations. Stories sustain us, they teach us, they protect us, and they join us to others.

Glossary of Terms
(marked with * in text)

Dialogic Reading: A method that Russ Whitehurst pioneered of reading picture books interactively with very young children by asking questions about the pictures, following in and expanding on children's responses.

Expressive language: Children's spoken language, as opposed to the words they understand but do not use in speech.

Mental state words: All words that refer to a person's internal states, such as desires, emotions, or thoughts (*wanna, angry, remember*).

Rich Reading: My method of reading books interactively with children of all ages, from toddlers (adapted from Dialogic Reading) to teenagers. With toddlers and younger preschoolers, the question-confirm-extend cycle occurs on every page, whereas with older preschoolers and school-age children, questions can occur less frequently, mainly at the end of the book-sharing session. With adolescents, Rich Reading can involve reading the same book at different times, or reading different books at the same time, but always discussing them, and remaining open to your child's perspective.

Rich Reminiscing: My method of sharing family stories interactively with children and adolescents of all ages, developed with colleagues Robyn Fivush and Catherine Haden. With younger children, the focus is mostly on your child's recent experiences. As your children get older, you can share stories about experiences they had apart from you, as well as experiences from their own lives that they don't remember (for example, the story of the day he or she was born). With older children and adolescents, you can share your own childhood stories and your family history. It's best at all ages to keep your story sharing interactive by asking questions and responding to your child. With older children and adolescents, it's important to let them tell at least half the story, and try to end on a positive note.

Rumination: Thinking repeatedly about a negative event without finding a solution.

Story Sharing: My umbrella term for my **Rich Reading** and **Rich Reminiscing** methods, which are similar in the way they are practiced, but differ in topic and genre (a book vs. a family story).

Temperament: A young child's tendency to be shy or sociable, focused or inattentive, active or placid, calm or excitable, happy and easygoing, or negative and difficult.

Theory of mind: An understanding of one's own and others' mental states, including desires, emotions, thoughts, dreams, and imaginings. A full-fledged theory of mind entails understanding that others can have beliefs and desires that differ from, and even conflict with, the child's beliefs and desires. Also called an "understanding of mind."

Whānau: A Māori concept of extended family and friends.

Working memory: The ability to hold information in mind for a short period of time before forgetting it, writing it down, or committing it to longer-term memory.

Notes

Introduction Notes

1. Fivush, R., Haden, C. A., & Reese, E. (2006). Elaborating on elaborations: Role of maternal reminiscing style in cognitive and socioemotional development. *Child Development, 77,* 1568–1588.
2. Le Guin, U. (1979). A citizen of Mondath. In S. Wood (Ed.), *Language of the night: Essays on fantasy and science fiction* (p. 31). New York: Putnam Books.
3. McNaughton, S. (1995). *Patterns of emerging literacy: Processes of development and transition.* Auckland: Oxford University Press.
4. Cox, L. (1993). *Kotahitanga.* Auckland: Oxford University Press.
   Reese, E., Hayne, H., & MacDonald, S. (2008). Looking back to the future: Māori and Pakeha mother-child birth stories. *Child Development, 79,* 114–125.
   Rewi, P. (2010). *Whaikōrero: The world of Māori oratory.* Auckland: Auckland University Press.
5. Tapsell, P. (2002). Marae and tribal identity in urban Aotearoa/New Zealand. In J. Moddell (Ed.), "Moral Communities," Special Issue of *Pacific Studies, 25,* 141–171.
6. Reese, E. (in press). Culture, narrative, and imagination. In M. Taylor (Ed.), *Oxford handbook of imagination.* New York: Oxford University Press.
7. For a fascinating account of storytelling traditions in indigenous Costa Rican communities, see Cuneo, C. N., McCabe, A. K., & Melzi, G. (2008). Mestizaje: Narratives of Dominican American children: Diversity among Latinos and links with other traditions. In A. McCabe, A. Bailey, & G. Melzi (Eds.), *The development of Latino narration* (pp. 237–272). New York: Cambridge University Press (quote from p. 252).
8. Fung, H., Miller, P. J., & Lin, L. C. (2004). Listening is active: Lessons from the narrative practices of Taiwanese families. In M. W. Pratt & B. H. Fiese (Eds.), *Family stories and the life course: Across time and generations* (pp. 303–326). Mahwah, NJ: Erlbaum.
9. Cuneo, C. N., McCabe, A. K., & Melzi, G. (2008). Mestizaje: Narratives of Dominican American children: Diversity among Latinos and links with other traditions. In A. McCabe, A. Bailey, & G. Melzi (Eds.), *The development of Latino*

narration (pp. 237–272). NY: Cambridge University Press. See http://www.literacynet.org/lp/hperspectives/llorona.html for the legend of la Llorona.

10. Harwood, R. L., Miller, J. G., & Irizarry, N. L. (1995). *Culture and attachment: Perceptions of the child in context.* New York: Guilford Press.

11. Reese, E., & Fivush, R. (1993). Parental styles of talking about the past. *Developmental Psychology, 29,* 596–606.

12. Cleveland, E. S., & Reese, E. (2008). Children remember early childhood: Long-term recall across the offset of childhood amnesia. *Applied Cognitive Psychology, 22,* 127–142.

13. Reese, E., & Newcombe, R. (2007). Training mothers in elaborative reminiscing enhances children's autobiographical memory and narrative. *Child Development, 78,* 1153–1170.

14. Mullis, I. V. S., Martin, M. O., Kennedy, A. M., & Foy, P. (2007). *PIRLS 2006 International Report: IEA's progress in international reading literacy study in primary schools in 40 countries.* Boston: Lynch School of Education, Boston College.

15. Kraemer, H., Stice, E., Kazdin, A., Offord, D., & Kupfer, D. (2001). How do risk factors work together? Mediators, moderators and independent variables. *The American Journal of Psychiatry, 158,* 848–856.

Chapter 1 Notes

1. Hart, B., & Risley, T. R. (1995). *Meaningful differences in the everyday experiences of young American children.* Baltimore: Brookes.

2. Carpenter, M., Nagell, K., & Tomasello, M. (1998). Social cognition, joint attention, and communicative competence from 9 to 15 months of age. *Monographs of the Society for Research in Child Development, 63,* 255.

3. Hoff, E. (2006). How social contexts support and shape language development. *Developmental Review, 26,* 55–88.

4. Whitehurst, G. J., Falco, F., Lonigan, C. J., Fischel, J. E., DeBaryshe, B. D., Valdez-Menchaca, M. C., & Caulfield, M. (1988). Accelerating language development through picture-book reading. *Developmental Psychology, 24,* 552–558.

5. Russian psychologist Lev Vygotsky based his theory of children's cognitive development on the deepening link between thinking and language in early childhood (Vygotsky, L. S. [1986]. *Thought and language* (A. Kozulin, Ed.). Cambridge, MA: The Massachusetts Institute of Technology Press), and Katherine Nelson expanded on that theory in her 1996 book, *Language in cognitive development: Emergence of the mediated mind.* New York: Cambridge University Press.

6. The connection between early language and later reading is evident across the preschool to primary school years. Kendeou, P., van den Broek, P., White, M. J., & Lynch, J. S. (2009). Predicting reading comprehension in early elementary school: The independent contributions of language and decoding skills. *Journal of Educational Psychology, 101,* 765–778.

In our longitudinal NZ study, we found that toddler language (as measured by parent reports and standardized vocabulary assessments) predicts reading accuracy and comprehension in adolescence (rs ranged from .30 to .56, $N = 51$). These correlations all remained significant even after controlling for mothers' education and language levels, both powerful predictors of children's language and reading development.

7. Menting and colleagues showed that the link between children's language skill and their later externalizing problems was mediated by peer rejection, but only for boys. In other words, boys' poor language skills lead to peer rejection, which in turn leads to externalizing behavior. Menting, B., van Lier, P. A. C., & Koot, H. M. (2011). Language skills, peer rejection, and the development of externalizing behavior from kindergarten to fourth grade. *The Journal of Child Psychology and Psychiatry, 52,* 72–79. See also Niobe Way's (2011) book, *Deep Secrets: Boys' Friendships and the Crisis of Connection.* Cambridge, MA: Harvard University Press.

8. In one study, mothers rated the behavior problems of toddlers with expressive language delays and typically developing toddlers, and researchers observed mother-toddler dyads in a toy clean-up situation (n = 34 in each group; average age 27 months). Toddlers with language delays displayed more negative behavior (crying, screaming, hitting, and throwing toys) in the toy clean-up; mothers also conversed with them less than they did with the typically developing toddlers. Mothers rated the toddlers with language delays as being lower on "acceptability," meaning that they weren't reaching mothers' expectations for their physical, intellectual, or emotional development. Caulfield, M. B., Fischel, J. E., DeBaryshe, B. D., & Whitehurst, G. J. (1989). Behavioral correlates of expressive language disorder. *Journal of Abnormal Child Psychology, 17,* 187–201.

9. Dale, P. S., & Fenson, L. (1996). Lexical development norms for young children. *Behavioral Research Methods, Instruments, and Computers, 28,* 125–127. Fifty percent of US children used these words by the following ages: "love" (22 months); "wanna" (23 months); "like" (25 months); "scared" (26 months); "sad" and "mad" (27 months); "think" and "pretend" (30 months).

10. For instance, children with autism, who have great difficulty with shared attention and communication, also lack mental state words in their vocabularies, even after they have reached the intellectual age of a 4-year-old. Happe, F. G. E. (1995). The role of age and verbal ability in the theory of mind task performance of subjects with autism. *Child Development, 66,* 843–855.

11. Whitehurst et al. (1988), see note 4.

12. Torppa, M., Tolvanen, A., Poikkeus, A-M., Eklund, K., Lerkkanen, M-K., Leskinen, E., & Lyytinen, H., (2007). Reading development subtypes and their early characteristics. *Annals of Dyslexia, 57,* 3–32.

13. Sachs, J. (1983). Topic selection in parent-child discourse. *Discourse Processes, 2,* 145–153.

14. Dale & Fenson (1996), see note 9. Age in months at which 50% of children are producing the word: child's name (19 mo.), "mine" (19 mo.), "me" (20 mo.), "I" (22 mo), "my" (23 mo.), "myself" (30 mo.); two-word combinations (19 mo.)

15. Reese, E. (1999). What children say when they talk about the past, Study 2. *Narrative Inquiry, 9,* 215–242. You will notice a pattern among child language researchers of studying their firstborn children. There's a reason for this pattern, as I'm sure all of you with more than one child will know. With the second or third child, there's simply no time to be recording every precious first word on a tape recorder or in a diary!

16. Piaget, J. (1952). *The origins of intelligence in children.* New York: Norton.

17. Barr, R., Dowden, A., & Hayne, H. (1996). Developmental changes in deferred imitation by 6- to 24-month-old infants. *Infant Behavior and Development, 19,* 159–170.

18. Miller, P. J., & Sperry, L. L. (1988). Early talk about the past: The origins of conversational stories of personal experience. *Journal of Child Language, 15,* 293–315: 58% of the 2-year-olds' stories were about negative events. In a follow-up study comparing children from working-class and middle-class communities in Chicago, in contrast, positive events predominated among children's stories from both communities. However, children from working-class neighborhoods still told more stories of physical harm (animal death, accidents) than did children from middle-class communities. When middle-class children narrated these tales, they were stories of "owies" (similar to Ben's) or of falling down at the playground, whereas the working-class children told tales of more dramatic events such as an older brother's sled crashing while they were a passenger. Burger, L. K., & Miller, P. J. (1999). Early talk about the past revisited: Affect in working-class and middle-class children's co-narrations. *Journal of Child Language, 26,* 133–162.

19. Reese (1999), Study 1, see note 15.

20. AAP Council on Communications and Media (2011); see also Australia's *Get Up and Grow* campaign.

21. Infants look more often to programs that feature children or puppets, and that contain singing, music, or sound effects.

    Huston, A. C., & Wright, J. C. (1983). Children's processing of television: The informative functions of formal features. In J. Bryant & D. R. Anderson (Eds.), *Children's understanding of television: Research on attention and comprehension* (pp. 35–68). New York: Academic.

    Schmitt, K. L., Anderson, D. R., & Collins, P. A. (1999). Form and content: Looking at visual features of television. *Developmental Psychology, 35,* 1156–1167.

    In a home-based study, Barr and colleagues noted that 12- to 18-month-old toddlers looked at a Baby Mozart video 60–70% of the time. Toddlers looked more at the video when they were older and had previously viewed similar videos. They also looked more when parents asked questions and described the video during coviewing.

    Barr, R., Zack, E., Garcia, A., & Muentener, P. (2008). Infants' attention and responsiveness to television increases with prior exposure and parental interaction. *Infancy, 13,* 30–56.

22. Barr, R. (2010). Transfer of learning between 2D and 3D sources during infancy: Informing theory and practice. *Developmental Review, 30,* 128–154.

23. Ganea, P. A., Pickard, M. B., & DeLoache, J. S. (2008). Transfer between picture books and the real world. *Journal of Cognition and Development, 9,* 46–66.

    Krcmar, M., Grela, B., Lin, K. (2007). Can toddlers learn vocabulary from television? An experimental study. *Media Psychology, 10,* 41–63.

    Simcock, G., & DeLoache, J. S. (2006). Get the picture? The effects of iconicity on toddlers' re-enactment from picture. *Developmental Psychology, 42,* 1352–1357.

    Simcock, G., & Dooley, M. (2007). Generalization of learning from picture books to novel test conditions by 18- and 24-month-old children. *Developmental Psychology, 43,* 1568–1578.

    Tare, M., Chiong, C., Ganea, P., & DeLoache, J. (2010). Less is more: How manipulative features affect children's learning from picture books. *Journal of Applied Developmental Psychology, 31,* 395–400.

24. Robb, M. B., Richert, R. A., & Wartella, E. A. (2009). Just a talking book? Word learning from watching baby videos. *British Journal of Developmental Psychology, 27,* 27–45.

25. Linebarger, D. L., & Walker, D. (2005). Infants' and toddlers' television viewing and language outcomes. *American Behavioral Scientist, 48,* 624–645.

Note that correlational studies such as this one cannot tell us about the causal effects of toddlers watching certain programs over others on their language development. For instance, the toddlers who watched more *Arthur* and *Clifford* may also have parents who read books to them more often, so these findings could reflect other influences on children's language besides their TV watching.

26. Barr, R., Lauricella, A., Zack, E., & Calvert, S. L. (2010). Infant and early childhood exposure to adult-directed and child-directed television programming. *Merrill-Palmer Quarterly, 56,* 21–48.

Zimmerman, F. J., & Christakis, D. A. (2007). Associations between content types of early media exposure and subsequent attention problems. *Pediatrics, 120,* 986–992.

Note that Christakis and colleagues also found a strong correlation between the overall amount of screentime in infancy and toddlerhood and later attention difficulties, but that study failed to control for critical variables that are associated with TV watching (poverty level and mothers' achievement). When these critical variables were controlled, the link between TV watching in early childhood and later attention problems disappeared. Christakis, D. A., Zimmerman, F. J., DiGiuseppe, D. L., & McCarty, C. A. (2004). Early television exposure and subsequent attentional problems in children. *Pediatrics, 113,* 708–713.

27. Vandewater, E. Z., Bickham, D. S., Lee, J. H., Cummings, H. M., Wartella, E. A., & Rideout, V. J. (2005). When the television is always on: Heavy television exposure and young children's development. *American Behavioral Scientist, 48,* 562–577.

Mothers experiencing depression allow their infants and toddlers to watch twice as much child-directed programming as do mothers without depression, and depressed mothers are less likely to interact with their babies and toddlers during these TV watching sessions. Bank, A. M., Barr, R., Calvert, S. L., Parrott, W. G., McDonough, S. C., & Rosenblum, K. (2012). Maternal depression and family media use: A questionnaire and diary analysis. *Journal of Child and Family Studies, 21,* 208–216. doi: 10.1007/s10826-011-9464-1

Kirkorian, H. L., Pempek, T. A., Murphy, L. A., Schmidt, M. E., & Anderson, D. R. (2009). The impact of background television on parent-child interaction. *Child Development, 80,* 1350–1359.

Schmidt, M. E., Pempek, T. A., Kirkorian, H. L., Frankenfield Lund, A., & Anderson, D. A. (2008). The effects of background television on the toy play behavior of very young children. *Child Development, 79,* 1137–1151.

28. Fidler, A. E., Zack, E., & Barr, R. (2010). Television viewing patterns in 6- to 18-month-olds: The role of caregiver-infant interactional quality. *Infancy, 15,* 176–196.

Strouse, G., O'Doherty, K., & Troseth, G. (2011). *Dialogic video: Influence of dialogic reading techniques on preschoolers' learning from video stories.* Paper presented at Institute for Educational Studies Conference.

29. Nelson, K. (1989/2006). *Narratives from the crib.* Boston, MA: Harvard University Press.

30. Ganea, Pickard, & DeLoache (2008), see note 23; Tare, Chiong, Ganea, & DeLoache (2010), see note 23.

31. Ainsworth, M. D. S., Blehar, M. C., Waters, E., & Wall, S. (1978). *Patterns of attachment: a psychological study of the Strange Situation.* Hillsdale, NJ: Erlbaum.
    Bowlby, J. (1969). *Attachment and loss: Volume one: Attachment.* London: Hogarth Press.
32. http://www.helpguide.org/mental/parenting_attachment.html; http://www.ahaparenting.com/parenting-tools/attachment-parenting/Pros-and-cons
33. Crain-Thoreson, C., & Dale, P. S. (1999). Enhancing linguistic performance: Parents and teachers as book reading partners for children with language delays. *Topics in Early Childhood Special Education, 19,* 28–39.
    Huebner, C. E. (2000). Promoting toddlers' language development: A randomized-control trial of a community-based intervention. *Journal of Applied Developmental Psychology,* 21, 513–535.
    Whitehurst et al. (1988), see note 4.
34. Cutspec, P. A. (2004). Influences of dialogic reading on the language development of toddlers. *Bridges: Practice-Based Research Syntheses, 2,* 1–12.
35. Harris, P. (1996). Desires, beliefs, and language. In P. Curruthers & P. Smith (Eds.), *Theories of theories of mind* (pp. 200–220). Cambridge, UK: Cambridge University Press.
    Perkins, C. (2011). *"Me," "my," "mine": Maternal mental state talk, children's social understanding and the role of the self-concept.* Unpublished PhD thesis, University of Otago, Dunedin, New Zealand.
    Taumoepeau, M., & Ruffman, T. (2006). Mother and infant talk about mental states relates to desire language and emotion understanding. *Child Development, 77,* 465–481.
    Taumoepeau, M., & Ruffman, T. (2008). Stepping stones to others' minds: Maternal talk relates to child mental state language and emotion understanding at 15, 24 and 33 months. *Child Development, 79,* 284–302.
36. Reese, E. (2012). The tyranny of shared book-reading. In S. Suggate & E. Reese (Eds.), *Contemporary debates in childhood education and development* (pp. 59–68). UK: Routledge Press.
    Analogy of book-reading to broccoli-eating for some children: Scarborough, H. S. & Dobrich, W. (1994). On the efficacy of reading to preschoolers. *Developmental Review, 14,* 245–302.
37. Peggy Miller and her colleagues have documented young children's emotional attachments to stories. Often these intense attachments are to stories with themes of separation or other problems that the children are currently encountering in real life. Children appear to use the stories to seek solace and understanding. Parents often encourage the attachment at the beginning, but fairly quickly the attachment can become irritating, frustrating, and even worrying for parents. As one mother said about her daughter's fascination with the Cinderella story, "Well, I've heard about Cinderella almost every day for over a year, and I've had to read the bloody story as often as I could stomach it . . . and maybe a little more. I just couldn't do it anymore!!" (Alexander et al., 2001, p. 388). Alexander, K. J., Miller, P. J., & Hengst, J. A. (2001). Young children's emotional attachments to stories. *Social Development, 10,* 374–398.
    Miller, P. J., Hoogstra, L., Mintz, J., Fung H., & Williams, K. (1993). Troubles in the garden and how they get resolved: A young child's transformation of his

favorite story. In C. A. Nelson (Ed.), *Memory and affect in development* (Vol. 26, pp. 87–114). Hillsdale, NJ: Erlbaum.

38. Correlational and experimental research with toddlers documents the benefits of an elaborative reminiscing style for toddlers' narrative and memory development.

Farrant, K., & Reese, E. (2000). Maternal style and children's participation in reminiscing: Stepping stones in children's autobiographical memory development. *Journal of Cognition and Development, 1,* 193–225.

Haden, C. A., Ornstein, P. A., Rudek, D. J., & Cameron, D. (2009). Reminiscing in the early years: Patterns of maternal elaborativeness and children's remembering. *International Journal of Behavioural Development, 33,* 118–130.

Harley, K., & Reese, E. (1999). Origins of autobiographical memory. *Developmental Psychology, 35,* 1338–1348.

Peterson, C., Jesso, B., & McCabe, A. (1999). Encouraging narratives in preschoolers: An intervention study. *Journal of Child Language, 26,* 49–67.

Reese, E., & Newcombe, R. (2007). Training mothers in elaborative reminiscing enhances children's autobiographical memory and narrative. *Child Development, 78,* 1153–1170.

39. Lewis, M., & Brooks-Gunn, J. (1979). *Social cognition and the acquisition of self.* New York: Plenum.

40. Reese & Newcombe (2007), see note 38; Taumoepeau, M., & Reese, E. (in press). Maternal reminiscing style, elaborative talk, and children's theory of mind: A training study. *First Language.*

41. Fivush, R., Gray, J. X., & Fromhoff, F. A. (1987). Two-year-olds talk about the past. *Cognitive Development, 2,* 393–409; Reese (1999), see note 15.

42. When age ranges are given, they represent the norms for which 90% of US children have achieved the relevant milestone.

Ainsworth, M. D. S., Blehar, M. C., Waters, E., & Wall, S. (1978). *Patterns of attachment: a psychological study of the Strange Situation.* Hillsdale, NJ: Erlbaum.

Barr, R., Dowden, A., & Hayne, H. (1996). Developmental changes in deferred imitation by 6- to 24-month-old infants. *Infant Behavior and Development, 19,* 159–170.

Bowlby, J. (1969). *Attachment and loss: Volume one: Attachment.* London: The Hogarth Press.

Bus, A. G., & Van IJzendoorn, M. H. (1988). Mother-child interactions, attachment and emergent literacy: A cross-sectional study. *Child Development, 59,* 1262–1272.

Fenson, L., Dale, P.S., Reznick, J. S., Bates, E., Thal, D. J., Pethick, S. J., ... Stiles, J. (1994). Variability in early communicative development. *Monographs of the Society for Research in Child Development, 59,* 242.

Lewis, M., & Brooks-Gunn, J. (1979). *Social cognition and the acquisition of self.* New York: Plenum.

Newcombe, R., & Reese, E. (2004). Evaluations and orientations in mother-child reminiscing as a function of attachment security: A longitudinal investigation. *International Journal of Behavioral Development, 28,* 230–245.

Thompson, R. A., & Nelson, C. A. (2001). Developmental science and the media: Early brain development. *American Psychologist, 56,* 5–15.

Chapter 2 Notes

1. Leach, P. (2003). *Your baby and child* (p. 431). London: Dorling Kindersley Limited.
2. Hoff, E. (2006). How social contexts support and shape language development. *Developmental Review, 26*, 55–88.
3. Freeman, D. (1968). *Corduroy.* New York: Scholastic.
4. Note that when Jenkins and Astington tested the links between theory of mind and preschoolers' play over time, even after controlling for children's language skill, they found that theory of mind predicted children's later ability to plan and engage in pretend play with peers. Their earlier pretend play, however, did not predict their later theory of mind.

   Jenkins, J. M., & Astington, J. W. (2000). Theory of mind and social behavior: Causal models tested in a longitudinal study. *Merrill-Palmer Quarterly, 46*, 203–220.

   Wimmer, H., & Perner, J. (1983). Beliefs about beliefs: Representations and constraining functions of wrong beliefs in children's understanding of deception. *Cognition, 13*, 103–128.
5. Note that in Adrián et al. (2007) with 3- to 7-year-old children, there was no difference with respect to whether mothers talked about the characters' mental states or their children's mental states in predicting theory of mind. Critically, this study controlled for children's language and earlier theory of mind abilities. This finding contrasts with the earlier findings of Taumoepeau and Ruffman (2006, 2008) with mothers' talk with toddlers, in which it was mothers' references to the child's own desires specifically that were helpful for children's emotion understanding. It is possible that at older ages, talking about others' mental states is equally beneficial to talking about the child's mental states. See also Ruffman, Slade, and Crowe (2002) and Adrián, Clemente, Villaneuva, and Rieffe (2005).

   Adrián, J. E., Clemente, R. A., & Villanueva, L. (2007). Mothers' use of cognitive state verbs in picture-book reading and the development of children's understanding of mind: A longitudinal study. *Child Development, 78*, 1052–1067.

   Adrián, J. E., Clemente, R. A., Villanueva, L., & Rieffe, C. (2007). Parent-child picture book reading, mothers' mental state language and children's theory of mind. *Journal of Child Language, 32*, 673–686.

   Ruffman, T., Slade, L., & Crowe, E. (2002). The relation between children's and mothers' mental state language and theory of mind understanding. *Child Development, 73*, 734–751.

   Taumoepeau, M., & Ruffman, T. (2006). Mother and infant talk about mental states relates to desire language and emotion understanding. *Child Development, 77*, 465–481.

   Taumoepeau, M., & Ruffman, T. (2008). Stepping stones to others' minds: Maternal talk relates to child mental state language and emotion understanding at 15, 24 and 33 months. *Child Development, 79*, 284–302.
6. Taumoepeau, M., & Reese, E. (in press). Maternal reminiscing style, elaborative talk, and children's theory of mind: A training study.
7. Singer, D. G., & Singer, J. L. (1992). *The house of make-believe: Children's play and the developing imagination.* Cambridge, MA: Harvard University Press.
8. Trionfi, G., & Reese, E. (2009). A good story: Children with imaginary companions create richer narratives. *Child Development, 80*, 1301–1313.

Nicoloupoulou (2005) and Engel (2005) discuss the importance of children's play in their storytelling. Imaginary companion play (see Taylor, 1999) is especially evident in firstborn children, perhaps because they more often play alone.

Engel, S. (2005). The narrative worlds of what is and what if. *Cognitive Development, 20,* 514–525.

Nicoloupoulou, A. (2005). Play and narrative in the process of development: Commonalities, differences and interrelations. *Cognitive Development, 20,* 495–502.

Taylor, M. (1999). *Imaginary companions and the children who create them.* New York: Oxford University Press.

9. American Academy of Pediatrics: Council on Communications and Media. (2011). Policy statement: Children, adolescents, obesity, and the media. *Pediatrics, 128,* 201–208.

Anderson, D. R., Huston, A. C., Schmitt, K. L., Linebarger, D. L., & Wright, J. C. (2001). Early childhood television viewing and adolescent behavior: The recontact study. *Monographs of the Society for Research in Child Development, 66*(1), 1–147.

Note that Anderson et al. found that the long-term effects of TV watching in early childhood differed for boys and girls. For boys, their high school grades were higher if they watched more educational programming in early childhood, but for girls, their grades in high school were lower if they watched more entertaining programming. Educational programming in early childhood was not as beneficial for girls as for boys, and entertainment programming was not as harmful for boys as for girls. This study was not experimental, so we can not assume that these differences in early childhood viewing resulted in differences in academic achievement. For instance, the time that preschoolers spend watching educational TV is linked to other positive activities such as playing outside and engaging in pretend play (Skouteris & McHardy, 2009).

Skouteris, H., & McHardy, K. (2009). Television viewing habits and time use in Australian preschool children. *Journal of Children and Media, 3,* 80–89.

10. Crawley, A. M., Anderson, D. R., Wilder, A., Williams, M., & Santomero, A. (1999). Effects of repeated exposures to a single episode of the television program *Blue's Clues* on the viewing behaviors and comprehension of preschool children. *Journal of Educational Psychology, 91,* 630–637.

Linebarger, D. L., Kosanic, A., Greenwood, C. R., & Doku, N. S. (2004). Effects of viewing the television program *Between the Lions* on the emergent literacy skills of young children. *Journal of Educational Psychology, 96,* 297–308.

Linebarger, D. L., & Piotrowski, J. (2009). TV as storyteller: How exposure to television narratives impacts at-risk preschoolers' story knowledge and narrative skills. *British Journal of Developmental Psychology, 27,* 47–69.

Linebarger, D. L., & Walker, D. (2005). Infants' and toddlers' television viewing and language outcomes. *American Behavioral Scientist, 48,* 624–645.

Kendeou, P., Bohn-Gettler, C., White, M. J., & van den Broek, P. (2008). Children's inference generation across different media. *Journal of Research in Reading, 31,* 259–272.

Rice, M. L., Huston, A. C., Truglio, R., & Wright, J. C. (1990). Words from "Sesame Street": Learning vocabulary while viewing. *Developmental Psychology, 26,* 421–428.

Uchikoshi, Y. (2006). Early reading in bilingual kindergartners: Can educational television help? *Scientific Studies of Reading, 10,* 89–120.

See http://katiemcmenamindesign.com, an excellent website for parents of preschoolers that reviews the latest products and research on the vast array of media available for young children.

11. Alexander, K. J., Miller, P. J., & Hengst, J. A. (2001). Young children's emotional attachments to stories. *Social Development, 10,* 374–398.

12. Crawley et al. (1999) demonstrated repeated viewing of *Blues' Clues* episodes helps strengthen children's comprehension; see note 10.

13. But note that Simcock, Garrity, and Barr (2011) demonstrated that 18- and 24-month-olds imitate a series of actions slightly better from a TV demonstration than from a storybook demonstration, probably due to the additional cues via TV, but their memory for actions learned from a live model is still superior to either books or TV (see Brito, Barr, McIntyre, & Simcock, 2011). Also, Strouse, O'Doherty, and Troseth (2011) demonstrated that when adults paused a televised storybook reading to ask questions, preschoolers benefited in similar ways to Dialogic Reading in terms of their vocabulary and story comprehension.

Brito, N., Barr, R., McIntyre, P., & Simcock, G. (2012). Long-term transfer of learning from books and video during toddlerhood. *Journal of Experimental Child Psychology, 111,* 108–119.

Simcock, G., Garrity, K., & Barr, R. (2011). The effect of narrative cues on infants' imitation from television and picture books. *Child Development, 82,* 1607–1619.

Strouse, G., O'Doherty, K., & Troseth, G. (2011). *Dialogic video: Influence of techniques on preschoolers' learning from video stories.* Paper presented at Institute for Educational Studies conference.

14. Barr, R., Zack, E., Garcia, A., & Muentener, P. (2008). Infants' attention and responsiveness to television increases with prior exposure and parental interaction. *Infancy, 13,* 30–56.

Low, J., & Durkin, K. (2001). Individual differences and consistency in maternal talk style during joint story encoding and retrospection: Associations with children's long-term recall. *International Journal of Behavioral Development, 25,* 27–36.

15. Reese, E., Haden, C. A., Baker-Ward, L., Bauer, P., Fivush, R., & Ornstein, P. A. (2011). Coherence of personal narratives across the lifespan: A multidimensional model and coding method. *Journal of Cognition and Development, 12,* 424–462.

16. Reese, E., & Brown, N. (2000). Reminiscing and recounting in the preschool years. *Applied Cognitive Psychology, 14,* 1–17.

17. Reese, E., & Cox, A. (1999). Quality of adult book-reading style affects children's emergent literacy. *Developmental Psychology, 35,* 20–28.

18. Stanovich, K. E. (1986). Matthew effects in reading: Some consequences of individual differences in the acquisition of literacy. *Reading Research Quarterly, 21,* 360–407.

19. Taumoepeau & Ruffman (2008), see note 5.

Slaughter, V., Peterson, C. C., & Mackintosh, E. (2007). Mind what mother says: Narrative input and theory of mind in typical children and those on the autism spectrum. *Child Development, 78,* 839–858.

20. Whitehurst, G. J., Epstein, J. N., Angell, A. L., Payne, A. C., Crone, D. A., & Fischel, J. E. (1994). Outcomes of an emergent literacy intervention in Head Start. *Journal of Educational Psychology, 86,* 542–555.

Zevenbergen, A. A., & Whitehurst, G. J. (2003). Dialogic reading: A shared picture book reading intervention for preschoolers. In A. Van Kleeck, S. A. Stahl, & E. B. Bauer (Eds.), *On reading books to children: Parents and teachers.* Mahwah, NJ: Erlbaum.

21. Heath, S. B. (1982). What no bedtime story means: Narrative skills at home and school. *Language in Society, 11,* 49–76.

22. Bettelheim, B. (1976). *The uses of enchantment.* New York: Knopf.

23. DeLoache, J. S., Simcock, G. & Macari, S. (2007). Planes, trains, automobiles and tea sets: Extremely intense interests in very young children. *Developmental Psychology, 43,* 1579–1586.

Johnson, K. E., Alexander, J. M., Spencer, S., Leibham, M. E., & Neitzel, C. (2004). Factors associated with the early emergence of intense interests within conceptual domains. *Cognitive Development, 19,* 325–343.

24. Robertson, S. J. (2009). *The role of genre, gender and enjoyment in children's language and literacy development.* Unpublished MA thesis. Dunedin, New Zealand: University of Otago.

25. Peterson, C., & McCabe, A. (1994). A social interactionist account of developing decontextualized narrative skill. *Developmental Psychology, 30,* 937–948.

26. Reese, E., & Cleveland, E. (2006). Mother-child reminiscing and children's understanding of mind. *Merrill-Palmer Quarterly, 52,* 17–43.

Reese, E. (1995). Predicting children's literacy from mother-child conversations. *Cognitive Development, 10,* 381–405.

Bohn-Gettler, C. M., Rapp, D. N., van den Broek, P., Kendeou, P., & White, M. J. (2011). Adults' and children's monitoring of story events in the service of comprehension. *Memory and Cognition, 39,* 992–1011.

27. Note that in this study, there was no link with children's emotion understanding when parents simply labeled emotions for their preschoolers or discussed the consequences of emotions.

Van Bergen, P., Salmon, K., Dadds, M. R., & Allen, J. (2009). The effects of mother training in emotion-rich, elaborative reminiscing on children's shared recall and emotion knowledge. *Journal of Cognition and Development, 10,* 162–187.

Van Bergen, P., & Salmon, K. (2010). The association between parent-child reminiscing and children's emotion knowledge. *New Zealand Journal of Psychology, 39,* 51–56.

28. Newcombe, R., & Reese, E. (2004). Evaluations and orientations in mother-child reminiscing as a function of attachment security: A longitudinal investigation. *International Journal of Behavioral Development, 28,* 230–245.

Reese, E., & Newcombe, R. (2007). Training mothers in elaborative reminiscing enhances children's autobiographical memory and narrative. *Child Development, 78,* 1153–1170.

29. Fivush, R. (2001). Owning experience: The development of subjective perspective in autobiographical memory. In C. Moore & K. Lemmon (Eds.), *The self in time: Developmental perspectives* (pp. 35–52). Hillsdale, NJ: Erlbaum.

30. Fiese, B. H., & Bickham, N. L. (2004). Pin-curling grandpa's hair in the comfy chair: Parents' stories of growing up and potential links to socialization in the

preschool years. In M. W. Pratt & B. H. Fiese (Eds.), *Family stories and the life course* (pp. 259–277). Mahwah, NJ: Erlbaum.

Reese, E. (1996). Conceptions of self in mother-child birth stories. *Journal of Narrative and Life History, 6,* 23–38.

31. Anglin, J. M. (1993). Vocabulary development: A morphological analysis. *Monographs of the Society for Research in Child Development, 58* (10, Serial No. 238).

Carlson, S. (2005). Developmentally sensitive measures of executive function in preschool children. *Developmental Neuropsychology, 28,* 595–616.

Eder, R. (1990). Uncovering young children's psychological selves: Individual and developmental differences. *Child Development, 61,* 849–863.

Fivush, A., Haden, C. & Adam, S. (1995). Structure and coherence of preschoolers' personal narratives over time: Implications for childhood amnesia. *Journal of Experimental Child Psychology, 60,* 32–56.

Friedman, W. J. (2003). The development of a differentiated sense of the past and the future. In R. Kail (Ed.), *Advances in child development and behaviour* (Vol. 31, pp. 229–269). San Diego: Academic Press.

Hartup, W. W., & Stevens, N. (1999). Friendships and adaptation across the life span. *Current Directions in Psychological Science, 8,* 76–69.

Povinelli, D. J., & Simon, B. B. (1998). Young children's understanding of briefly versus extremely delayed images of the self: Emergence of the autobiographical stance. *Developmental Psychology, 34,* 188–194.

Reese, E., Haden, C. A., Baker-Ward, L., Bauer, P., Fivush, R., & Ornstein, P. A. (2011). Coherence of personal narratives across the lifespan: A multidimensional model and coding method. *Journal of Cognition and Development, 12,* 424–462.

Thompson, R. A., & Nelson, C. A. (2001). Developmental science and the media: Early brain development. *American Psychologist, 56,* 5–15.

Wimmer, H., & Perner, J. (1983). Beliefs about beliefs: Representation and constraining function of wrong beliefs in young children's understanding of deception. *Cognition, 13,* 103–128.

Chapter 3 Notes

1. Rodda, E. (2003). *Forests of silence.* Scholastic Sagebrush.
2. Linguist William Labov wrote a seminal paper with colleague Jacob Waletzky on classic narrative high-point structure in stories of personal experiences. Other approaches to narrative include psychologist Nancy Stein and colleagues' "story schema" theory that the best narratives are goal-oriented, in which a character is presented with a problem that must be solved. Once children master these classic story templates, they show better comprehension and memory for the stories they hear and read.

Labov, W., & Waletzky, J. (1967/1997). Narrative analysis: Oral versions of personal experience. In J. Helm (Ed.), *Essays on the verbal and visual arts* (pp. 12–44). Seattle: University of Washington Press. (Reprinted in *Journal of Narrative and Life History, 7,* 3–38).

Stein, N., & Glenn, C. (1979). An analysis of story comprehension in elementary school children. In R. Freedle (Ed.), *New directions in discourse processing* (pp. 53–120). Norwood, NJ: Ablex.

3. Sendak, M. (1963). *Where the wild things are.* New York: Harper & Row.

4. Adams, M. J. (1990). *Beginning to read: Thinking and learning about print.* Cambridge, MA: MIT Press.

5. Dostoevsky, F. (1866/1956). *Crime and punishment.* New York: Random House.

6. Jennings, P. (2004). *The Rascal series.* Auckland, Penguin NZ.

7. Dickinson, O. K., & Tabors, P. O. (2001). *Beginning literacy with language: Young children learning at home and school.* Baltimore: Brookes.
   Spira, E. G., Storch Bracken, S., & Fischel, J. E. (2005). Predicting improvement after first grade reading difficulties: The effects of oral language, emergent literacy and behavior skills. *Developmental Psychology, 41,* 225–234.

8. This gender difference is more pronounced for the narratives that boys and girls tell about personal experiences than in their fictional stories, or in their retellings of stories from books. For instance, colleague Emily Cleveland and I found that New Zealand 5-1/2-year-old girls told longer stories of their early experiences than did boys, and Robyn Fivush, Catherine Haden, and colleagues found that differences in the quality of US girls' and boys' personal narratives emerged as early as age 3-1/2. When researchers ask children to make up a story about a wordless picture book, however, they typically do not find differences between boys' and girls' stories.
   Cleveland, E. S., & Reese, E. (2008). Children remember early childhood: Long-term recall across the offset of childhood amnesia. *Applied Cognitive Psychology, 22,* 127–142.
   Fivush, A., Haden, C. & Adam, S. (1995). Structure and coherence of preschoolers' personal narratives over time: Implications for childhood amnesia. *Journal of Experimental Child Psychology, 60,* 32–56.
   Hoff-Ginsberg, E. (1997). Frog stories from four-year-olds: Individual differences in the expression of referential and evaluative content. *Journal of Narrative and Life History, 7,* 223–227.

9. Eder, R. (1990). Uncovering young children's psychological selves: Individual and developmental differences. *Child Development, 61,* 849–863.

10. Harter, S. (1999). *The construction of the self: A developmental perspective.* New York: Guilford Press.

11. Bird, A., & Reese, E. (2006). Emotional reminiscing and the development of an autobiographical self. *Developmental Psychology, 42,* 613–626.

12. Reese, E., Bird, A., & Tripp, G. (2007). Children's self esteem and moral self: Links to parent-child conversations about emotion. *Social Development, 16,* 460–478.

13. Rothbart, M. K., & Derryberry, D. (2002). Temperament in children. In C. von Hofsten & L. Baeckman (Eds.), *Psychology at the turn of the millennium: Social, developmental and clinical perspectives* (Vol. 2, pp. 17–35). Florence, KY: Taylor & Francis/Routledge.

14. Allan, N. P., & Lonigan, C. J. (2011). Examining the dimensionality of effortful control in preschool children and its relation to academic and socioemotional indicators. *Developmental Psychology, 47,* 905–915.
    Spira, Storch Bracken, & Fischel (2005), see note 7.

15. Bird, A., Reese, E., & Tripp, G. (2006). Parent-child talk about past emotional events: Associations with child temperament and goodness-of-fit. *Journal of Cognition and Development, 7,* 189–210.

16. Hudson, J. A. & Shapiro, L. R. (1991). From knowing to telling: The development of children's scripts, stories, and personal narratives. In A. McCabe &

C. Peterson (Eds.), *Developing narrative structure* (pp. 89–136). Hillsdale, NJ: Erlbaum.

Reese, E., Suggate, S., Long, J., & Schaughency, E. (2010). Children's oral narrative and reading skills in the first three years of instruction. *Reading and Writing, 23,* 627–644.

17. de Hamel, J. (1996). *Hemi and the shortie pyjamas.* Auckland: Puffin Books.

18. Sameroff, A. J., & Haith, M. M. (Eds.). (1996). *The five to seven year shift: The age of reason and responsibility.* Chicago: University of Chicago Press.

19. Fivush, A., Haden, C. & Adam, S. (1995). Structure and coherence of preschoolers' personal narratives over time: Implications for childhood amnesia. *Journal of Experimental Child Psychology, 60,* 32–56.

20. For an excellent overview of this topic, see Siegler, R. S., & Alibali, M. W. (2004). *Children's thinking* (4th edition). Upper Saddle River, NJ: Prentice-Hall.

21. Peterson, C., & McCabe, A. (1983). *Developmental psycholinguistics: Three ways of looking at a child's narrative.* New York: Plenum.

22. Beck, S. R., & Riggs, K. J. (in press). Counterfactuals and reality. To appear in M. Taylor (Ed.), *Oxford handbook of imagination.* NY: Oxford University Press.

23. Paolini, C. (2002). *Eragon.* NY: Random House.

24. Psychologist Monique Sénéchal conducted an excellent review of the research on how parents can help their children learn to read. She concluded that simply listening to your child read helps their eventual reading success, but it's even better if you help your child more directly by offering them specific advice on how to decode a word, to figure out from the context what it means, and to praise your child's early reading efforts.

    Sénéchal, M. (2006). *The effect of family literacy interventions on children's acquisition of reading: From kindergarten to Grade 3.* Portsmouth, NH: National Center for Family Literacy, RMC Research Corporation.

25. Rubin, D. C. (2000). The distribution of early childhood memories. *Memory, 8,* 265–269. See also Cleveland and Reese (2008) from note 8.

26. Anglin, J. M. (1993). Vocabulary development: A morphological analysis. *Monographs of the Society for Research in Child Development, 58* (10, Serial No. 238).

    Bird, A., & Reese, E. (2006). Emotional reminiscing and the development of an autobiographical self. *Developmental Psychology, 42,* 613–626.

    Bird, A., Reese, E., & Tripp, G. (2006). Parent-child talk about past emotional events: Associations with child temperament and goodness-of-fit. *Journal of Cognition and Development, 7,* 189–210.

    Eder, R. (1990). Uncovering young children's psychological selves: Individual and developmental differences. *Child Development, 61,* 849–863.

    Harter, S. (1998). The development of self-representations. In N. Eisenberg & W. Damon (Eds.), *Handbook of child psychology* (5th ed., Vol. 3, pp. 553–617). New York: Wiley.

    Hartup, W. W., & Stevens, N. (1999). Friendships and adaptation across the life span. *Current Directions in Psychological Science, 8,* 76–69.

    Koh, J. B. K., & Wang, Q. (2012). Development of self. *Cognitive Science, 3,* 513–524.

    Marcus, G. F. (1995). Children's over-regularization of English plurals: A quantitative analysis. *Journal of Child Language, 22,* 447–459.

Peterson, C., & McCabe, A. (1983). *Developmental psycholinguistics: Three ways of looking at a child's narrative.* New York: Plenum.

Reese, E., Haden, C. A., Baker-Ward, L., Bauer, P., Fivush, R., & Ornstein, P. A. (2011). Coherence of personal narratives across the lifespan: A multidimensional model and coding method. *Journal of Cognition and Development, 12,* 424–462.

Sameroff, A. J., & Haith, M. M. (Eds.). (1996). *The five to seven year shift: The age of reason and responsibility.* Chicago: University of Chicago Press.

Spira, E. G., Storch Bracken, S., & Fischel, J. E. (2005). Predicting improvement after first grade reading difficulties: The effects of oral language, emergent literacy and behavior skills. *Developmental Psychology, 41,* 225–234.

Suggate, S. P., Schaughency, E. A., & Reese, E. (2011). The contribution of age and formal schooling to oral narrative and pre-reading skills. *First Language, 31,* 379–403.

Thompson, R. A., & Nelson, C. A. (2001). Developmental science and the media: Early brain development. *American Psychologist, 56,* 5–15.

Chapter 4 Notes

1. Bucher, K., & Manning, M. L. (2006). *Young adult literature exploration, evaluation, and appreciation.* Upper Saddle River, NJ: Pearson Education.

2. McKenna, M. C., Kear, D. J., & Ellsworth, R. A. (1995). Children's attitude toward reading: A national survey. *Reading Research Quarterly, 30,* 934–956.

3. Emery, R. (2004). *The truth about children and divorce: Dealing with the emotions so you and your children can thrive* (pp. 98–99). New York: Viking Penguin.

4. Lecce, S., Zochi, S., Pagnin, A., Palladino, P., & Taumoepeau, M. (2010). Reading minds: The relation between children's mental state knowledge and their meta-knowledge about reading. *Child Development, 81,* 1876–1893.

5. Chall, J. S. (1983). *Stages of reading development.* New York: Harcourt Brace.
   The latest term for these children, who constitute 13.4% of the population of school-aged children in America, is "late emerging poor readers."
   Struthers, P., Schaughency, E., & Reese, E. (2011). *Better serving all children: Partnering parents and teachers to tailor strategies to support individual learner needs in reading acquisition.* Paper presented at the 4th Educational Psychology Forum, Massey University, Albany, NZ.
   Chall, J., & Jacobs, V. (2003). Poor children's fourth-grade slump. *American Educator,* Spring. Available at: http://www.aft.org/pubs-reports/american_ Educator/spring2003/chall.html.
   Catts, H. W., Compton, D., Tomblin, J. B., & Bridges, M. S. (2011). Prevalence and nature of late-emerging poor readers. *Journal of Educational Psychology.* Advance online publication. doi: 10.1037/a0025323.
   Suggate, S. P., Lenhard, W., Neudecker, E., & Schneider, W. (2012). *Vocabulary acquisition from independent reading, shared reading, and story telling.* Manuscript under review.

6. Alonzo, J., Basaraba, D., Tindal, G., & Carriveau, R. S. (2009). They read, but how well do they understand? *Assessment for Effective Intervention, 35,* 34–44.

7. Hofferth, S. L. (2009). Media use vs. work and play in middle childhood. *Social Indicators Research, 93,* 127–129.

Hofferth, S. L. (2010). Home media and children's achievement and behavior. *Child Development, 81,* 1598–1619.

Rideout, V. J., Foehr, U. G., & Roberts, D. F. (2010). *Generation M2: Media in the lives of 8- to 18-year-olds.* Menlo Park, CA: Henry J. Kaiser Family Foundation.

8. Swing, E., Gentile, D. A., Anderson, C. A., & Walsh, D. A. (2010). Television and video game exposure and the development of attention problems. *Pediatrics, 126,* 214–221.

9. Holtz, P., & Appel, M. (2011). Internet use and video gaming predict problem behavior in early adolescence. *Journal of Adolescence, 34,* 49–58; see also Hofferth (2010), see note 7.

10. Berman, R. A. (2008). The psycholinguistics of developing text construction. *Journal of Child Language, 35,* 735–771.

11. Reese, E. (in press). Culture, narrative, and imagination. In M. Taylor's (Ed.), *Oxford handbook of imagination.* New York: Oxford University Press.

12. Hayne, H., & MacDonald, S. (2003). The socialization of autobiographical memory in children and adults: The roles of culture and gender. In R. Fivush & C. A. Haden (Eds.), *Autobiographical memory and the construction of a narrative self: Developmental and cultural perspectives* (pp. 99–120). Mahwah, NJ: Erlbaum.

13. Bohn, A., & Berntsen, D. (2008). Life story development in childhood: The development of life story abilities and the acquisition of cultural life scripts from late middle childhood to adolescence. *Developmental Psychology, 44,* 1135–1147.

14. Michaels, S. (2001). Sharing time: Children's narrative styles and differential access to literacy. *Language in Society, 10,* 423–442.

15. Habermas, T., & de Silveira, C. (2008). The development of global coherence in life narratives across adolescence: Temporal, causal and thematic aspects. *Developmental Psychology, 44,* 707–721.

16. Friedman, W. J., Reese, E., & Dai, X. (2010). Children's memory for the times of events from the past years. *Applied Cognitive Psychology, 25,* 156–165.

17. Yan, C., White, N., Ball, V., & Reese, E. (2009). *Life stories and well-being in middle-childhood and adolescence.* Poster presented at Society for Research in Child Development, Denver, CO.

18. Trelease, J. (2006). *The read-aloud handbook* (6th ed.). New York: Penguin.

Trelease, J., & Reading Tree Productions. (2011). *Trelease on reading.* Retrieved from http://www.trelease-on-reading.com/.

19. Frattaroli, J. (2006). Experimental disclosure and its moderators: A meta-analysis. *Psychological Bulletin, 132,* 823–865.

Pennebaker, J. W., & Seagal, J. D. (1999). Forming a story: The health benefits of narrative. *Journal of Clinical Psychology, 55,* 1243–1254.

For tips to use with older adolescents, see Pennebaker, J. (2004). *Writing to heal: A guided journal for recovering from trauma and emotional upheaval.* Oakland, CA: New Harbinger.

20. Reynolds, M., Brewin, C. R., & Saxton, M. (2000). Emotional disclosure in school children. *Journal of Child Psychology and Psychiatry, 41,* 151–159.

Fivush, R., Marin, K., Crawford, M., Reynolds, M., & Brewin, C. R. (2007). Children's narratives and well-being. *Cognition and Emotion, 21,* 1414–1434.

21. Fivush, R., Marin, K., McWilliams, K., & Bohanek, J. G. (2009). Family reminiscing style: Parent gender and emotional focus in relation to child well-being. *Journal of Cognition and Development, 10,* 210–235.

Fivush, R., Bohanek, J. G., & Marin, K. (2010). Patterns of family narrative co-construction in relation to adolescent identity and well-being. In K. C. McLean & M. Pasupathi (Eds.), *Narrative development in adolescence: Advancing responsible adolescent development* (pp. 45–63). New York: Springer.

Marin, K., Bohanek, J. G., & Fivush, R. (2008). Positive effects of talking about the negative: Family narratives of negative experiences and preadolescents' perceived competence. *Journal of Research in Adolescence, 18,* 573–593.

Sales, J. M., & Fivush, R. (2005). Social and emotional functions of mother-child reminiscing about stressful events. *Social Cognition, 23,* 70–90.

22. Rosenthal, C. J. (1985). Kinkeeping in the familial division of labor. *Journal of Marriage and Family, 47,* 965–974.

23. Yan et al. (2009), see note 17.

24. Reese, E., Bird, A., & Tripp, G. (2007). Children's self-esteem and moral self: Links to parent-child conversations regarding emotion. *Social Development, 16,* 460–478.

25. Pratt, M. W., & Fiese, B. H. (Eds.). (2004). *Family stories and the life course.* Mahwah, NJ: Erlbaum.

26. Bohanek, J. G., Fivush, R., Zaman, W., & Lepore, C. (2009). Narrative interaction in family dinnertime conversations. *Merrill-Palmer Quarterly, 55,* 488–515.

27. Peterson, C., & McCabe, A. (1983). *Developmental psycholinguistics: Three ways of looking at a child's narrative.* New York: Plenum.

28. For more on blended family trees, see Melinda Blau's excellent book on coparenting in separated families: Blau, M. (1993). *Families apart: Ten keys to successful co-parenting.* New York: Perigee.

29. Anglin, J. M. (1993). Vocabulary development: A morphological analysis. *Monographs of the Society for Research in Child Development, 58*(10, Serial No. 238).

Broderick, P. C., & Korteland, C. (2002). Coping style and depression in early adolescence: Relationships to gender, gender role, and implicit beliefs. *Sex Roles, 46,* 201–213.

Chrysochoou, E., Bablekou, Z., Tsigilis, N. (2011). Working memory contributions to reading comprehension components in middle childhood children. *The American Journal of Psychology, 124,* 275–289.

Compas, B. E., Connor-Smith, J. K., Saltzman, H., Thomsen, A. H., & Wadsworth, M. E. (2001). Coping with stress during childhood and adolescence: problems, progress, and potential in theory and research. *Psychology Bulletin, 127,* 87–127.

Damon, W., & Hart, D. (1988). *Self-understanding in childhood and adolescence.* Cambridge, UK: Cambridge University Press.

Friedman, W. J., Reese, E., & Dai, X. (2010). Children's memory for the times of events from the past years. *Applied Cognitive Psychology, 25,* 156–165.

Hartup, W. W., & Stevens, N. (1999). Friendships and adaptation across the life span. *Current Directions in Psychological Science, 8,* 76–69.

Kail, R. (1991). Processing time declines exponentially during childhood and adolescence. *Developmental Psychology, 27,* 259–266.

Koh, J. B. K., & Wang, Q. (2012). Development of self. *Cognitive Science, 3,* 513–524.

Nolen-Hoeksema, S. (2001). Gender differences in depression. *Current Directions in Psychological Science, 10,* 173–176.

Porter, J. N., Collins, P. F., Muetzel, R. L., Lim, K. O., & Luciana, M. (2011). Associations between cortical thickness and verbal fluency in childhood, adolescence, and adulthood. *Neuroimage, 55,* 1865–1877.

Speece, D. L., Ritchey, K. D., Silverman, R., Schatschneider, C., Walker, C. Y., & Andrusik, K. N. (2010). Identifying children in middle childhood who are at risk for reading problems. *School Psychology Review, 39,* 258–276.

Twenge, J. M., & Campbell, W. K. (2001). Age and birth cohort differences in self-esteem: A cross-temporal meta-analysis. *Personality and Social Psychology Review, 5,* 321–344.

This dip in self-esteem was only apparent when interpersonal aspects of self-esteem are measured. This point is interesting because self-esteem problems predict later depression, and girls appear to react more often to interpersonal problems by becoming depressed compared to boys (Nolen-Hoeksema, 2001). For instance, girls are more likely to become depressed over the breakup of a relationship or a conflict with friends than are boys.

Chapter 5 Notes

1. These days, because of the lower age of puberty and the extended period of dependence on parents, children as young as 10 are classified as adolescents, and those aged 18–25 are termed "emerging adults." For the purposes of family story sharing, I will use an age range for adolescence from 12 to 18 because the most significant changes in life story development happen in those years, and because teenagers in many Western countries leave home by age 18. Sometimes in this chapter I will use "teenager" interchangeably with "adolescent" because many 12-year-olds in contemporary society have already entered puberty.

   Arnett, J. J. (2000). Emerging adulthood: A theory of development from the late teens through the twenties. *American Psychologist, 55,* 469–480.

2. Larson, R. W., Richards, M. H., Moneta, G., Holmbeck, G., & Duckett, E. (1996). Changes in adolescents' daily interactions with their families from ages 10 to 18: Disengagement and transformation. *Developmental Psychology, 32,* 744–754.

3. Allen, J. P., Hauser, S. T., Bell, K. L., & O'Connor, T. G. (1994). Longitudinal assessment of autonomy and relatedness in adolescent–family interactions as predictors of adolescent ego development and self-esteem. *Child Development, 65,* 179–194.

   Allen, J. P., Hauser, S. T., O'Connor, T. G., Bell, K. L. (2002). Prediction of peer-rated adult hostility from autonomy struggles in adolescent-family interactions. *Development and Psychopathology, 14,* 123–137.

4. Some adolescents, however, particularly those learning English as a second language, still struggle with reading for a variety of reasons: small vocabularies, poor working memory, and slow word-recognition skills.

   Lesaux, N. K, & Kieffer, M. J. (2010). Exploring sources of reading comprehension difficulties among language minority learners and their classmates in early adolescence. *American Educational Research Journal, 47,* 596–632.

5. Nippold, M. A., Duthie, J. K., & Larsen, J. (2005). Literacy as a leisure activity: Free-time preferences of older children and young adolescents. *Language, Speech, and Hearing Services in Schools, 36,* 93–102.

   Rideout, V. J., Foehr, U. G., & Roberts, D. F. (2010). *Generation M2: Media in the lives of 8- to 18-year-olds.* Menlo Park, CA: Henry J. Kaiser Family Foundation.

6. McHale, S. M., Crouter, A. C., & Tucker, C. J. (2001). Free-time activities in middle childhood: Links with adjustment in early adolescence. *Child Development, 72*, 1764–1778.
   This study was correlational, but even when time spent alone was taken into account, time spent reading still predicted higher levels of depression in early adolescence.
7. Anderson, C. A., & Bushman, B. J. (2001). Effects of violent video games on aggressive behavior, aggressive cognition, aggressive affect, physiological arousal, and prosocial behavior: A meta-analytic review. *Psychological Science, 12*, 353–359.
8. Rideout et al. (2010), see note 5.
9. O'Keeffe, G. S., Clarke-Pearson, K., & Council on Communications and Media. (2011). The impact of social media on children, adolescents, and families. *Pediatrics, 127*, 800–804.
10. McLean and Pratt (2006) call this process "meaning-making," whereas Habermas and de Silveira (2008) term it "causal coherence." In our research (Chen, McAnally, Wang, & Reese, 2012), we find that the two types of insight are strongly linked to each other. Pasupathi and Wainryb (2010) talk about a parallel development from age 12 to 16 in which adolescents interpret the events of their lives with increasing insight and precision.
    Chen, Y., McAnally, H., Wang, Q., & Reese, E. (2012). The coherence of critical event narratives and adolescents' psychological functioning. *Memory, 20*, 667–681.
    Habermas, T., & de Silveira, C. (2008). The development of global coherence in life narratives across adolescence: Temporal, causal and thematic aspects. *Developmental Psychology, 44*, 707–721.
    McLean, K. C., & Pratt, M. W. (2006). Life's little (and big) lessons: Identity statuses and meaning-making in the turning point narratives of emerging adults. *Developmental Psychology, 42*, 714–722.
    Pasupathi, M., & Wainryb, C. (2010). Telling the whole story: Facts and interpretations in autobiographical memory narratives from childhood through adolescence. *Developmental Psychology, 46*, 735–746.
11. Bohn, A., & Berntsen, D. (2008). Life story development in childhood: The development of life story abilities and the acquisition of cultural life scripts from late middle childhood to adolescence. *Developmental Psychology, 44*, 1135–1147.
    Reese, E., Chen, Y., McAnally, H., & Wang, Q. (2010). *Life stories of New Zealand European and Chinese adolescents.* Paper presented in T. Habermas (Chair), Adolescent Narrative Identity in Dialogue and Monologue, Goethe University, Frankfurt A.M., Germany.
12. McLean, K. C., & Breen, A. V. (2009). Processes and content of narrative identity development in adolescence: Gender and wellbeing. *Developmental Psychology, 45*, 702–710.
    McLean, K. C., & Mansfield, C. D. (2012). The co-construction of adolescent narrative identity: Narrative processing as a function of adolescent age, gender, and maternal scaffolding. *Developmental Psychology, 48*, 436–447.
13. Burt, C. D. B. (1994). An analysis of a self-initiated coping behavior: Diary-keeping. *Child Study Journal, 24*, 171–190.
    Habermas, T., & Bluck. S. (2000). Getting a life: The emergence of the life story in adolescence. *Psychological Bulletin, 126*, 748–769.

14. Soliday, E., Garofalo, J. P., & Rogers, D. (2004). Expressive writing intervention for adolescents' somatic symptoms and mood. *Journal of Clinical Child and Adolescent Psychology, 33,* 792–801.
15. Boniel-Nissim, M., & Barak, A. (2011). The therapeutic value of adolescents' blogging about social-emotional difficulties. *Psychological Services.* Advance online publication. doi: 10.1037/a0026664.
16. McLean & Breen (2009), see note 12.
    McLean, K. C., Breen, A. V., & Fournier, M. A. (2010). Constructing the self in early, middle, and late adolescent boys: Narrative identity, individuation, and well-being. *Journal of Research on Adolescence, 20,* 166–187.
17. Mansfield, C. D., McLean, K. C., & Lilgendahl, J. P. (2010). Narrating traumas and transgressions: Links between narrative processing, wisdom, and well-being. *Narrative Inquiry, 20,* 246–273.
    Reese, E., Haden, C. A., Baker-Ward, L., Bauer, P., Fivush, R., & Ornstein, P. A. (2011). Coherence of personal narratives across the lifespan: A multidimensional model and coding method. *Journal of Cognition and Development, 12,* 424–462.
18. Chen, McAnally, Wang, & Reese (2012), see note 10; Habermas & De Silveira (2008), see note 10; McLean & Breen (2009), see note 12.
19. Nippold et al. (2005), see note 5.
    Chiu, M. M., & McBride-Chang, C. (2006). Gender, context, and reading: A comparison of students in 43 countries. *Scientific Studies of Reading, 10,* 331–362.
20. McLean & Breen (2009), see note 12; Reese, E., & McAnally, H. (2012). *Predicting adolescent well-being from family storytelling practices.* Manuscript in preparation.
21. Research on the best ways to converse with teenagers about their experiences is surprisingly still in its infancy. We don't have any hard experimental evidence at this point, so the advice I offer here is based on high-quality correlational studies with adolescents:
    Habermas, T., Negele, A., & Mayer, F. B. (2010). Honey, you're jumping about: Mothers' scaffolding of their children's and adolescents' life narration. *Cognitive Development, 25,* 339–351.
    McLean, K. C., & Mansfield, C. D. (2011). The co-construction of adolescent narrative identity: Narrative processing as a function of adolescent age, gender, and maternal scaffolding. *Developmental Psychology, 48,* 436–447.
    Weeks, T. L., & Pasupathi, M. (2010). Autonomy, identity, and narrative construction with parents and friends. In K. C. McLean & M. Pasupathi (Eds.), *Narrative development in adolescence: Creating the storied self* (pp. 65–92). R. J. R. Levesque (Series Editor), *Advancing responsible adolescent development.* New York: Springer Science.
    Zaman, W., & Fivush, R. (2011). When I was a little girl…: Gender differences in adolescents' intergenerational and personal stories. *Journal of Research on Adolescence, 21,* 703–716.
    Only two studies so far of parent-adolescent storytelling and well-being are longitudinal:
    Fivush, R., Bohanek, J. G., & Marin, K. (2010). Patterns of family narrative coconstruction in relation to adolescent identity and well-being. In K. C. McLean & M. Pasupathi (Eds.), *Narrative development in adolescence: Creating the storied self*

(pp. 45–63). R. J. R. Levesque (Series Editor), *Advancing responsible adolescent development*. New York: Springer Science.

Reese & McAnally (2012), see note 20.

22. McLean & Mansfield (2011), see note 21. Unfortunately no research exists yet on family story sharing between fathers and older teenagers.

23. Pratt, M. W., Norris, J. E., van de Hoef, S., Arnold, M. L. (2001). Stories of hope: Parental optimism in narratives about adolescent children. *Journal of Social and Personal Relationships, 18,* 603–623.

24. Norris, J. E., Kuiack, S., & Pratt, M. W. (2004). As long as they go back down the driveway at the end of the day: Stories of the satisfactions and challenges of grandparenthood. In M. W. Pratt & B. H. Fiese (Eds.), *Family stories and the life course: Across time and generations.* (pp. 353–374). Mahwah, NJ: Erlbaum.

Reese, E., & Fivush, R. (2008). Collective memory across the lifespan. *Memory, 16,* 201–212.

Pratt, M. W., Norris, J. E., Lawford, H., & Arnold, M. L. (2010). What he said to me stuck: Adolescents' narratives of grandparents and their identity development in emerging adulthood. In K. C. McLean & M. Pasupathi (Eds.), *Narrative development in adolescence: Creating the storied self* (pp. 93–112). R. J. R. Levesque (Series Editor), *Advancing responsible adolescent development*. NY: Springer Science.

Zaman & Fivush (2011), see note 21.

25. The order in which the teenagers told their mothers' and fathers' stories in our study was counterbalanced, such that half of the girls told their mothers' stories first and then dads' stories, and half of the boys told their dads' stories first and then their mothers' stories, just in case the order of the story affected the level of detail.

See also Zaman & Fivush (2011), see note 21.

26. Thorne, A., McLean, K. C., & Dasbach, A. (2004). When parents' stories go to pot: Telling personal transgressions to teenage kids. In M. W. Pratt & B. E. Fiese (Eds.), *Family stories and the lifecourse: Across time and generations,* (pp. 187–209). Mahwah, NJ: Erlbaum.

27. Mackey, K., Arnold, M. L., & Pratt, M. W. (2001). Adolescents' stories of decision making in more and less authoritative families: Representing the voices of parents in narrative. *Journal of Adolescent Research, 16,* 243–268.

28. Dumas, T. M., Lawford, H., Tieu, T-T., & Pratt, M. W. (2009). Positive parenting in adolescence and its relation to low point narration and identity status in emerging adulthood: A longitudinal analysis. *Developmental Psychology, 45,* 1531–1544.

29. Rideout, V. J., Foehr, U. G., & Roberts, D. F. (2010). *Generation M2: Media in the lives of 8- to 18-year-olds.* Menlo Park, CA: Henry J. Kaiser Family Foundation.

30. Broderick, P. C., & Korteland, C. (2002). Coping style and depression in early adolescence: Relationships to gender, gender role, and implicit beliefs. *Sex Roles, 46,* 201–213.

Fabricius, W. V., Schwanenflugel, P. J., Kyllonen, P. C., Barclay, C. R., & Denton, S. M. (1989). Developing theories of the mind: Children's and adults' concepts of mental activities. *Child Development, 60,* 1278–1290.

Grotevant, H. D., & Cooper, R. C. (2005). Individuality and connectedness in adolescent development. In U. E. Elisabeth & A. E. Skoe, (Eds.) *Personality development in adolescence: A cross national and lifespan perspective.* London and New York: Routledge.

Habermas, T. (2007). How to tell a life: The development of the cultural concept of biography. *Journal of Cognition and Development, 8,* 1–31.

Hartup, W. W., & Stevens, N. (1999). Friendships and adaptation across the life span. *Current Directions in Psychological Science, 8,* 76–69.

Koh, J. B. K., & Wang, Q. (2012). Development of self. *Cognitive Science, 3,* 513–524.

Kuhn, D. (2006). Do cognitive changes accompany developments in the adolescent brain? *Perspectives on Psychological Science, 1,* 59–67.

Lesaux, N. K, & Kieffer, M. J. (2010). Exploring sources of reading comprehension difficulties among language minority learners and their classmates in early adolescence. *American Educational Research Journal, 47,* 596–632.

Nolen-Hoeksema, S. (2001). Gender differences in depression. *Current Directions in Psychological Science, 10,* 173–176.

Pasupathi, M., & Wainryb, C. (2010). On telling the whole story: Facts and interpretations in autobiographical memory narratives from childhood through adolescence. *Developmental Psychology, 46,* 735–746.

Spear, L. P. (2000). The adolescent brain and age-related behavioral manifestations. *Neuroscience and Biobehavioral Reviews, 24,* 417–463.

Chapter 6 Notes

1. Fivush, R., Haden, C.A., & Reese, E. (2006). Elaborating on elaborations: The role of maternal reminiscing style in cognitive and socioemotional development. *Child Development, 77,* 1568–1588.

2. Dunn, J., & Cutting, A. (1999). Understanding others, and individual differences in friendship interactions in young children. *Social Development, 8,* 201–219.
   Hughes, C., & Dunn, J. (1998). Understanding mind and emotion: Longitudinal associations with mental-state talk between young friends. *Developmental Psychology, 34,* 1026–1037.

3. Reese, E., & Newcombe, R. (2007). Training mothers in elaborative reminiscing enhances children's autobiographical memory and narrative. *Child Development, 78,* 1153–1170.
   Taumoepeau, M., & Reese, E. (in press). Maternal reminiscing style, elaborative talk, and children's theory of mind: A training study. *First Language.*

4. Bybee, J. (1998). The emergence of gender differences in guilt during adolescence. In J. Bybee's (Ed.), *Guilt and children* (pp. 113–125). San Diego: Academic Press.
   Yan, C., White, N., Ball, V., & Reese, E. (2009). *Life stories and well-being in middle-childhood and adolescence.* Poster presented at the Society for Research in Child Development, Denver, CO.

5. Yan, C. (2011). *Narrative identity and well-being from middle childhood to late adolescence: A developmental, cross-cultural perspective.* Unpublished PhD thesis, University of Otago, Dunedin, New Zealand.

6. Buckner, J. P., & Fivush, R. (2000). Gendered themes in family reminiscing. *Memory, 8,* 401–412.
   Fivush, R., Marin, K., McWilliams, K., & Bohanek, J. G. (2009). Family reminiscing style: Parent gender and emotional focus in relation to child well-being. *Journal of Cognition and Development, 10,* 210–235.

7. Zaman, W., & Fivush, R. (2011). When I was a little girl…: Gender differences in adolescents' intergenerational and personal stories. *Journal of Research on Adolescence, 21,* 703–716.

8. Rosenthal, C. J. (1985). Kinkeeping in the familial division of labor. *Journal of Marriage and Family, 47,* 965–974.

   Ross, M., & Holmberg, D. (1990). Recounting the past: Gender differences in the recall of events in the history of a close relationship. In M. P. Zanna & J. M. Olson (Eds.), *The Ontario symposium: Vol. 6. Self-inference processes* (pp. 135–152). Hillsdale, NJ: Erlbaum.

9. Fiese, B. H., & Bickham, N. L. (2004). Pin-curling grandpa's hair in the comfy chair: Parents' stories of growing up and potential links to socialization in the preschool years. In M. W. Pratt & B. H. Fiese (Eds.), *Family stories and the life course* (pp. 259–277). Mahwah, NJ: Erlbaum.

   Zaman, W., & Fivush, R. (2011). When I was a little girl…: Gender differences in adolescents' intergenerational and personal stories. *Journal of Research on Adolescence, 21,* 703–716.

10. Bird, A., Reese, E., & Tripp, G. (2006). Parent-child talk about past emotional events: Associations with child temperament and goodness-of-fit. *Journal of Cognition and Development, 7,* 189–210.

11. Skowronek, J. S., Leichtman, M. D., & Pillemer, D. B. (2008). Long-term episodic memory in children with attention-deficit/hyperactivity disorder. *Learning Disabilities Research and Practice, 23,* 25–35.

    In one study, adolescents with ADHD reached the performance of those without ADHD when a memory task was made emotionally more salient by including pictures depicting people with emotional expressions. Krauel, K., Duzel, E., Hinrichs, H., & Santel, S. (2007). Impact of emotional salience on episodic memory in attention-deficit/hyperactivity disorder: A functional magnetic resonance imaging study. *Biological Psychiatry, 61,* 1370–1379.

12. Klein, S. B., Gangi, C. E., & Lax, M. L. (2011). Memory and self-knowledge in young adults with ADHD. *Self and Identity, 10,* 213–230.

13. Bird, Reese, & Tripp (2006), see note 10.

14. Children with a difficult temperament are more likely to become depressed as adolescents and young adults, but the good news is that with positive coping skills, they can lessen or avoid altogether the possibility of depression. The coping strategies that they will need depend on the stressor. For uncontrollable and chronic stressors, such as parental discord or chronic pain, the healthiest coping mechanisms are to accept the situation and to use distraction and positive thinking to reframe one's thoughts about the stressor. Children who are able to use these strategies cope better with their parents' depression and are less likely to experience depression themselves. Compas, Bruce E., Connor-Smith, J., & Jaser, S. (2004). Temperament, stress reactivity, and coping: Implications for depression in childhood and adolescence. *Journal of Clinical Child and Adolescent Psychology, 33,* 21–31.

15. Dale, P. S., Crain-Thoreson, C., Notari-Syverson, A., & Cole, K. (1996). Parent-child book reading as an intervention technique for young children with language delays. *Topics in Early Childhood Special Education,16,* 213–235.

16. Tompkins, V., & Farrar, M. J. (2011). Autobiographical memory and book narratives with children with specific language impairment. *Journal of Communication Disorders, 44,* 1–22.

17. Wetherell, D., Botting, N., & Conti-Ramsden, G. (2007). Narrative in adolescent specific language impairment (SLI): A comparison with peers across two different narrative genres. *International Journal of Language and Communication Disorders, 42,* 583–605.

18. Grotevant, H. D., & Cooper, R. C. (2005). Individuality and connectedness in adolescent development. In U. E. Elisabeth & A. E. Skoe, (Eds.), *Personality development in adolescence: A cross national and life span perspective.* London and New York: Routledge.

19. Pratt, M. W., Norris, J. E., Lawford, H., & Arnold, M. L. (2010). What he said to me stuck: Adolescents' narratives of grandparents and their identity development in emerging adulthood. In K. C. McLean & M. Pasupathi (Eds.), *Narrative development in adolescence: Creating the storied self* (pp. 93–112). R. J. R. Levesque (Series Editor), *Advancing responsible adolescent development.* New York: Springer Science.

20. Reese, E., & Fivush, R. (2008). Collective memory across the lifespan. *Memory, 16,* 201–212.

21. Artioli, F., Cicogna, P. C., Occhionero, M., & Reese, E. (2012). The people I grew up with: The role of sociodemographic factors on early memories in an Italian sample. *Memory, 20,* 189–197.

22. Pratt, Norris, Lawford, & Arnold (2010), see note 19.

23. Norris, Kuiack, and Pratt (2004) list many other wonderful ways for grandparents to share their lives with their grandchildren, such as using a grandchild's war videogames as a launching pad for a story about a grandparent's own real-life wartime experiences. When grandparents engage with their grandchildren in their favorite activities, such as gardening or cooking, the family stories will emerge naturally and effortlessly.

    Norris, J. E., Kuiack, S., & Pratt, M. W. (2004). As long as they go back down the driveway at the end of the day: Stories of the satisfactions and challenges of grandparenthood. In M. W. Pratt & B. H. Fiese (Eds.), *Family stories and the life course: Across time and generations.* (pp. 353–374). Mahwah, NJ: Erlbaum.

24. Bengtson, V. L. (2001). Beyond the nuclear family: The increasing importance of multigenerational bonds. *Journal of Marriage and Family, 63,* 1–16.
    Bongaarts, J. (2001). Household size and composition in the developing world in the 1990s. *Population Studies, 55,* 263–279.

25. McKenzie, S., & Carter, K. (2010). Measuring whānau: A review of longitudinal studies in New Zealand. *MAI Review, 3,* 1–11.

26. Yarosz, D. J. & Barnett, W.S. (2001). Who reads to young children?: Identifying predictors of family reading and activities. *Reading Psychology, 22,* 67–81.
    Raikes, H., Pan, B. A., Luze, G., Tamis-LeMonda, C., Brooks-Gunn, J., Constantine, J., … Rodriguez, E. (2006). Mother-child book-reading in low-income families: Correlates and outcomes during the first three years of life. *Child Development, 77,* 924–953.

27. Reese, E. (2012). The tyranny of shared book-reading. In S. Suggate & E. Reese (Eds.), *Contemporary debates in childhood education and development.* Milton Park, Abingdon, Oxon, UK: Routledge Press.

28. Melzi, G., Schick, A. R., & Kennedy, J. L. (2011). Narrative elaboration and participation: Two dimensions of maternal elicitation style. *Child Development, 82,* 1282–1296.

29. Wang, Q., Doan, S. N. & Song, Q. (2010). Talking about internal states in mother-child reminiscing influences children's self-representations: A cross-cultural study. *Cognitive Development, 25,* 380–393.

Wang, Q., & Fivush. R. (2005). Mother-child conversations of emotionally salient events: Exploring the functions of emotional reminiscing in European-American and Chinese families. *Social Development, 14,* 473–495.

Leyva, D., Reese, E., Grolnick, W., & Price, C. (2008). Elaboration and autonomy support in low-income mothers' reminiscing: Links to children's autobiographical narratives. *Journal of Cognition and Development, 9,* 363–389.

Melzi, G., & Fernández, C. (2004). Talking about past emotions: Conversations between Peruvian mothers and their preschool children. *Sex Roles, 50,* 641–657.

Miller, P. J., Sandel, T. L., Liang, C-H., & Fung, H. (2001). Narrating transgressions in Longwood: The discourses, meanings, and paradoxes of an American socializing practice. *Ethos, 29,* 159–186.

Wang, Q. (2006). Relations of maternal style and child self-concept to autobiographical memories in Chinese, Chinese Immigrant, and European American 3-year-olds. *Child Development, 77,* 1794–1809.
30. Miller et al. (2001, p. 170), see note 29.
31. Growing Up in New Zealand (2010). *Before we are born: A longitudinal study of New Zealand children and their families.* Auckland: University of Auckland.
32. See Beth O'Malley (2008) *LifeBooks: Creating a treasure for the adopted child.* Winthrop, MA: Adoption-Works Press.

Chapter 7 Notes

1. See Anne Pellowski's books on storytelling traditions around the world for more ideas: Pellowski, A. (1991). *The world of storytelling: A practical guide to the origins, development and applications of storytelling.* Portland, OR: Wilson.
   Pellowski, A. (2005). *Drawing stories from around the world and a sampling of European handkerchief stories.* Westport, CT: Libraries Unlimited.
2. Bohanek, J. G., Fivush, R., Zaman, W., Lepore, C. E., Merchant, W., & Duke, M. P. (2009). Narrative interaction in family dinnertime conversations. *Merrill-Palmer Quarterly, 55,* 488–515.
3. If you are an adventurous family, see the website http://www.familyadventureproject.org/2011/10/10-lessons-from-10-years-adventuring.html for inspiration.
4. Marvin, C. (1994). Cartalk! Preschool children's conversations en route home from school. *Language and Hearing Services in the Schools, 25,* 146–155.
5. See William Pollack's book: Pollack, W. (1998). *Real boys: Rescuing our sons from the myths of boyhood.* New York: Random House.
6. Gross, J., & Hayne, H. (1998). Drawing facilitates children's verbal reports of emotionally laden events. *Journal of Experimental Psychology: Applied, 4,*163–179.
7. Fivush, R. (2004). The silenced self: Constructing self from memories spoken and unspoken. In D. R. Beike, J. M. Lampinen, & D. A. Behrend (Eds.), *The self and memory* (pp. 75–94). New York: Psychology Press.
   Sales, J. M., Fivush, R., Parker, J., & Bahrick, L. (2005). Stressing memory: Long-term relations among children's stress, recall and psychological outcome following Hurricane Andrew. *Journal of Cognition and Development, 6,* 529–545.
8. Bird, A., & Reese, E. (2008). Autobiographical memory in childhood and the development of a continuous self. In F. Sani (Ed.), *Individual and collective*

self-continuity: Psychological perspectives (pp. 43–54). New York: Psychology Press.

9. McAdams, D. P. (2006). The redemptive self: Generativity and the stories Americans live by. *Research in Human Development, 3,* 81–100.

10. Reese, E., Haden, C. A., Baker-Ward, L., Bauer, P., Fivush, R., & Ornstein, P. A. (2011). Coherence of personal narratives across the lifespan: A multidimensional model. *Journal of Cognition and Development, 12,* 424–462.

11. See Robert Emery's excellent books on this topic, including thoughtful advice on how to break the news of an impending separation to your children: Emery, R. (2012). *Renegotiating family relationships: Divorce, child custody, and mediation.* New York: Guilford Press.

    Emery, R. (2004). *The truth about children and divorce: Dealing with the emotions so you and your children can thrive.* New York: Viking Penguin.

    For lists of books that therapists use in bibliotherapy, see http://www.clpgh.org/research/parentseducators/parents/bibliotherapy.

Index